Pressure Groups in British Politics

Pearson Education

We work with leading authors to develop the
strongest educational materials in politics,
bringing cutting-edge thinking and best learning
practice to a global market.

Under a range of well-known imprints, including
Longman, we craft high quality print and
electronic publications which help
readers to understand and apply their content,
whether studying or at work.

To find out more about the complete range of our
publishing please visit us on the World Wide Web at:
www.pearsoneduc.com

Pressure Groups in
British Politics

Bill Coxall

An imprint of **Pearson Education**

Harlow, England · London · New York · Reading, Massachusetts · San Francisco
Toronto · Don Mills, Ontario · Sydney · Tokyo · Singapore · Hong Kong · Seoul
Taipei · Cape Town · Madrid · Mexico City · Amsterdam · Munich · Paris · Milan

Pearson Education Limited
Edinburgh Gate
Harlow
Essex CM20 2JE
England

and Associated Companies throughout the world

Visit us on the World Wide Web at:
www.pearsoneduc.com

First published 2001

ISBN 0 582 28994 7 PPR

British Library Cataloguing-in-Publication Data
A catalogue record for this book can be obtained from the British Library

Library of Congress Cataloging-in-Publication Data
Coxall, W.N.
    Pressure groups in British politics / Bill Coxall.
        p. cm.
    Includes bibliographical references and index.
    ISBN 0-582-28994-7
    1. Pressure groups--Great Britain. I. Title.
JN329.P7 C69 2001
322.4'3'0941--dc21

                                                              00-052017

10 9 8 7 6 5 4 3 2 1
05 04 03 02 01

Typeset by 43 in 10/12pt Sabon
Printed in Great Britain by Henry Ling Ltd., at the Dorset Press, Dorchester, Dorset

Contents

Bill Coxall

Bill Coxall was educated at Oxford University and the London School of Economics before completing his doctorate. He taught in schools before lecturing in history at Eastbourne College of Education. He was a founder member of the Politics Association and Reviews Editor of the Association's journal, *Teaching Politics*. Bill wrote numerous articles and books. He died aged 61 after a brief illness. This book is dedicated to his wife Hazel, and their children Edward, Anne and Jonathan.

Acknowledgements

The team at Pearson Education is grateful to Lynton Robins for his invaluable help in completing Chapter 8 on behalf of Bill Coxall, and for his assistance in stepping in and seeing the book through to publication.

The publishers are grateful to the following for permission to reproduce copyright material:

Figure 2.1 from Talking Politics in *The Guardian*, 21 August 1989, © The Guardian, Ian Swift; Figure 4.1 from Talking Politics in *The Guardian*, Spring 1996, © The Guardian, Peter Clarke; Figure 5.1 © Lynton Robins; Figure 6.1 from Talking Politics in *The Guardian*, Autumn 1990, © Bill Robinson; Figure 7.1 from *The Guardian*, 17 November, 1998, © The Guardian, Martin Argles; Figure 7.2 from Donga in Disguise in *The Guardian*, 18 September, 1996, © Robin Mayes; Table 2.1 from Social Trends 24, National Statistics, © Crown Copyright 2000; Table 4.1 from Measurement of Change in Pressure Group Politics in *Talking Politics* 5.1 p.19 © R. Baggott (1992); Tables 5.1, 5.2 and 5.3 from *Parliament and Pressure Politics*, O.U.P., (Rush, M. 1990); Table 6.2 from *The Sceptical Electorate*, © Ashgate Publishing Limited (Curtice, J. and Jowell, R. 1995).

While every effort has been made to trace the owners of copyright material, in a few cases this has proved impossible and we take this opportunity to offer our apologies to any copyright holders whose rights we may have unwittingly infringed.

Introduction

Sadly, *Pressure Groups in British Politics* will be Bill Coxall's final contribution to the literature of political science. Typically, it is concerned with educating another generation of students in the detail of British political life. On this occasion, Bill returned to a topic he first wrote about over 20 years ago with a new book which reflects the great advances made in understanding the changing nature, activities and processes that today characterise the world of pressure groups.

Chapter 1 makes sense of the diversity that faces those who research the 'anonymous empire' by exploring the contested areas of defining and categorising pressure groups. This is followed by a brief historical analysis which examines the role of pressure groups within the political system as Britain moved from the corporatist flavoured postwar years into the 1980s and 1990s where free-market rhetoric provided the new ingredient. Groups themselves were under pressure from governments which saw them in terms of serpents strangling their efforts to be efficient as well as interfering with free working of the marketplace.

The European Union is the focus of Chapter 3. The various strategies available for groups seeking inclusion and advantage are examined together with examples of success and failure. The opportunities for pressure group activity that are provided by constitutional and institutional arrangements in Britain are examined in Chapter 4. Also included in this chapter is the useful notion that some pressure groups become accepted as legitimate participants in the policy process, eventually becoming part of an established policy community. The consequences of such a policy community being destabilised is examined by means of a case study.

Chapter 5 confronts the question of why pressure groups, which are generally realistically informed on the power structure of Britain's political system, bother to lobby parliament. In fact their motives may be 'lower order' ones; lobbying MPs may help put an issue on a future political agenda or provide 'belt and braces' insurance when other activities have priority.

Chapter 6 examines another dynamic of pressure group development, the rise of new social movements. Numerous examples illuminate the growth of a relatively new kind of political participation which takes place mostly outside what has become thought of as the 'normal' process.

How can pressure groups and social movements be assessed in terms of whether or not they alter policy or change attitudes and beliefs? Chapter 7 lists the factors that may provide a group with political clout, such as financial resources, influential membership and the potential to damage government, before proceeding to consider the vexed question of how influence is measured in practice.

The final chapter provides a conclusion which reviews the contribution of pressure groups and social movements to Britain's parliamentary democracy. Expressed in the bluntest terms, do pressure groups disperse power throughout sections of society that would otherwise have little or no influence, or do pressure groups do no more than marginally increase the size of the élite charged with control over the mass of Britain's citizens? Is it possible that 'traditional' pressure groups bolster élites whereas new social movements attack élites?

Readers of this book will, then, find salient pressure group themes explored in an accessible way and the most crucial questions discussed in some depth. Each chapter stimulates further study through guided reading, case studies and examination questions.

Lynton Robins

CHAPTER 1

What are pressure groups?

The activities of pressure groups are seldom far from the headlines. Recently, for example, pressure groups have campaigned to promote or prevent new road-building, to ban or retain handguns, to abolish or preserve fox-hunting and to reform or preserve the constitution. The Trades Union Congress looked for some modest concessions from the Labour Government and both it and the employers' group, the Confederation of British Industry, backed the government's decision to join a single European currency. Church leaders pressed the government to exempt religions from the European Convention on Human Rights on the grounds that it could force parishes to marry homosexual couples and ordain women and even force church schools to employ non-Christian headteachers. Oxford and Cambridge universities lobbied to retain the state subsidies which give them about £2000 per student more than other universities. Museum directors called on Prime Minister Tony Blair to intervene in order to prevent the imposition of museum charges. Backers of a £500 million public lottery game said to be 'as addictive as cocaine' sought to persuade the government to delay a ban on it for two years so that they could recover their money. The British Airports Authority pushed hard for a fifth terminal at Heathrow Airport whilst Hacan, the group opposing it, claimed that a fifth terminal would lead to an unacceptable doubling of the number of passengers. The death of Diana, Princess of Wales gave added prominence to the international campaign to ban landmines. Pro-choice campaigners honoured the thirtieth anniversary of the Abortion Act whilst their pro-life opponents lobbed flowers off Westminister Bridge in protest and Cardinal Hume urged the Prime Minister to change Labour's policy on abortion. Gay groups campaigned to lower the age of consent for homosexuals to 16. Finally disability groups opposed the proposed cuts in disablement benefits.

Such an extensive review of pressure group actions is worthwhile in order to demonstrate both the extent and seriousness of the groups' involvement in contemporary British society. First, their concerns range from international and European to the national and local and the interests they seek to advance or protect include business, trade unions, the churches, educational establishments, welfare claimants, the environment, animals, women and minorities. They are to be found at all levels of British society and play a vital role in shaping political decisions. More people now belong to pressure groups than to political parties and in recent decades, as their membership and professionalism have increased, their importance has grown. Second, the review shows the considerable degree to which pressure groups are involved in society's most serious political conflicts – for example, over Britain's place in Europe, the reform of the welfare state, the role of women, the protection of the environment, animal welfare, and much more. Pressure groups help to shape the central political issues of the distribution of society's resources and the nature of the society itself.

In examining the role of pressure groups in the political system, this book aims to shed light on what the political scientist S.E. Finer described as an 'anonymous empire'. Successive chapters define them, look at their development since 1945, consider their relations with Europe, government, parliament and public opinion, examine the factors shaping their political influence, and analyse their importance for democracy. This chapter introduces the subject: it defines pressure groups, describes the different ways in which they have been characterised by political scientists, considers their functions within the political system, examines the targets of their activities, and offers a brief overview of their role in a democracy. It begins by considering the groups themselves. What are pressure groups?

Defining pressure groups

Pressure groups are like political parties in that they aim to influence the making and implementation of political decisions. However, pressure groups do not seek to do this by standing for election in order to form the government as parties do, but by lobbying decision-makers, by seeking to influence them directly or indirectly in a particular direction. Groups like the Pro-Life Alliance which aimed to repeal the 1967 Abortion Act and put forward 53 candidates in the 1997 general election, or the Referendum Party which put forward a massive 547 candidates in that election, are only apparent exceptions to this rule. For these groups had no hope of forming a government; rather they stood for publicity, to make a political point for a cause – respectively, against abortion and for a referendum on Europe. They may therefore be regarded as pressure groups seeking to *influence* public policy rather than as parties which want to *exercise power directly*. These examples also illustrate a second difference between pressure groups and political parties. Typically, pressure groups have narrower concerns than political parties. Whereas parties normally have a comprehensive perspective taking in all aspects of public policy, pressure groups have partial outlooks limited to a specific field of concern. Pressure groups often dissolve as soon as they have achieved their purpose, as the Referendum Party promised to do once a referendum on Britain's future in Europe had taken place and as do many local campaigning groups.

Definition 1.1   **Pressure group**

A pressure group is any organisation that aims to influence public policy by seeking to persuade decision-makers by lobbying rather than by standing for election and holding office.

Pressure groups and the political system

Unlike political parties in that they do not stand for election in order to form a government, pressure groups nonetheless fulfil similar functions to parties in the political system. Alongside parties, pressure groups are the major agencies of participation, representation and political education.

Participation: for most people, pressure groups are now a more important means of political participation than parties. Whereas party membership declined in the postwar period, pressure group membership grew rapidly, especially after the 1960s, with the result that combined party membership is now numbered in hundreds of thousands but total pressure groups membership is numbered in millions, with environmental groups alone possessing between 4 and 5 million members in the early 1990s. A particular significance of pressure groups is to provide a means of political participation between elections. An excellent example is the anti-poll tax movement which arose out of nothing in the late 1980s and galvanised a huge range of opinion from the extreme left to Conservatives and the ordinarily non-political in an ultimately successful campaign to overthrow the tax.

Representation: whereas parties play a directly representative role in democracies through elections, pressure groups also play a representative role through their capacity to organise and express the opinions of specific parts of the electorate to government at all levels. For example, pressure groups are the means by which the views of a wide range of particular interests and causes such as public sector workers, insurance companies, building societies, motorists, pensioners, law reformers and promoters of animal welfare can be represented to government. The authority with government of the organisations representing these sections of opinion depends to some extent on the size of their membership and, in the case of sectional groups, their ability to speak for the bulk of their potential membership, i.e. all or most small businessmen, doctors, lecturers, railwaymen or cabin crew.

Political education: pressure groups enrich democratic societies by developing and propagating information over a wide range of subjects. It pays pressure groups to engage in first-class research because their authority with decision-makers stems from the quality of their expertise as well as from the size of their memberships. Without pressure groups, far less would be known by the general population about matters such as organophosphate poisoning, the difficulties of the disabled, the control of foxes, marine pollution or the dangers of nuclear war. Pressure groups issue constant challenges to citizens to form opinions on issues and provide information which helps them make up their minds. Along with parties, they contribute to the continuous debate of democratic politics.

Types of pressure group

Pressure groups are not all of a kind and can be distinguished according to: (1) the nature of their membership; and (2) their strategies towards and relations with government.

(1)   The nature of pressure groups' membership: sectional and cause groups

Greenpeace, the Trades Union Congress, the Brewers and Licensed Victuallers Association, the Confederation of British Industry, Women Against Rape, Amnesty International, the Child Poverty Action Group, the Police Federation and the Campaign against Terminal 5 at Heathrow (Hacan) are all pressure groups, but of different types. The main distinction usually made is between groups that emerge out of the performance of a particular function such as a trade or occupation and groups that are formed to promote a particular cause. The former are usually referred to as *sectional* or *interest* groups whilst the latter are described as *cause*, *attitude* or *promotional* groups. The terms employed throughout this book are 'sectional' and 'cause'. Thus, the Trades Union Congress, the Brewers and Licensed Victuallers Association, the Confederation of British Industry and the Police Federation are sectional groups whilst Greenpeace, Women Against Rape, Amnesty International, the Child Poverty Action Group and Hacan are cause groups. Membership of a sectional group is restricted to those belonging to a particular business, trade, occupation or profession, e.g. brewers, policemen or to a particular section, e.g. trade unionists or businessmen; membership of a cause group is open to all those sharing a particular set of values or believing in a particular cause, e.g. safeguarding the environment (Greenpeace) or alleviating child poverty (Child Poverty Action Group). The purpose of sectional groups is to protect the self-interest of their members whilst that of cause groups is to further a particular cause, often involving the interests of others. Some writers further distinguish between cause groups in terms of the kind of causes they promote, e.g. welfare, environmental, animal rights, political, international, and so on. The sectional/cause group distinction may on occasion be blurred. For example, sectional groups such as the British Medical Association (BMA) often promote causes such as anti-smoking which they consider of benefit to the public generally whilst cause groups such as the Campaign for the Advancement of State Education draw largely for their membership on teachers in state schools who stand to gain professionally from the success of this cause. In addition, some groups such as local amenity or 'nimby' (not in my backyard) campaigns are difficult to classify since they draw upon motives that are both altruistic and also protective of an interest. For the most part, however, the distinction between sectional and cause groups is a useful classification which is employed frequently throughout this book.

Definition 1.2 Sectional group

A sectional pressure group represents the self-interest of a particular economic or social group in society: examples are the Confederation of British Industry (CBI), the Trades Union Congress (TUC) and the British Medical Association (BMA).

Definition 1.3 Cause group

A cause group is formed to promote a particular cause based on a set of shared attitudes, values or beliefs: examples are Greenpeace, the Child Poverty Action Group and Amnesty International.

---

(2) Pressure group strategies: insider and outsider groups

Increasingly used in addition to the sectional/cause group categorisation of pressure groups is the insider/outsider typology developed by Wyn Grant in the late 1970s (Grant, 1995, pp. 15–23). These terms describe groups in terms of their strategies and their relationship with government. Thus, *insider* groups are regarded as legitimate by government and involved in consultation on a regular basis. For example, the National Farmers Union is automatically consulted by governments when agricultural policy is under discussion. Insider groups meet continually with ministers and civil servants and in return for their insider status are expected to keep to 'the rules of the game'. Abiding by the rules of the game involves:

- providing accurate, well-researched, reliable information, and at all costs avoiding exaggeration
- presenting its case competently using moderate language

- being prepared to keep confidences and not 'go public' if negotiations appear to be going against it
- being willing to compromise, avoid threats and accept the outcome of the bargaining process.

Insider groups gain their insider status for a variety of reasons. They may speak for organisations that are part of the state itself like the local authority associations and the Association of Chief Police Officers (ACPO) or closely allied to it like the Church of England with its traditional role in education. Or they may represent a key economic function, such as business organisations, the major financial institutions and the farming community. Or they may be recognised by government because they possess specialist information and expertise, e.g. professional associations, or because they speak for a large membership on a key issue or possess the backing of public opinion.

In contrast, *outsider* groups either do not wish to be regarded as legitimate by government or are unable to gain recognition. They are often campaigning groups outside the political mainstream. An example is Compassion in World Farming. Outsider groups therefore work outside the political process. Shut out from influence in Whitehall by choice or necessity, they have fewer strategies available and must focus on achieving change through public opinion.

Grant further subdivides both insider and outsider groups into three categories: 'high profile' insider groups like the CBI and the BMA are prepared to reinforce their close relations with government by cultivating public opinion; 'low profile' insiders rely entirely on behind-the-scenes contacts with government; and 'prisoner' groups find it difficult or impossible to break away from government because they are part of the public sector like the local authority associations or entirely dependent on government for funding like the Family Fund Trust, a charity set up by government which distributes government-provided money to families with severely disabled children. Of the outsider groups, 'potential' insiders seek and have the capacity to achieve insider status; examples include groups that are ideologically incompatible with a particular government but whose fortunes can change after a general election such as right-wing think-tanks under the Labour Government before 1979 or the trade unions in the Thatcher–Major years after 1979. Outsiders 'by necessity' are those groups that lack the skills and know-how required to become insiders whilst 'ideological' outsiders are groups whose goals or methods (or both) are in conflict with the political consensus such as direct action road protesters, animal liberationists and nuclear disarmers.

The division of groups into insiders and outsiders is a less straightforward classification than the sectional/cause typology and not always easy to use. First, it cuts across the sectional/cause group categories. Thus, whilst most insiders are probably sectional groups, not all sectional groups are insiders: for example, the trade unions were shut out from influence by the Conservative governments between 1979 and 1997. Similarly, most outsiders are cause groups, but not all cause groups are outsiders; for example, the Howard

League for Penal Reform has long enjoyed insider status with the Home Office. The Royal Society for the Protection of Birds (RSPB) is a classic example of a cause goup with insider status which in 1993 managed to amend a bill to make it possible to secure convictions for the theft of birds' eggs on the evidence of a single witness. Second, Grant's typology has been criticised as confusing the two distinct dimensions of status and strategy. Grant writes: 'The insider/outsider distinction refers to a status that is achieved by the pursuit of a strategy. Strategy and status are very closely interlinked, so that pursuing an insider strategy is a precondition of winning insider status' (Grant, 1995, p. 15). Problems arise with this because in practice groups often seek influence on policy by engaging in consultations with government and pursuing media campaigns simultaneously. For example, the Brewers' Society campaign against reforms of the industry in 1989 involved pressure on government, parliament, party and public opinion at the same time, whilst the influence of the World Wildlife Fund on government policy towards deforestation and the World Bank in 1991 only occurred after a large-scale card-writing campaign to MPs had put pressure on the government to consult the WWF (Baggott, 1995, p. 19). Should these groups be described as insiders or outsiders? Both sought and achieved consultation with government over policy (suggesting an insider designation) but also employed strong public campaigns which were, moreover, crucial to their success (suggesting an outsider designation). Nonetheless, despite certain difficulties, by directing attention to the influence groups have on public policy, the insider/outsider typology forms a useful additional tool of analysis.

Definition 1.4   Insider group

An insider group is regarded as legitimate by government and consulted on a regular basis.

Definition 1.5   Outsider group

An outsider group either does not wish to become involved in a consultative relationship with public policy-makers or is unable to gain recognition.

Pressure politics

Pressure groups are the main focus of this book but the concept of pressure, whilst including pressure groups, also extends well beyond them. This is because *pressure*, which may be described as the effort by a group to achieve influence by various means of persuasion, occurs within all social organisations. Groups of people adopt differing views and try to persuade decision-makers to adopt them in such widely diverse organisations as government departments, churches, schools, universities, trade unions and private companies. An example is the movements to advance the rights and interests of gays and women within the Church of England. This process occurs within pressure groups themselves, as indicated, for example, by the attempts of radicals to infiltrate moderate organisations like the National Trust and the RSPCA. In other words, the term 'pressure' can describe a (very widespread) type of activity as well as being attached to a kind of organisation. Pressure groups differ from the kinds of (usually) informal and transient groupings found within institutions both by being formally organised and by aiming to influence public decisions, but the process of pressure in each case is similar. Moreover, it is worth underlining that pressure group policies themselves are shaped by a process of internal pressure politics of this nature.

Primary and secondary groups

One further point may be made before considering the role played by pressure groups in the political system. So far pressure groups have been discussed as if the main purpose of all of them is political lobbying. However, this is not the case. For example, the reason for existence of a group such as Charter 88 is to lobby for a political cause, whereas the main function of firms in manufacturing industry is to produce goods, the main function of trade unions is to defend the workplace interests of their members and the main function of motoring organisations is to provide a service for their members. There is a distinction then between *primary groups* whose sole purpose is to engage in political lobbying and *secondary groups* which are not primarily political but which may also adopt political standpoints or make political representations. The term 'pressure group' as used throughout this book therefore encompasses both primary and secondary groups but this basic distinction needs to be borne in mind.

Pressure group targets in British politics

How do pressure groups in Britain seek to achieve their aims? Something has already been said on this topic in the discussion of insider and outsider groups but it is useful to provide a more systematic, albeit brief, outline in order to prepare for the fuller discussion throughout the book. The selection of targets by groups can be considered from two perspectives: the *policy process* and *pressure points*. In terms of the policy process, groups may seek to influence political decisions at one or more of the following stages:

BOX 1.1

Categorising pressure groups

Re-read the opening paragraph and then do the following exercise.

1. Identify the pressure groups involved in the various campaigns that are mentioned as *sectional* or *cause* groups: for example, sectional groups are likely to want new road-building whilst cause groups wish to prevent it.

2. State how you think the following groups might be involved in the campaigns mentioned: the British Roads Federation, the RSPCA, the British Shooting Sports Council, the Society for the Protection of the Unborn Child, the Countryside Alliance, the Snowdrop Campaign, Alarm UK, the British Field Sports Society, the Society of Motor Traders and Manufacturers, Abortion Law Reform Association, Stonewall, the League Against Cruel Sports. For example, the British Field Sports Society wish to preserve fox-hunting whilst the League Against Cruel Sports wish to ban it.

3. In the opening passage, identify five organisations that follow insider strategies and three kinds of campaign that follow outsider strategies.

4. Re-read the section above on primary and secondary groups and then say which of the groups mentioned in Question 2 are *primary* groups and which are *secondary* groups.

- creation of the political agenda
- policy formation
- policy implementation.

An example drawn from the animal welfare movement helps to show what can be involved. The animal rights campaigner Richard Ryder has described the steps to reform the animal experimentation law between 1969 and 1986. He argues that 'at least three ingredients were required for success: a high level of public concern; a well-argued case; and direct contact with Ministers'. The campaign began with public awareness at a low level but this gradually changed for the following reasons:

- the very high level of public interest shown in Ryder's own book *Victims of Science* (1975)
- a story which appeared in the *Sunday People* in 1975 about ICI forcing beagles to smoke tobacco substitute which revealed to the media that the public were more receptive to such stories than previously thought
- a letter-writing campaign to ministers, MPs and the media by animal welfarists
- the gradually changing image of animal welfarists themselves from 'the Edwardian image of old ladies in hats' to more youthful campaigners.

By itself the public campaign to raise awareness would not have brought success without the parallel successful effort to make a good impression on government, amongst which the following features were of particular significance:

- the aim of the campaign was reform, not abolition, and the fact that it was couched in moderate, scientific and well-reasoned terms by experienced and qualified people drawn from well-established groups such as the RSPCA and the National Anti-Vivisection Society helped make it persuasive to the political parties
- Ryder's call for a determinate number (five) of specific, achievable reforms including the strengthening of the Inspectorate, the development of humane alternatives and the introduction of licence fees focused the campaign on clear and attainable objectives
- the achievement of good relationships with sympathetic ministers, who included a former Labour Cabinet minister, Douglas Houghton, a Labour Cabinet minister, Merlyn Rees, and a future Conservative Cabinet minister, David Mellor, gave the campaign the necessary 'friends in high places'.

In its later stages the campaign to reform the animal experimentation law was much assisted by the greater publicity given to animal welfare generally by the successful campaign of Greenpeace, the International Fund for Animal Welfare (IFAW) and the RSPCA to stop the slaughter of Scottish seals (1978). But the major breakthrough came in 1979 when the campaigners 'put animals into politics' by persuading the major parties to include animal welfare policies in their election manifestos. The election pledge by the Conservative Party to 'update' the legislation of animal experiments led to the Animals (Scientific Procedures) Act (1986).

Thus, starting from a very low level of public interest and politicians' cynicism, the animal welfare movement had been influential at the first two stages of the policy process. First, it had placed animal welfare on the political agenda and, second, by making sound, well-reasoned proposals for reform, it had made a large contribution to policy formation (Ryder, cited in Garner, 1996a, pp. 166–93).

Finally, there is the policy implementation and enforcement stage. With regard to *implementation*, much legislation is carried out through statutory instruments, where an Act of Parliament gives ministers the powers to make regulations to implement it. This process involves considerable consultation with pressure groups, with draft regulations sent to affected groups for comment. *Enforcement* also often involves groups. For example, in addition to its lobbying activities, the RSPCA also has a service role which includes not only running clinics and animal hospitals but also employing inspectors to police the anti-cruelty laws. Although the RSPCA has no legal enforcement role and receives no government funds, it does do important work in identifying and prosecuting those who mistreat animals on behalf of the state. The organisation does not itself have powers of arrest but works closely with the police (Garner, 1993b, p. 338).

Another perspective on pressure group behaviour is to consider *pressure points*, that is, the points in the political system that form targets for groups (Baggott, 1995, pp. 23–4). This is the approach adopted in the organisation of this book. Broadly, pressure groups have a wide range of potential targets but their main emphasis is conditioned by the nature of the political system. Three features of the British political system are worthy of note here. First, despite the impact of devolution the British system remains unitary rather than federal. This means that power is concentrated at the centre rather than divided between the federal and state governments, as in the United States or Germany. Nevertheless, dependent upon geographical interests, increasing pressure group activity will focus on the devolved legislatures of Scotland, Wales and Northern Ireland. Second, Britain's parliamentary system involves the almost total domination of parliament by the government of the day. In the United States, the separation of powers between the executive and legislature creates two powerful institutions, the Presidency and Congress. In Britain, power resides essentially in the government which almost invariably gets its way within parliament. The third feature is the growing authority of the European Union which now forms an important source of laws binding on British subjects.

The major contrast, as already seen in the discussion of insider and outsider groups, is between a strategy targeting *government* – at local, national or international level – and one targeting *public opinion*. The animal lobby provides examples of campaigns aimed at a large number of targets. Thus, moderate, well-established groups such as the RSPCA and the National Anti-Vivisection Society have sought influence with *government* by getting parties to adopt election pledges and since 1989 under the aegis of the Political Animal Lobby (PAL) by political donations to parties. Animal welfare groups have also gained representation on government advisory committees; for example, three members of the Animal Procedure Committee set up to advise the Home Secretary on animal experimentation under the 1986 Animals (Scientific Procedures) Act are drawn from animal welfare interests. Animal welfare campaigners have also targeted *local councils* to ban hunting and circuses on their land; have pressured *parliament* to introduce anti-hunting and other legislation; and since 1980 the Eurogroup for Animal Welfare, formed by the RSPCA, has lobbied *European institutions*. Most animal groups, however, aim to influence government indirectly by *public campaigns* to change public opinion, with groups like Animal Aid encouraging consider-able grass-roots activity. Press advertisements, petitions, demonstrations, mass rallies and stunts all play a role in gaining publicity for the cause. Other groups bypass the political arena by pressurising *consumers*, for example to buy 'cruelty-free' cosmetics or to stop buying fur coats, or engage in legal *direct action*, for example the disruption of hunts by the Hunt Saboteurs, or illegal *direct action* like the raids on animal laboratories and factory farms by the Animal Liberation Front (Garner, 1993b, pp. 340–9).

Pressure groups and democracy

The mainstream view of pressure groups held by Western liberals is that there is a close relationship between groups and democracy. Their very right to exist is based on a fundamental democratic principle – freedom of association: the right of individuals to join together freely to form associations to promote their interests and purposes. Whereas under dictatorship this freedom is normally suppressed, in democracy it is fundamental. At the same time, a wide variety of active pressure groups denoting a vigorous associative life has been seen as a key indicator of a healthy democracy. Thus, democracy is a precondition for groups and a lively range of groups is an important indicator that democracy is functioning effectively.

More specifically, liberal *pluralists* argue that pressure groups contribute in the following ways to democracy:

- they improve government by providing specialised information and placing important items on the political agenda
- they enhance the quality of public debate by channelling informed opinion to the news media
- they provide additional agencies for political participation which are particularly important between elections
- they offer a means for the representation of minorities, thereby helping to ensure that society averts the threat of 'the tyranny of the majority'
- they contribute to the monitoring and surveillance of government by criticism and by exposing information it would rather keep secret
- they form a source of countervailing power to government, thereby constituting an unofficial opposition alongside the official opposition provided by political parties
- they help to disperse power through society and to counteract major concentrations of power in large sectional interests.

Quotations

Pressure groups permit citizens to express their views on complex issues which affect their lives ... Numerical democracy ... finds it difficult ... to take account of the intensity of opinion on a particular issue. Democracy cannot be reduced simply to a head-counting exercise: it must also take account of the strength of feelings expressed, and the quality of arguments advanced.

(Wyn Grant, *Pressure Groups, Politics and Democracy in Britain*, 2nd edn, 1995, pp. 23–4)

I was one of those imprisoned for protesting at Twyford Down. Sometimes, when the shady avenues of bureaucracy have been exhausted, there is no choice but to throw yourself in front of the digger.

(Emma Must, Alarm UK, *The Guardian*, 27 December 1994)

However, starting with major political theorists such as Hobbes and Rousseau, some political analysts have argued that, far from being a symptom of democratic vitality, pressure groups undermine democracy. One of their main points is that pressure groups thwart the implementation by governments of policies for which the electorate has voted at general elections by lobbying in favour of sectional, or partial, interests. The sort of incident such critics have in mind occurred in November 1997 when the Labour Government abandoned the ban on tobacco advertising it had published in its manifesto after vigorous lobbying from the Formula One chief, Bernie Ecclestone, who had donated £1 million to party funds. A similar episode occurred in 1994 when United Biscuits, one of the Conservative Party's largest corporate donors, was among the companies that successfully persuaded the Conservative Government to scrap the restrictions on the movement of heavy lorries in London. In both cases, therefore, the public interest in better health and less pollution was blocked by large sectional interests operating behind the scenes. Whereas parties seek to offer comprehensive visions, pressure groups offer only partial ones. Critics have other arguments too. One is that with large business groups enjoying far superior access to decision-makers than other causes and interests, vast inequalities exist in groups' opportunities for influence. Pressure groups do not occupy a level playing field. Critics also argue that many groups are far from democratic themselves and that the views they press on public officials are often far from representative of those held by their members. The debate on how far groups enhance or detract from democracy will be raised again later but should be borne in mind throughout the book.

Quotations

The formidable specialist expertise of many lobbyists has made them an invaluable resource for a generalist civil service which has sometimes become their captive. Vested interests – farmers, teachers, police officers, whoever – are locked in fatal embrace with Whitehall, corrupting the process of disinterested government.

(Melanie Phillips, *The Observer*, 24 March 1996)

Brent Spar (the episode in 1995 when Greenpeace lobbied successfully against Shell's plan for the deep-sea dumping of its oil rig) shows how politics is going and, however seductive the appeal of single-issue campaigning, that way marks a failure not a triumph of democracy.

(Hugo Young, *The Guardian*, June 1995)

Summary

- A pressure group is any organisation that seeks to influence public policy by lobbying decision-makers rather than, like a political party, standing for election and forming a government.

- Pressure groups are very numerous in democratic societies. They are involved in the most serious conflicts and play a key role in shaping society's values and distributing its resources.

- Pressure groups serve the three very important democratic functions of political participation, political representation and political education. Their combined membership nowadays is greater than that of political parties; they express a wide range of opinions to government; and they enhance the quality of public debate.

- Two main ways of categorising pressure groups have been developed: according to the nature of the membership and according to their relations with government. In terms of membership, a distinction is usually made between *sectional* groups which represent the self-interest of a particular social group or section and *cause* groups which promote a particular social cause based on shared attitudes or values. With regard to relations with government, the basic distinction is between *insider* groups which are regarded as legitimate by government and are consulted on a regular basis and *outsider* groups which either do not want consultative status or are unable to achieve it.

- The concept of pressure includes pressure groups but extends beyond them since it occurs in all organisations. However, pressure groups differ from the kind of informal and usually impermanent groupings that arise within organisations by being formally organised, operating openly and aiming to influence public decisions.

- The term pressure group as employed throughout this book includes both *primary* groups whose sole purpose is to exercise political pressure and *secondary* groups whose main purpose is not political but who may adopt political standpoints or engage in political lobbying from time to time.

- The search for political influence by pressure groups can be considered from two perspectives: the *policy process* and *pressure points*. According to the first perspective, groups may be seen as seeking influence at one or more of three stages: creation of the political agenda; policy formation; and policy implementation.

- According to the pressure point perspective, pressure group behaviour is analysed in relation to the points of the political system that they target. In Britain's unitary, executive-dominated system of government, many groups focus especially on the executive. However, in the choice of targets, much depends on the nature of the group and influence may also be sought through devolved and local government, quangos, parliament and the courts. The institutions of the European Union are of increasing importance for sectional and environmental groups. Groups that lack or are unable to achieve legitimacy with government or insider groups that need public support to strengthen their campaigns target public opinion.

- Liberal *pluralist* analysts hold sympathetic views of pressure groups, regarding them as very valuable in enhancing the quality of governmental decision-making, public participation and political debate. They focus especially on the role of groups in forming bastions of countervailing power and additional sources of political opposition to government. However, other commentators adopt a less favourable view of pressure groups, drawing attention to the way in which they can thwart the wishes of the public as expressed through elections and can distort the democratic process by skewing decisions towards already powerful sections of society such as business.

Further reading

Wyn Grant (1995) *Pressure Groups, Politics and Democracy in Britain*, 2nd edn (London: Macmillan) is an authoritative overview. Martin J. Smith (1995) *Pressure Politics* (Manchester: Baseline Books) provides an excellent brief introduction whilst Rob Baggott (1995) *Pressure Groups Today* (Manchester: Manchester University Press) offers a useful, longer survey. Key interpretative essays and valuable comparative material are to be found in Jeremy J. Richardson (ed.) (1993) *Pressure Groups* (Oxford: Oxford University Press).

CHAPTER 2

Pressure groups since 1945

This chapter examines the historical development of pressure group politics in postwar Britain. Particular emphasis is given to the evolving relations between the main sectional groups and government and to the rapid development of cause groups, especially in the context of new social movements. There are three main phases in postwar pressure group politics: (1) 1945–1960, a period of close relations between government and the main producer groups but relatively limited cause group activity; (2) 1960–1979, a phase of even closer, so-called corporatist relations between government, business and trade unions and the emergence of new cause groups in the fields of welfare, women's rights and the environment; and (3) 1979–1997, when corporatism was overturned and the government severely curtailed the power of the unions whilst popular participation and protest through new social movements expanded. The chapter ends with a brief look at groups' relations with New Labour after 1997, with special reference to contrasts and continuities with earlier phases.

Phase (1) 1945–1960

Close relations between the state and the large producer groups and professional associations began during the war when the state took over total responsibility for the economy, including industrial and agricultural production, an emergency hospital service and other aspects of the nation's health. This transformation of a previously non-interventionist state into an interventionist war-fighting machine had implications for key sectional groups such as those representing business, trade unionists, farmers and doctors, whose cooperation was necessary for the effectiveness of the national war effort. In particular, the war massively increased the status of organised labour. Ernest Bevin, the general secretary of the Transport and General Workers Union, was quickly appointed Minister of Labour by Churchill. A towering figure, Bevin ensured the trade unions were involved in all aspects of labour policy. A National Joint Advisory Council with representatives from both employers and unions was established and a large number of government departments either created new consultative bodies involving the unions or brought the unions onto existing bodies.

After 1945, a new phase in the peacetime relations between the main sectional and professional interests and government began. The main reason for the new group–government relationship was the responsibility assumed by postwar governments for management of the economy and the creation of the welfare state. The adoption by postwar governments (Labour, 1945–51 and Conservative, 1951–64) of commitments: (1) to manage a mixed economy (four-fifths private enterprise, one-fifth publicly owned) on Keynesian lines; (2) to pursue full employment as a primary goal of economic policy; and (3) to administer a welfare state involving 'cradle to grave' social security, a taxation-financed National Health Service free at the point of use, a national education service and a large-scale housing programme, created a 'new world' for pressure groups. It automatically enhanced the social status and political bargaining power of the producer and professional groups upon whose cooperation the government relied in order to be able to deliver its economic and social policy promises to the electorate. Naturally enough, in these circumstances, a broad spectrum of business, commercial, financial, professional and trade union interests became involved in permanent consultative relationships with government. A tacit bargain to the mutual advantage of groups and government was struck. Government gained from the organised groups the advice and cooperation it needed in order to be able to carry out its policies effectively whilst, for their part, the groups derived the chance to influence government policies in their own interests.

Government and the unions

Organised labour was among the main beneficiaries of this 'new world'. The election of a Labour Government in 1945 enabled the trade unions to maintain the close relationship with government established during the war. Labour was sometimes described as 'two-thirds trade union pressure group, one-third political party' and the unions had played a prominent role in shaping its policies. Although normally respectful of middle-class professional leadership in the parliamentary party, in practical and formal terms, the unions largely dominated the party, providing the bulk of its finances and possessing the majority of votes at conference. In 1945, the unions sponsored 120 Labour MPs, of whom 29 were appointed to Government and six to the Cabinet. A key feature of the new close government–union relationship was regular consultation between government and unions on a wide range of social, economic and industrial issues, with union representation on government committees rising from 12 in 1939 to 60 ten years later. The union movement – which claimed to act on behalf of a working class that still constituted almost three-quarters of society – had become a major estate of the realm, assuming an unprecedented degree of influence and responsibility.

Government and unions both gained from their close cooperation. The government gained:

- Avoidance of large-scale industrial conflict: the trade unions acquiesced in the continuation of wartime restrictions on the right to strike (Order 1305).
- Wage restraint: between 1948 and 1950, the TUC accepted a voluntary wage freeze in return for dividend limitation by business.

The trade union movement gained:

- Policies beneficial to the working class such as the welfare state, full employment, nationalisation and a commitment to 'fair shares'.
- Repeal of the Trades Disputes Act (1946). Passed to damage the unions in the aftermath of the 1926 General Strike, this legislation introduced a system whereby trade unionists had to signal active support for their union's political fund by 'contracting in'. The 1946 Act repealed this legislation, substituting 'contracting out', whereby unionists indicated they wished not to contribute to the political levy, for 'contracting in'.
- Broad acceptance of the principle of free collective bargaining with employers for wages which was central to the unions' reason for existence.

This system of good government–trade union relations continued under the Conservatives after 1951, with the party generally accepting that conciliation of the unions was necessary in the interests of both industrial peace and electoral success. Thus, national economic recovery depended upon industrial peace whilst electoral success for the Conservatives demanded that they move away from their image as the party of hostility to organised labour and of mass unemployment acquired in the 1930s. Cultivation of good relations with the representatives of business and especially labour was as necessary to Conservative governments as to Labour in order to avoid social conflict. Successive ministers of Labour, Walter Monckton and Ian Macleod, therefore, were given the tasks of maintaining close relations with the TUC and defusing possible strike action – generally achieved by sympathetic consideration of union demands by courts of inquiry. Previous talk of curbing union power, for example by new anti-picketing laws or ballots for election of union officials or before strikes, was quickly forgotten. Leading Conservatives, like Labour before them, continued to put their faith in fostering voluntary agreements in industry rather than compulsion through legislation. Typical of this approach were the informal meetings in 1956 at which Conservative ministers exhorted representatives from the TUC and the main employers' organisations to restrain wage and price increases. However, as industrial relations deteriorated (strike activity doubled between 1953 and 1959), inflationary pressures increased and full employment became more difficult to maintain, Conservative disquiet about leaving industrial relations and wage bargaining to voluntary union–employer agreements mounted. Nonetheless, down to the early 1960s, Conservative governments continued to believe in exhortation of trade unions to moderate their wage claims rather than in a nationally imposed wages policy or wage freeze. This approach was summed up by Ian Macleod in 1958 when he maintained that 'only in a partnership independent of politics between the three great partners – government, trade unions and employers – was there any real lasting hope for good, sound industrial relations' (cited in Dorey, 1995, p. 50).

Government and other leading groups

Government relations with *business* were complicated postwar by the political weakness of business which made it hard for government to enter partnership with it (Grant, 1993, p. 18). First, down to 1965, peak representation of business was divided between several employers' organisations, of which the main ones were the British Employers' Confederation (BEC, 1919) and the Federation of British Industries (FBI, 1916). Second, business was not then – and is not now – a monolithic entity but rather is internally divided and, largely because of these internal divisions, it found difficulty both in defining its interests and in deciding upon a common political strategy. For example, there are important differences of interest and outlook between the manufacturing, financial and retailing sectors; between the nationalised industries and the private sector; betweeen large and small firms; and – within manufacturing – between individual companies and sectors.

Nonetheless, business formed strong relationships with postwar governments both at the levels of peak representation and of individual industries and firms. Labour put both the BEC and the FBI on its Economic Planning Board and, when making plans for its wage freeze (1948), consulted closely with the FBI and with other peak organisations, the National Union of Manufacturers and Associated British Chambers of Commerce. Business agreed to voluntary limitation of dividends between 1948 and 1950 but persuaded Labour to relax the controls on prices within a few months (Beer, 1965, p. 206). Down to the late 1980s, another important way in which government conducted its relations with business was through sponsorship divisions with different sectors of industry located in the various departments, especially the Department of Trade. Sponsorship divisions gave every industry and practically every product a point of contact in Whitehall. In the words of a CBI booklet (1987), sponsor departments constituted 'the most important relationship that the majority of businessmen will ever have with government'. Their role was to act as informed but not uncritical lobbyists for their industries within Whitehall. A sponsorship department existed to help its industry achieve success: to that end, the sponsoring department identified and aggregated the views of its industry and tried to ensure that government policies promoted its interests. In carrying out this function, sponsorship to some extent compensated for 'the inadequacies of an often incoherent system of business representation' (Grant, 1993, pp. 53–4). The Conservative governments of the 1950s maintained most of the Labour legacy of business representation including the Economic Planning Board and sponsorship divisions. From the point of view of business in this era, government economic management through the manipulation of interest rates and hire purchase was seen as detrimental to research, development planning and investment. In addition, business had to tolerate governments' determination to maintain good relations with the TUC; it complained that its tax burden was too heavy and that it was being starved of capital by the nationalised industries' easy access to government funds.

Other representative groups such as farmers and doctors formed close relationships with specific government departments which came later to be described by the term *policy networks* (Marsh and Rhodes, 1992). The concept of policy networks describes a range of relations between pressure groups and government departments on a continuous line from *policy communities* at one extreme to *issue networks* at the other. Policy communities involve close, continuous, stable relations between government officials and a very limited number of groups; participants tend to share the same ideology and the communities are insulated from other networks and the public. At the other extreme, issue networks describes a government–group relationship involving a much larger number of groups; discontinuous, not particularly close contacts between officials and groups; relatively open access with groups moving in and out of the policy process; and greater conflict over policies and values. After 1945, policy networks were established in many policy areas including transport, power, education, agriculture and health.

Definition 2.1   Policy networks

This is the idea that policy-making in modern government is compartmentalised in a series of distinct policy areas, each with its specific range of groups and each with its own pattern of relationships between civil servants and groups. The term policy network is a generic term which encompasses a range of different relationships between officials and groups from the close, stable relations of a policy community at one extreme to the looser, less continuous, less close relations of an issue network at the other.

Agriculture, where the Ministry of Agriculture, Fisheries and Food (MAFF) developed a very close relationship with the National Farmers Union (NFU), forms a classic example of a policy community. The main features of this relationship were the close involvement of the NFU in all aspects of agricultural policy-making and in particular in the Annual Price Review which set the level of agricultural subsidies for the year ahead; the exclusion from the policy process of groups that might challenge the NFU such as the Country Landowners Association and the National Union of Agricultural Workers; and the broad agreement between officials and farmers' representatives on the twin goals of increasing agricultural productivity and achieving reasonable living standards for farmers. The background to this relationship was the wartime need to increase agricultural production which strengthened the farmers' bargaining position and the way in which the NFU exploited this position by developing its membership in order to become the main representative of farmers and by impressing on MAFF its ability to keep to 'the rules of the game' (Smith, 1995, pp. 34–5).

A policy community also developed in the *health service*. Before and during the war, many institutions and groups had significant interests in health care, including local authorities, insurance companies and charities as well as the medical profession. The main reason for the growth in the postwar political influence of doctors – as with farmers – was large-scale state intervention, especially the creation of the National Health Service (1948). Yet when a comprehensive national health service was first mooted during the war to replace the the former inadequate, patchy provision, the British Medical Association fiercely resisted the idea. It believed that the interests of its members were better suited by the pre-war system in which private insurance paid the fees of doctors for approximately half the population, leaving doctors free to charge private practice fees for the other half (Glennerster, 1995, p. 47). The main fear of doctors was being forced to become a state-salaried profession. Hence, negotiations between Labour and the medical profession over the establishment of the NHS were bitter and drawn out and involved significant concessions both to hospital consultants and to general practitioners (GPs). Thus, when the hospitals were nationalised, consultants were guaranteed a secure income by the national government, the power to award themselves permanent merit awards and in addition the right to continue drawing income from private patients. Doctors remained private professional people owning their practices but being paid capitation fees for their NHS patients. One historian has wondered whether 'a harder bargain might have been struck' by Labour with consultants and doctors on the grounds that in the 1940s 'the medical profession was as much in need of state finance as the NHS was in need of its expertise' (Lowe, 1993, p. 174). What is clear is that just as the need of the state for efficiently produced cheap food made farmers powerful after the war, so the need of governments for effective delivery of national health care made doctors powerful. In the case of the doctors, the mutual dependence of government and doctors was institutionalised in the relations between the Ministry of Health and the representatives of the doctors, the BMA, and to a lesser extent, of the consultants, the Royal College of Surgeons. The shared assumptions of the participants in the health policy community were the central importance of the national health service and the need to involve the self-employed, self-regulating medical profession in the making and administration of health policy (Smith, 1995, p. 37).

BOX 2.1

Postwar political ideologies on pressure groups

Three ideological attitudes fed into the widespread acceptance of the legitimacy of pressure group politics by the two main parties between the 1940s and the 1970s: pluralist liberalism, reformist labourism and one nation Conservatism.

Pluralist liberalism (see also Chapter 1) is the most influential perspective on pressure groups in Western democracies and has influenced both the Labour and Conservative parties. It holds that pressure groups make a vital contribution to a healthy democratic society in (at least) two important ways. They do this because they form:

- vigorous intermediary institutions between government and the individual, thereby providing tough barriers against an overmighty executive
- important channels of participation and representation, facilitating the communication of both the intensity of popular feeling on particular issues and the variety of popular opinions.

The pluralist perception of the legitimacy of pressure group activity has penetrated deeply into the British political culture. Indeed, this has often been described as an associative culture, in which large numbers of people derive satisfaction from joining voluntary groups in order to pursue a wide variety of social purposes from sport to charitable activity. Such activity gains its legitimacy in large part from being based on the liberal principle of freedom of association.

Reformist labourism, the belief in the gradualist, parliamentary route to socialism held by the British Labour party, absorbed the liberal pluralist view of the legitimacy of groups. However, it added to this perspective a strong conviction of the value of collective effort to improve the position of the weakest groups in society. The party formed the political wing of this collective effort whilst the trade unions constituted the industrial wing. As a labourist rather than a Marxist party, Labour believed that the situation of the working class could be improved by the party achieving a parliamentary majority through winning elections and then using the power of the state to implement policies beneficial to the working class such as welfarism and full employment. In government, the party's statist outlook entailed government responsibility for national economic management, nationalisation of key industries and administration of an expanded welfare system; all of these responsibilities drew it into permanent negotiations and consultation with a large range of both public and private sector groups.

One nation Conservativism: Traditional, moderate or one nation Conservatism was the dominant strand in Conservatism for 30 years beginning in the late 1940s. Basically, it represented a reaction against the libertarian, free market strand of Conservatism which had been influential pre-war and was to become dominant under Mrs Thatcher. It accepted the need for government social and economic intervention as a 'middle way' between a free market economy and socialist planning. In its composition, by the mid-twentieth century, the Conservative Party, although formerly a landed party, had become mainly representative of business and the higher professions. One nation Conservatism drew upon a traditional Tory view of society as composed of a range of differing but equally legitimate interests such as business, trade, farming, shopkeeping, and the professions, each with a natural right to be represented in government. By the

BOX 2.1 (CONTINUED)

second quarter of the twentieth century manual labour had been added to these legitimate interests. In this vein, a leading Conservative in 1948 expressed his belief in 'a balanced society ... in which the greatest number and variety of legitimate interests are all welcome and have an assured place' and urged Conservatives to 'deliberately encourage such groups and associations and make maximum use of them to carry out government policy' (Sir David Eccles, cited in Beer, 1965, p. 77). One nation Conservatives also drew upon the traditional Conservative idea that voluntary groups are valuable because, as well as providing outlets for human altruism, they foster in the individual a sense of community and of belonging to society, thereby improving social cohesion and preventing the disintegration of society into a collection of isolated units.

Questions

Read the first section of this chapter and the above passage, then answer the following questions.

1. What elements in their parliamentary composition and in their ideologies disposed both Labour and the Conservatives after 1945 to look favourably on the representation of groups – especially the main producer groups – in government?
2. What advantages and dangers were there (a) for government and (b) for pressure groups in the system of close government–group consultation established after 1945?
3. What do you understand by *sponsorship divisions*? How do you think they were of benefit to industry?
4. Describe the concept of *policy networks* in your own words and give a postwar example, being careful to mention both its main features and the reason for its emergence.

Now read the passage on the Conservatives' relationships with sectional interests (pp. 32–36, below), then answer these questions.

5. From the perspective of New Right ideology, what was wrong with the way postwar governments down to 1979 conducted relations with the major sectional interests?
6. Describe the main changes in the relations between government and pressure groups brought about by Conservative governments after 1979.
7. Did any pressure groups gain in status and influence under the Conservatives (1979–97)? If so, which ones and why?

Phase (2) 1960–1979

In this period, the comparative decline of the British economy became a serious political issue. Britain's share of world manufactures fell from 25.5 per cent in 1950 to about 11 per cent in 1970 and its rate of economic growth in these two decades, although good in comparison with its own historical standards, was far lower than the growth rates achieved in the EEC, the USA and Japan. The consequences of the decline in the international competitiveness of its economy was seen in a sharp deterioration in the early 1960s of Britain's balance of payments and a steady rise in rates of inflation and unemployment. The response of both major parties (Conservative, 1959–64 and 1970–74 and Labour, 1964–70 and 1974–79) was a combination of intensified economic intervention and the modernisation of institutions. The consequences for the large producer groups were considerable: first, the representatives of employers and unions were drawn into even closer relationships with the government; and second, there was intense political pressure on the trade unions for voluntary reform followed by the attempt at legislative reform of industrial relations in the early 1970s.

The corporatist phase of economic management

The change of direction towards tripartite economic management by government, business and unions originated in a Federation of British Industry conference at Brighton in 1960 (Grant, 1993, p. 30). Within two years, the first major institution of what later came to be described as corporatist government had been established by the Conservatives: the National Economic Development Council (NEDC, 1961). The NEDC brought together representatives of the employers and the unions with civil servants and Cabinet ministers with the aim of forging agreement on measures to increase the economic growth rate. Over the following 18 years of its active existence (it was not in fact formally wound up until the early 1990s), it provided a forum for the discussion of Britain's economic problems and possible solutions to them. Under frequent discussion were a wide range of factors including investment, productivity, restrictive practices and the level of wage settlements. At the same time, a 'pay pause' (July 1961) formed the prelude to the introduction of a formal incomes policy which Prime Minister Macmillan and some leading ministerial colleagues had concluded was 'necessary as a permanent part of our economic life' (Macmillan, cited in Dorey, 1995, p. 72). A National Incomes Commission (NIC) was set up to review incomes policy issues.

Labour continued this strongly interventionist line after 1964. Its 12-point Statement of Intent (1964) contained joint pledges by government, management and unions to work together 'to achieve and maintain a rapid increase in output and real income combined with full employment'. This preceded the establishment of the National Board for Prices and Incomes (1964), another highly interventionist body aimed at curbing price and wage increases. The attempt to regulate prices and incomes through voluntary or statutory policies lasted from 1961 to 1977 and was followed by the unilateral government imposition of limits on pay increases between 1977 and 1979 by the Labour

Government which collapsed in a wave of strikes in the winter of 1978–79 (the 'Winter of Discontent'). The philosophy underlying this corporatist phase of government was summed up by the Conservative Prime Minister Edward Heath when he told the 1972 Conservative Conference that 'the trade unions and employers (must) fully share with the government the benefits and obligations of running the economy' (cited in Kavanagh and Morris, 1994, p. 61). The corporatist phase involving the effort to run the economy by a tripartite partnership of government, employers and unions was interrupted only once in these years – between 1970 and 1972, when Heath sought to reverse the previous state interventionist trend by allowing market forces a greater role in determining prices, incomes and investment and reducing the role of the state. But faced with company bankruptcies, rising unemployment and trade union hostility following his government's industrial relations legislation, Heath was forced into a 'U-turn' and this brief interlude ended with a return to the corporatist attempt to build a new partnership with the TUC and CBI. The high point of 'corporatist' politics was the 'social contract' (1974–75) between Labour and the unions by which the party promised to maintain living standards in return for union restraint on wage claims.

Definition 2.2 **Corporatism**

Corporatism refers to a form of sectional group relationships with government in which the major sectional groups representing employers and trade unions work together with government in the making and implementation of industrial and economic policy.

The corporatist phase of government–group relations was widely deemed a failure. The representative bodies such as the NEDC and the PICB tended to deteriorate into mere 'talking shops' and generally lacked both executive power and moral authority. In practice, the tripartite relationship fell short of fully fledged corporatism for two main reasons. First, the Treasury kept tight control of government economic policy and second, the main sectional bodies had weak central organisations which were unable to enforce national agreements on their members. For these and other reasons, many commentators prefer the term 'neo-corporatism' to describe a government–producer groups relationship which had corporatist aspects but fell short of the system of state–producer group relations in 1930s fascist Italy. Although prices and incomes policies achieved some successes, overall they too have generally been accounted a failure. The major difficulty facing the corporatist group–government relationship was the inability of the CBI and TUC to secure anything more than the short-term compliance of their members to the agreements they made with government. The Confederation of British Industry (1965) always found difficulty in speaking for a disparate variety of businesses effectively whilst the TUC proved unable to control its shop floor membership. The basic difficulties were cultural, the long-standing and deeply ingrained preference of both business and trade unions for a voluntary system of industrial relations rather than a legally-enforced one. The fundamental role of unions is to improve the pay and conditions of their members whilst that of businesses is to make profits for their shareholders. Hence, they were 'reluctant partners' in corporatist government because government intervention often made these objects more difficult to achieve. By the late 1970s, the political search had begun for an alternative method of government. Corporatism had politicised industrial relations and economic policy-making, involved government in well-publicised defeats by the major sectional interests and led to charges that Britain had become 'ungovernable'.

Governments sought to make economic partners of the unions in the 1960s and 1970s but they also in this period came to perceive the unions as the main cause of Britain's economic decline. Politicians criticised trade unions for producing increases in wages unjustified by rises in productivity, for 'restrictive practices' that prevented management introducing necessary changes in working patterns and staffing levels and for their unofficial strikes, i.e. strikes that not only were not approved by the union leaderships but were often made against their advice (Dorey, 1995, p. 70). However, attempts to reform Britain's system of industrial relations failed. First, Labour's proposals to curb the unions' power to strike in its white paper 'In Place of Strife' (1969) broke down in the face of opposition from the unions, the Parliamentary Labour Party and from within the Cabinet. Then, Heath's Industrial Relations Act (1971), which included a provision for legally enforceable collective wage agreements, was rendered a 'dead letter' by a combination of union resistance and inconsistent judicial decisions. By the late 1970s the trade unions were widely seen by the public as 'overmighty' institutions which had 'defeated' successive governments – Labour and the Conservatives over industrial relations reform in 1969 and 1972; the Conservatives in 1974 – when faced by a miners' strike Heath had lost an election on the issue of 'Who rules? Government or unions?'; and Labour in 1979 when the unions had broken through its pay policy in the 'Winter of Discontent'. In the public perception, a new approach to the trade unions was necessary too.

Cause groups and new social movements

Political participation surged after the late 1950s, bringing a significant increase in diversity and pluralism. New social movements were launched, older ones virtually reinvented and a large number of new cause groups founded. This period saw large numbers enlisting in the movements for peace, second wave feminism and the protection of the environment and joining the lobbies aimed at relieving poverty, enhancing civil liberties and reforming the law on abortion and other 'conscience' issues.

The first major postwar pressure group was the *Campaign for Nuclear Disarmament* (1958). The product of the the the age of nuclear deterrence and the Cold War between the superpowers, CND touched a pacifist vein of sentiment with a long tradition. With a largely middle-class, youthful membership it represented a break with the prevalent pragmatic, deferential, hard-to-mobilise political culture and at its peak was a genuine mass movement able to attract 100 000 in 1961 to the finale of its annual Aldermaston to London march. It captured the Labour Party for unilateral nuclear disarmament in 1960 but declined after the nuclear tests ban and the Cuban missile crisis (1962), which suggested that the superpowers would back down rather than engage in nuclear war. The peace movement focused on the moral indefensibility of nuclear weapons together with the strong possibility of the world sliding into nuclear holocaust sooner or later if states continued to possess them. *Second wave feminism* surfaced in the late 1960s, developing out of the student movement of that era together with the emergence of a new generation of better-educated women disappointed with the progress made by women since the war. The immediate postwar generation of women had benefited from the family allowances and health reforms of the 1940s and had fought for equal pay, which was achieved for women civil servants and teachers in the mid-1950s. The Equal Pay Committee then disbanded, believing that there was not enough support to continue the campaign into industry. Thus, by the late 1960s, 'first wave' liberal feminism which had worked for the suffrage in the 1900s, helped gain welfare reforms in the 1940s and achieved equal pay in some professions in the 1950s, appeared to have run out of steam.

It was re-energised and extended by 'second wave feminism' which began with the first of a series of Women's Liberation conferences at Ruskin College, Oxford in 1970. This and later conferences agreed to campaign for seven basic demands:

- equal pay
- equal education and opportunity
- 24-hour nursery provision
- free contraception and abortion on demand (all agreed in 1970)
- financial and legal independence for women
- no discrimination against lesbians (1974)
- protection against sexual harassment (1978).

The main aims of women's liberation were to politicise sexuality, sexual preference, sexual issues (abortion, contraception) and gender relations, all of which had hitherto been seen as lying within the sphere of private relationships. A loosely structured movement lacking the formal framework associated with male-dominated organisations and with a large number of local branches, women's liberation made some legislative progress in the

1970s. This included the Equal Pay Act (1970), the Sex Discrimination Act (1975), which established the Equal Opportunities Commission to promote awareness of sexism and support test cases, the Employment Protection Act (1975), which introduced rights to maternity leave and to return to work thereafter, and the Domestic Violence Act (1977), which made prosecution easier in the case of violence against women. Although some ground was lost in the 1980s, and the new feminism still had much to achieve in the 1990s when significant inequalities remained in politics, at work and in the home, the movement had transformed attitudes to the role of women in society (Thane, 1994, pp. 392–410; Byrne, 1994, pp. 442–59).

A third social movement, *environmentalism*, achieved expression both through the Ecology Party (1973) and through environmental pressure groups. From the early 1960s there was rising public concern about all three aspects of the environmental movement – preservation of the countryside as an amenity, nature conservation and animal welfare. This led to increases in the membership of old-established groups such as the National Trust (1895), the Council for the Protection of Rural England (1926), the Ramblers Association (1935) and the Royal Society for the Protection of Birds (1889) and the formation of a new generation of campaigning groups such as Friends of the Earth (1970) and Greenpeace (1971) (Figure 2.1). Traditional animal welfare organisations such as the Royal Society for the Prevention of Cruelty to Animals (RSPCA, 1824) and the League against Cruel Sports (1926) were joined by a range of radical direct action organisations such as the Hunt Saboteurs Association (1964) and the Animal Liberation Front (1976). An indication of the rapid expansion of the animal protection movement is that whereas only one new group was formed between 1945 and 1960, eleven new groups emerged in the 1960s and 1970s (Garner, 1993b, p. 333). All told, by 1980, almost a hundred national environmental groups and several thousand local ones were in existence with an estimated combined membership of 2.5–3 million (Lowe and Goyder, 1983, p. 1). Table 2.1 indicates the scale of the increase in membership of some leading environmental groups between the early 1970s and the early 1990s.

Definition 2.3   New social movement

New social movements are radical groups which challenge the existing social and political order on behalf of excluded sections of the population or currently ignored issues. They are often more loosely structured than traditional groups and aim to shift the political agenda and change policies by long-term campaigns aimed at transforming public awareness. Since the 1960s, they have been the main agencies of political participation and mobilisation in Western democratic societies.

The social and moral issues left out by the reforms creating the welfare state in the late 1940s became the major concern of the immediate postwar

Figure 2.1 Friends of the Earth raising the issue of nitrate pollution of water.

Table 2.1 Some leading environmental groups, 1971–92

	1971	1980	1992
Greenpeace	–	10 000	411 000
Friends of the Earth	1 000	12 000	116 000
Ramblers Association	22 000	36 000	94 000
National Trust	–	950 000	2 152 000
Council for Protection of Rural England	21 000	27 000	46 000
World Wide Fund for Nature	12 000	51 000	209 000
Royal Society for the Protection of Birds	98 000	321 000	850 000

Source: *Social Trends* 24 (1994).

generation in the 1950s and 1960s. Reform of the laws on capital punishment, abortion, divorce and homosexuality – the so-called 'conscience' reforms – were called for by middle-class campaigning groups such as the National Campaign for the Abolition of Capital Punishment (1955), the Abortion Law Reform Association (1967), and the Committee for Homosexual Law Reform (1967), which targeted opinion-formers and the political élite. Liberalisation of the law proceeded on all these issues in the late 1960s, largely as a result of a favourably disposed Labour Home Secretary (Roy Jenkins) and of a Labour Government which allowed a free vote on them. Capital punishment was abolished in 1965, abortion on the NHS within 28 weeks of conception and on the consent of two doctors was legalised in 1967, homosexual acts between consenting adults aged 21 and over was permitted by law in the same year, whilst in 1969 the law on divorce was reformed to allow marriages that had broken down to be dissolved after three years by the consent of both parties. The abolition of capital punishment proceeded despite strong opposition of public opinion to the move whilst abortion law reform was contested fiercely by the Society for the Protection of the Unborn Child (1967).

Another notable development of the 1960s was the emergence of a number of pressure groups, often referred to collectively as the 'poverty lobby', whose aim was to remedy deficiencies in the welfare state. The Child Poverty Action Group (1966) campaigned on behalf of low earners and especially children in low income families, arguing for increased family allowances, Shelter (1966) aimed to raise funds for the homeless, and the Disablement Income Group (1966) emerged as a lobby for the disabled. Later, the Low Pay Unit developed out of the Child Poverty Action Group, focusing on the issue of low pay and leaving the original group to concentrate on the needs of poor families. The 1960s groups emerged against the background of consensual welfare politics

BOX 2.2

Explaining the growth of new social movements

A range of different explanations – social, economic, technological, cultural, political and movement-specific – have been offered for the rise of new social movements.

- *The decline of the working class and the emergence of a 'new middle class'.* In the first half of the twentieth century, the major structural division in society was between a numerically predominant but socially unprivileged working class and a dominant business and professional middle class. As a result, class division was a leading motive force in politics, and the labour movement made the political running. However, by the late twentieth century, the working class no longer constituted a majority of the population and the politics of collective solidarity was in decline, leaving political 'space' for people to pursue a politics based on gender, race, the environment, and concern for non-humans rather than on class. At the same time as the working class declined, a 'new middle class' emerged consisting mainly of public sector professionals ideologically predisposed to 'post-materialist values'.

- *Social and economic advance.* Postwar affluence and increased welfare have diminished the significance of a politics based on the satisfaction of material needs and opened the possibility of a new post-materialist politics based on lifestyle values. New social movements recruit from a better-educated, more economically secure generation which is more concerned with quality of life issues than with living standards. This is the argument of the US political scientist Ronald Inglehart; his research in six Western European countries in 1970 suggested that whilst materialist values still predominated in the over 25 age group, post-materialist values were slightly more common amongst 15–24 year olds (cited in Garner, 1996, p. 68). The link between the growth of environmentalism and economic prosperity seems to be confirmed by evidence suggesting that concern for the environment rises in economic booms such as the late 1980s but declines in economic recessions such as the early 1990s (Garner, 1996, p. 68).

- *Technological change.* Contemporary society has become an information society in which new technologies of data-storage and retrieval and of communicating information and opinion have contributed to the upsurge of campaigning pressure groups. In particular, the spread of a dynamic, intrusive mass media relentlessly searching for news stories underlies the rise of single-issue groups which target public opinion.

- *The rise of a new individualist politics.* Trust in Britain's traditional political parties declined from the 1970s, partly because of their seeming inability to solve problems of economic decline but also because of the emergence in the radical student protest movement in the late 1960s of a new politics based on individual freedom and self-fulfilment which had little regard for the old collectivist politics. The emergence of the new social movements was the consequence in part of the search for a more participatory, decentralised, anti-hiercharchical and localised form of politics to replace the existing hierarchical, centralised and Westminster-dominated one.

BOX 2.2 (CONTINUED)

- *Contemporary social failure.* Other interpretations stress a more movement- and cause-specific form of explanation: for example, for explanations of the growth of environmentalism, the new feminism and multi-culturalism, some argue that we need look no further than the facts that the environment was deteriorating and that much still needed to be done to improve the situation of women and the ethnic minorities. Similar arguments could be advanced for the post-1960s rise of the poverty, civil rights and international aid lobbies; i.e. that they emerged because poverty still existed, civil rights were deficient and there was a glaring contrast between a wealthy First World and a poor Third World.

Questions

1. In general, which *type* of explanation of the rise of new social movements do you find most convincing, and why: explanations based on structural factors such as social, economic and cultural change or explanations based on experience and observation of the real world, e.g. the worsening of environmental degradation, the continuation of gender inequality, the existence of racial prejudice, and so on?

2. Is it true that since 1945 a collectivist politics based on class and the satisfaction of material needs and dominated by the two major parties has been displaced by an individualist politics dominated by new social movements and single-issue pressure groups and based on the expression of post-materialist values?

3. Why, and how far, did new social movements become more attractive than political parties as agencies of political participation after the 1960s?

in which poverty was politically significant because of the belief – prevalent in government circles and widely shared by the public – that poverty was an evil which could in principle be alleviated and ought in practice to be remedied, if not abolished.

Phase (3) 1979–1997

The assault on corporatism

The implementation of the Thatcherite agenda of 'rolling back the frontiers of the state' brought Conservative governments after 1979 into serious conflict with the leading sectional interests and professional groups favoured by all previous postwar governments. According to New Right ideology which, with the Conservative victory in the 1979 general election, displaced the dominant social democratic Keynesian consensus, corporatism was the main reason for British economic decline rather than part of the solution to it. The economic case against corporatism was that it had overloaded the state with group demands, paralysing its capacity for effective action. In particular, it had helped bring about an excessive public sector and damagingly high levels of taxation to pay for it. It had produced a situation in which decisions that should have been made by the market were made by groups and government (e.g. on prices, incomes and a range of other matters). It had had an inflationary effect on the whole economy and was one of the the main factors in undermining Britain's ability to compete internationally. The political case against corporatism was: (1) that parliament was being bypassed and that territorial representation based on constituencies was being superseded by *functional* representation of the sectional interests; in other words, the national will as expressed in general elections and represented in parliament was being circumvented by secret, backstairs deals cobbled together by government, business and unions; (2) that citizens not represented by one of the powerful sectional and professional lobbies were losing out to those who were: for example, non-trade unionists were at a disadvantage compared with trade unionists, and consumer interests – pupils, parents, patients and shoppers – were ignored in favour of producer interests, teachers, doctors, farmers; and (3) that Britain was becoming 'ungovernable' as a consequence of the role of overmighty interests such as the trade unions in blocking legislation deemed necessary by the political élite and even in helping to bring down governments by their militancy (King, 1976).

Accordingly, the Conservative governments after 1979 did the following.

- Reasserted the authority of government over the major sectional interests by ending the corporatist system of tripartite consultation and moving to an arm's length relationship with employers and unions; tripartite institutions such as the National Economic Development Council were first sidelined and then abolished.
- Launched a successful legislative and political attack on the legal privileges and economic strength of the trade unions. It severely curtailed trade union powers by legislation (see Table 2.2); made careful preparations for (e.g. by ensuring large stockpiles of coal at power stations) and won major industrial confrontations, e.g. the 1984–85 Miners' Strike; banned trade unions at the government international surveillance headquarters GCHQ; and by prioritising curbing inflation over maintaining high employment allowed a sharp rise in unemployment (to over 3 million in 1986), which undermined union recruitment.

The Thatcherite agenda of 'rolling back the state' involved persistent efforts to curb public spending, to make the public sector more efficient and to reform education and the health service. Together with the general bias of New Right governments towards the private sector, these policies meant that – with the police as a significant exception – intermediate institutions and pressure groups linked to the public sector and public service ethos lost influence.

Table 2.2 Major industrial relations legislation, 1980–93

1980 Employment Act	Removed union immunity from prosecution for secondary picketing
1980 Employment Act	Restrictions on closed shop
1984 Trade Union Act	Required secret ballots before strikes
1988 Employment Act	Required secret ballots for the election of all members of trade union governing bodies
1990 Employment Act	Abolished the closed shop (the requirement that all workers belong to a union)
1992 Trade Union Act	Amalgamated collective employment rights legislation
1993 Trade Union Act	Further restricted ability of trade unions to call strikes (by requirement of 7-day notice of strike action and postal, not workplace, ballots on strikes)

Institutions and groups losing influence included the churches, the BBC and the local government associations; professional bodies such as the BMA, Law Society, civil service unions, and unions representing university lecturers and teachers; and the poverty lobby. Typical of this process was the way in which a classic insider group like the BMA adopted outsider tactics in the late 1980s over the government's refusal to negotiate over a new contract for GPs. It launched a public campaign against the Secretary for Health Kenneth Clarke with advertisements headed 'What do you call a man who ignores medical advice? Answer: Mr Clarke'. But the campaign made little impact and a new contract was imposed on doctors in 1990.

However, Conservative governments were not hostile to all pressure groups and ideological sympathisers gained influence. Thus, although by 1983 the Conservative Government's policies towards industry and general aloofness had goaded the Director General of the CBI into threatening 'a bare-knuckle fight' with it, its relations with other groups became closer. These included the right-wing Institute of Directors; the City, to whom the government turned for advice on deregulation of financial services; the merchant banks and insurance companies; energy producers including the major oil companies; the roads lobby, especially the British Roads Federation, favoured by a pro-car, anti-rail government; large retail groups; estate agents, advantaged by the government's encouragement of owner occupation, including the promotion of council house sales; and advertising agencies and the public relations industry, boosted by the huge expansion in parliamentary and political lobbying and by privatisation. Right-wing 'think-tanks' such as the Adam Smith Institute, the Institute of Economic Affairs and the Centre for Policy Studies influenced government policies on educational and health service reform, family policy and privatisation. Finally, the Conservatives made increased use of voluntary associations such as charities in the delivery of services and were also sympathetic to private health providers and independent schools which could assist in the implementation of their policies.

The rise and rise of new social movements

The explosion of political participation through new social movements and single issue cause groups continued through the 1980s and 1990s. In particular, in addition to a resurgence of the peace movement, there were important developments in multi-cultural and environmental politics.

- *The peace movement.* CND resurfaced in the late 1970s and early 1980s, reinvigorated by what was perceived as an escalation of the superpower nuclear arms race by the NATO decision to introduce a new generation of nuclear missiles in Europe. This phase recruited not only from the left-wing segment of the middle classes but also from women politicised by the new feminism, some of whom set up a peace camp at Greenham Common in Berkshire. At its peak in the mid-1980s, CND had about 85 000 members nationally whilst another 100 000 belonged to local CND or peace groups and mass demonstrations attracted up to 400 000 participants. The movement waned in the late 1980s following the superpower agreements to scale down their holdings of nuclear weapons and the collapse of the Soviet Union.

- *Multi-culturalism.* There were several episodes that ensured a high political profile for issues of freedom of speech, blasphemy, equality of citizenship, minority rights and the enforcement of the law on racial harassment. The Rushdie Affair (1989) came about when the Ayatollah Khomeini issued a *fatwa* against the author Salmon Rushdie for his book *The Satanic Verses*, which was considered to be offensive to Islam. In effect, this edict pardoned any Muslim who should kill Rushdie, which led to the author's retreat into a secret existence under constant police protection. One political result of the ensuing furore, which liberals saw in terms of the right of freedom of expression and many Muslims in terms of blasphemy against their religion, was to bring British Muslims together, an experience that helped produce the Muslim Parliament (1992), claimed to be the first representative body of British Muslims. The non-elected parliament was established by Dr Khalim Siddiqui to represent 'a non-territorial Islamic state' in Britain but was opposed by Dr Hesham el-Esawy, President of the Islamic Society for the Promotion of Racial Tolerance, on the grounds that it would intensify anti-Islamic feeling. The Muslim Council (1997) was launched to provide a focus and structure for cooperation within the Muslim community with the hope of attracting government funding for Muslim cultural and community centres. Finally, with racial incidents and racial harassment an everyday occurrence at street level, groups such as the Campaign against Racism and Fascism and the Anti-Nazi League sought to combat racism in society.

- *Protection of the environment.* (1) The environmental movement experienced a massive expansion, nearly doubling its membership to about 5 million and more than tripling its income to around £200 million. (2) Groups like Greenpeace moved towards a more moderate strategy based on research-based appeals to policy-makers, industry and public, and the provision of services and solutions whilst more radical groups such as Earth First! and Earth Liberation Front emerged to challenge traditional groups like Friends of the Earth. (3) Coordination of efforts grew with the issue of joint statements on government policy, e.g. on water and electricity privatisation, and Friends of the Earth cooperated with other groups on changes to the water privatisation bill. (4) Some shift in influence occurred on countryside matters away from traditionally dominant groups such as the NFU towards the conservation lobby. The erosion of farmers' influence was assisted by food 'scares' over salmonella in chickens and BSE in beef. (5) The environmental lobby in common with many sectional groups focused increasingly on the EU, with Greenpeace, Friends of the Earth and World Wildlife Fund all establishing offices in Brussels. (6) In the early 1990s, anti-roads protest dominated the headlines with 250 anti-road groups brought together in 1991 under the umbrella organisation Alarm UK. The government roads programme outlined in its 1989 White Paper was seen as unnecessary and too costly and after a series of well-publicised protests, the programme was scaled down in 1996. (7) The animal rights lobby achieved increasing prominence, with the issue receiving constant media attention through the activities of the Hunt Saboteurs, the campaign against animal experiments by the Animal Liberation Front and the protests at the ports against live animal exports in the mid-1990s.

Current trends and prospects: pressure groups and New Labour

It is still too soon to establish definitively whether the Blair Government will mark a new phase of government–group relations. But certain trends are already becoming clear.

New Labour, business and unions: the changing relationship

New Labour's adoption of neo-liberal, Thatcherite economics proceeded together with its determined attempt to reassure British business that New Labour believes in free markets and the right of management to manage. By the 1997 General Election, polls indicated that Labour was no longer seen as a threat by businessmen, a finding that was reinforced by some top company chairmen (Granada, Great Universal Stores) declaring support for Labour. A poll of businessmen showed that 80 per cent were not worried by the prospect of a Labour Government whilst 15 per cent actually thought businesses would do better under Labour. A key issue was Europe. Generally pro-EU, big business feared the election of a right-wing Conservative Government hostile to Europe, some of whose ministers would like Britain to withdraw from the EU. These fears seemed amply confirmed after the election when the new Conservative leader William Hague adopted the position that Britain should not join a single currency for at least a decade whilst, according to the CBI but not the Institute of Directors, big business opinion had hardened in favour of a British entry soon after the millennium (*The Guardian*, 6 and 10 November 1997). However, the CBI strongly disagreed with Labour on issues such as the minimum wage and the European Social Chapter – to which Labour signed up immediately after gaining power. Nonetheless, New Labour's relations with business were far closer than in past Old Labour administrations, a symbol of them being the appointment of a leading businessman, the chairman of BP, Sir David Simon, to a top government job in charge of trade and competitiveness policy.

An essential part of the 'modernisation' of Labour was the deliberate distancing of the party from the trade unions. The party's internal reforms in the 1990s steadily reduced union influence within the party at all levels – at Conference, on the National Executive Committee, in the appointment of leader and in the selection and sponsorship of parliamentary candidates (see Chapter 6). At the same time, in its public policy stance, New Labour was careful to stress that the unions could expect no special favours and that there would be no return to the corporatist era of settling the national economic problems between Prime Minister and TUC over 'beer and sandwiches' at No. 10. Conservative trade union legislation would remain on the statute book, leaving Britain, in Blair's words, with 'a more restricted trade union legislative framework than any country in the Western world'. On the other hand, the Labour Government *was* closer to the unions than the Conservatives had been between 1979 and 1997. Shortly after the election, the TUC general secretary was welcomed into Downing Street for private talks with a British Prime Minister for the first time for over a decade. By late 1997, New Labour had pleased the TUC by entering the Social Chapter, removing the ban on unions at GCHQ, and indicating its willingness to look favourably on a right to union recognition and greater employee rights at work. The appointment of the centre-left academic George Bain as chairman of the Low Pay Commission rather than Tony Blair's original choice, Whitbread chief executive Peter Jarvis, was hailed by union officials as their first lobbying achievement of the Labour Government. In addition, despite business promises to provide more money for Labour, the unions remained the party's chief paymasters. Although the trade unions' contribution to party funds dropped from 75 per cent to 50 per cent between 1986 and 1996, they still contributed over £11 million to Labour's 1997 election campaign.

The impact of changing social preferences

Meanwhile, other indications of the way in which a change in government had brought changing social preferences were the fierce struggles between pressure groups unleashed by Labour's manifesto promises of a ban on cigarette advertising, greater freedom for people to explore the open countryside and a free vote on a ban on hunting with hounds. By early 1998, Labour had been forced into a partial retraction of its promise on cigarette advertising after determined lobbying by the Formula One chief Bernie Ecclestone; it allowed landowners two years to achieve voluntary agreements on ramblers' rights of access to land; and it had been faced with a massive London demonstration of over 250 000 organised by the Countryside Alliance largely in defence of fox-hunting – the largest since CND rallies in the early 1980s. In terms of lifestyle politics, Labour developed further the libertarian politics of John Major's Conservative administration. Under Major, then Blair, gay and lesbian groups were no longer excluded as they were during the socially authoritarian years of unsympathetic Thatcher governments. The director of Stonewall informed the press that under New Labour there had been a 'sea change in attitude'. Although not initially successful, Labour set about repealing section 28 of a Local Government Act introduced by a Thatcher government which banned the 'promotion' of homosexuality in schools.

Summary

- The adoption by postwar governments of policies of Keynesian economic management and the welfare state enhanced the status of sectional business and union groups which became involved in close consultative relationships with government.

- From these new, consultative relationships, government gained the co-operation and advice it needed to carry out its policies whilst groups gained the chance to influence government policy in their own interests.

- Down to 1960, postwar governments relied on exhortation of employers and unions to restrain dividend, price and wage increases within a framework of voluntarist industrial relations and wage bargaining.

- Important sets of relations were established between government and sectional groups within individual departments. One such set of relationships was the *sponsorship divisions* to promote the interests of particular industries which the CBI later described as the most important relationship a businessman was likely to have with government.

- Other sectional interests such as farmers (NFU) and doctors (BMA) became part of *policy communities* inside, respectively, the Ministry of Agriculture,

Fisheries and Food (MAFF) and the Ministry of Health. A policy community is at one end of a spectrum of relationships between officials and group representatives within departments which goes by the generic term *policy networks*. It involves continuous, stable relationships between civil servants and a small number of groups, in which participants share the same broad policy objectives. By contrast, at the opposite end of the spectrum are *issue networks* which are characterised by discontinuous, less close relations between officials and a larger number of groups, open access and greater conflict over policy aims and values.

- Britain's economic decline was the main factor in bringing about increased government intervention in the economy after 1960, a phase of government–producer group relationships often described as *corporatist*. Corporatism involved very close collaboration between government, CBI and TUC in the making and implementation of economic policy, especially incomes policies. Governments' perception of 'irresponsible' trade unionism as a major factor in national decline led to attempts to reform industrial relations, but without success before 1979.

- A huge surge of political participation started in the early 1960s with the peace movement (CND) and continued in the early 1970s with the women's liberation movement and a growing popular interest in protection of the environment. Political lobbying brought about the so-called 'permissive society' reforms of the laws on abortion, divorce, homosexuality and capital punishment in the 1960s which also saw the formation of the 'poverty lobby' to correct what were seen as defects in the welfare state.

- After 1979, Conservative implementation of the New Right agenda of 'rolling back the state' and a free market economy led to a new phase of government–pressure group relations. The major sectional groups lost policy influence, being kept at arm's length by government which thereby ended corporatist relations. The trade unions were hit hard by government: their privileges were curbed by legislation, their membership was eroded by heavy unemployment and a large-scale miners' strike ended in heavy defeat. However, certain groups gained influence, mainly those who supported New Right ideology and those required to help implement government policies.

- New social movements continued to gain ground in the 1980s, with millions flocking to the causes of peace and environmentalism. In the 1990s, significant developments occurred in ethnic minority politics whilst environmental protesters were involved in direct action to stop new road-building and advance animal rights.

- New Labour came to power determined not to go back to the old corporatist-style government–sectional group relations of the 1970s. Its relations with business were closer and its attitude to the unions cooler than those of previous Labour administrations. Both CBI and TUC preferred

Labour to the Conservatives, the former because of its more sympathetic attitude to the EU, especially the single currency; the latter because Labour adopted the Social Chapter, allowed unions back to GCHQ, seemed prepared to introduce a minimum wage and held out the possibility of union recognition and enhanced employee rights at work.

Further reading

On postwar trade unions and their relations with government, D. Marsh (1992) *The New Politics of British Trade Unionism* (London: Macmillan) and R. Taylor (1993) *The Trade Union Question in British Politics* (Oxford: Blackwell) should be consulted. On postwar relations between government and the major sectional interests, see K. Middlemas (1979) *Politics in Industrial Society* (London: Andre Deutsch) and specifically on business, C. Miller (1991) 'Lobbying' in G. Jordan (ed.) *The Commercial Lobbyists* (Aberdeen: Aberdeen University Press) and W. Grant (1993) *Business and Politics in Britain*, 2nd edn (London: Macmillan). On postwar social movements, there are P. Byrne (1994) 'Pressure groups and popular campaigns' and P. Thane (1994) 'Women since 1945' in P. Johnson (ed.) *Twentieth Century Britain* (London: Longman); J. Lovenduski and V. Randall (1993) *Contemporary Feminist Politics* (Oxford: Oxford University Press); R. Garner (1993a) *Animals, Politics and Morality* (Manchester: Manchester University Press); and R. Garner (1996) *Environmental Politics* (London: Palgrave).

CHAPTER 3

Pressure groups and Europe

Pressure groups have always played a prominent part in the European Union, both in shaping its development and in influencing its decision-making on a day-to-day basis. The role of agricultural interests in the early 1970s and of business in the mid-1980s may be cited as two brief examples of the lobbying power of major interests both in defending and in creating a position of advantage within the Community. Thus, first, in the early decades of the Community, with the Common Agricultural Policy, a system of price support for farmers, accounting for the bulk of its budget and being the only policy that was decided at Community level, agricultural interests were the main interests represented at European level. When, as part of his plan to restructure European agriculture, the Commissioner in charge of agriculture, Sicco Mansholt, proposed a cut in price levels to force inefficient farmers off the land, his proposal was dubbed 'a psychological blunder' by the Community's farming pressure group. Worse, the plan triggered a major riot which effectively destroyed the proposal. In the words of one authority: '...the Council of Agricultural Ministers ... were accompanied to Brussels by 80 000 demonstrating farmers, who hung Mansholt in effigy, burned cars, tore up street signs, broke windows, killed one policeman, and injured 140 more of the 3 000 deployed to restrain them' (George and Sowemimo, 1996, p. 181). Second, in the 1980s, after years of little progress towards further integration, European business played a major part in the 'relaunching of Europe' by the Single European Act (1986). Fearful of the intensified economic competition from the United States, Japan and the newly industrialised countries of South East Asia, the leaders of the largest European companies pressed for the creation of a European single market, which eventually came into existence in 1992. As Justin Greenwood has observed: 'In the shape of the ERT (European Round Table – a select group of the leaders of Europe's largest firms), they helped provide the blueprint and much of the impetus for the single market, and, where member states faltered or showed signs of a loss of nerve, business was there encouraging, prodding, or, if necessary, threatening removal of investment' (Greenwood, 1997, p. 254). For European big business, an integrated European economy roughly similar in terms of GDP to that of the United States and 40 per cent larger than that of Japan improved conditions for their ability to compete in the global marketplace and they therefore lobbied hard – and successfully – for its creation. These are especially dramatic examples of Euro lobbying by major interests. Few groups possess the political clout of farmers and business. Nonetheless, lobbying Europe has increased in importance for most groups in the 1990s. This chapter examines several key themes: the growth of Euro lobbying since the Single European Act (1986); the main strategies employed by groups; how groups organise to lobby EU institutions; the targets of Euro lobbying; policy networks in the European Union; and the overall impact of group lobbying on the European Union.

The expansion of Euro lobbying

The Single European Act (SEA, 1986) and the Treaty of European Union (TEU, 1992 – often referred to as the Maastricht Treaty) marked a significant stage in the development of the European Community/Union after a long period of standing still. The effects of the two Acts were to extend the scope of Community/Union policy-making to areas previously the responsibility of national governments and, by reforming the decision-making process, to weaken the influence of national governments at European level. Thus, the Single European Act committed member states to completing a single European market (the free movement of goods, services, capital and labour within the EC) by the end of 1992, and strengthened European-level policy-making in a number of areas not mentioned or only touched upon in the original treaties – economic and political cohesion, research and technology, the environment and social policy. It also removed the need for unanimous decisions on the Council of Ministers by introducing qualified majority voting (QMV) in policies relating to the single market and strengthened the legislative powers of the European Parliament by giving it a right of second reading over legislation covered by qualified majority voting. The Treaty of European Union further extended the range of decisions the Council of Ministers could determine by majority votes to include the free movement of capital, transport, research and technology, the environment and social policy, and further increased the powers of the European Parliament (Mazey and Richardson, 1992, pp. 92–5). In addition, under the Agreement on Social Policy in the TEU, employers' organisations and trade unions (the 'social partners') gained important powers, including the right to be consulted by the European Commission on social policy and to conclude agreements themselves (Greenwood, 1997, p. 54).

The overall impact of these treaty developments transformed the policy-making system confronting pressure groups. Before the SEA, much lobbying of the European Community was conducted through national governments. Because power was concentrated in the Council of Ministers where each country possessed a veto, groups relied upon national administrations to defend their interests. It was also the case that, although EC law was supreme over national legislation, the scope of Community legislation was limited and hence many groups had little interest in the EC policy process. However, after 1986, with the move to QMV on a number of policies in the Council of Ministers, groups could no longer rely on their governments alone to defend their interests; rather, it made sense for them both to seek to influence EC policy-making at an earlier stage and to try to build coalitions with groups in other states when decisions reached the Council of Ministers. In addition, with the European Parliament being given the power of co-decision by the TEU, it became a greater focus for lobbying by public interest groups. The nature of the change should not be exaggerated: as already noted, interests have always played an important role in the European Community, especially in such sectors as coal, steel and agriculture. By 1980, 439 Euro-groups (transnational federations) existed and specific firms and industries were also active at European level. But the SEA and TEU, by shifting power away from national governments towards the EC/EU and by changing the institutional balance of power within the European institutions themselves, led to both an intensification of Euro lobbying and to an expansion in the diversity and range of interests represented at European level. By the early 1990s, according to the European Commission (1992), there were 525 Euro-groups in Brussels; approximately 3000 interest groups, a figure that includes firms, professions, employers' associations, trade unions, and a wide range of cause groups as well as the transnational associations and federations; and in all about 10 000 individuals involved in interest representation (Greenwood, 1997, p. 3).

The shift of power to the European Union

It is no longer possible to understand the policy process in ... the member states of the EC(EU) – and especially that of pressure groups in that process – without taking account of the shift in power to Brussels.

(S. Mazey and J. Richardson, in Richardson (ed.) (1993), p. 191)

BOX 3.1

The lobby to save duty free

The European Union set 1 July 1999 as the date for the ending of duty free shopping and the plan triggered an expensive last-ditch lobbying campaign in 1997–98 by an alliance of transport unions, ferry companies, port operators, airlines and airports – the International Duty Free Confederation (IDFC). The IDFC and its sister organisations

BOX 3.1 (CONTINUED)

in 15 EU states were lobbying to save a huge industry worth £12 billion a year worldwide (£4.6 billion in Europe, £1 billion in Britain) which employed 140 000 people throughout the EU. The lobby spent over £1 billion in early 1998 alone and appeared to be having some effect when EU transport ministers voted to commission a study into the possible effects of abolition, thereby deciding, much to the annoyance of the Brussels Commission, to reopen the matter seven years after the original proposal to terminate duty free. There was other support too: Ireland, where duty free began at Shannon airport in 1947, came out against abolition whilst some leading politicians (John Prescott (UK), Lionel Jospin (France) and Gerhard Schroeder, presidential candidate in Germany) favoured a review of the ban. There were also signs of disquiet in the British public, concerned about the loss of duty free jaunts to France and the possible increases in travel costs resulting from the ban.

The IDFC argued that duty free:

- provided a large number of jobs (140 000) which the EU should be protecting rather than destroying; one third would disappear if duty free ended

- helped keep fares down; travel costs between member states might rise significantly if duty free were banned

- enabled investment in better airports and new ships and planes whereas ending duty free would close half of local airports and make long-haul ferry services unviable

- furnished an international showcase for European products.

The EU Commission argued that:

- banning duty free was part of the long-term aim of the single market to prevent different tax and duty rates between member countries

- it was illogical to give travellers of a particular nationality (e.g. British) and certain types of travellers (e.g. by plane or ship) a comparative advantage over other nationals and types of traveller: for example, duty free existed between London and Paris but not between London and Manchester and there was duty free for travellers between London and Paris by ship or plane but not by rail or bus

- the duty free industry had had seven years to prepare for the end of the concession but had used the time to lobby against the change instead

- duty free was a confidence trick in that many duty free goods could be bought cheaper elsewhere, e.g. red wine, which was cheaper in France than on the ferries; airlines, airports and ferry operators should find other ways to invest their money

- all taxpayers bore the burden of a massive subsidy to certain sections of the travel industry (ferries, airlines) and a few regular travellers.

However, in May 1998, European Finance Ministers refused a reprieve for the ban with the result that duty free shopping ended on 1 July 1999. Mario Monti, the European Commissioner for the Single Market, summed up the decision as follows: 'The interests of a vast silent majority are being protected against the interests of a vocal minority'. The chief executive of BAA, the privatised airports operator, predicted a £10 increase in fares to enable airlines and airport operators to recoup their losses but many

BOX 3.1 (CONTINUED)

groups in Britain welcomed the decision including the National Institute of Economic and Social Research, the Consumers' Association, the Brewers' and Licensed Retailers' Association and the National Federation of Retail Newsagents.

(Sources: *The Economist*, 27 September 1997; *The Guardian*, 19 March and 27 May 1998; *The Observer*, 24 May 1998)

Questions

1. Identify the 'silent majority' who allegedly gain and the 'vocal minority' who lose from the ending of the ban on duty free.

2. Why, in your view, did the groups representing brewers and retail newsagents welcome the decision to end duty free shopping?

3. How far is it reasonable to describe the lobbying activities of the IDFC as 'a fire brigade campaign'?

Strategies of Euro lobbying

British pressure groups may seek influence in Europe either through the 'national route' or the 'European route' or through a combination of the two strategies. Use of the national route by a group involves seeking influence at either the policy formation stage or the policy implementation stage, or both. Influence at the policy formation stage may be sought at the point of final decision by lobbying the British government to press its case on the Council of Ministers. This route may appear attractive to a group because, in addition to lobbying on behalf of national interests at the Council of Ministers, governments also defend sectional interests there. Groups can use established channels (policy networks) to persuade ministers to adopt their case and they may also establish direct contact with British civil servants on COREPER, the committee of permanent representatives, who are often involved in brokering last-minute compromises between states as the basis for decisions by the Council of Ministers. British governments in the 1990s espoused sectional interests such as farmers, the fishing industry and industrialists (the CBI and Institute of Directors) at this final stage of European Union decision-making over respectively the beef crisis, fishing quotas and the opt-out from the TEU's Social Chapter.

A group may also use the national route at the *policy implementation* stage. The European Union has very weak enforcement powers and relies on member states to implement its directives. Implementation records of member states vary. On the single market, for example, Commission figures in early 1997 showed Britain as having one of the best records on implementation of directives – it was behind only Holland and Denmark and had translated

94.31 per cent of the 1423 edicts into law compared with France's 90.9 per cent and Germany's 89.95 per cent records. Nonetheless, influencing policies at the implementation stage remains a constant possibility for groups in all member states including Britain. As Grant points out: 'Because translating Union directives into action on the ground is the task of member states, a range of possibilities is opened up for exemption, delay and modification which can be highly beneficial to particular interests' (Grant, 1995, p. 102). At the implementation stage, trade associations may engage in 'damage-limitation' by trying to exempt a particular category of companies altogether from a directive or removing certain of a company's most sensitive products from a proposal or achieving as late a starting point as possible for the legislation (Sargent, 1993, cited in Grant, 1995, p. 102). The national route remains important, therefore, for two main reasons: (1) final decision within the EU remains with the Council of Ministers; and (2) implementation of EU directives is a matter for national governments.

The national route has a certain appeal to groups but also has drawbacks. Its advantages include the ability of groups to tap into well-established relationships with government through the use of existing policy networks; and, in particular, if the group represents an interest of strategic importance for the national economy, to enlist the natural sympathies of its own government. Equally, lobbying national government may appeal to small firms and public interest groups that lack the resources to adopt a Brussels strategy (Greenwood, 1997, p. 33). However, there are high risks for a group in being solely reliant on a national strategy. First, however closely the government may wish to identify with a group's interest, it always has to bear in mind the national interest, which may not warrant its total commitment to a specific sectional cause. Second, even where the government is totally committed to pushing a particular case, it may simply be outvoted on the Council of Ministers. Third, the government operates in a political environment within the European Union in which compromise is 'the name of the game'; concessions on one issue in return for past, present or possible future support on others are constantly required and it may be just 'tough luck' for an interest if its demands are bargained away in such situations. Fourth, and finally, there have been cases of group interests – especially on technical issues – being given away inadvertently by ministers who do not understand the full significance of the matter before them (Grant, 1995, p. 101). Rather than relying on the national route alone, many groups today seek to strengthen their lobbying position by combining it with the 'European route', or 'Brussels strategy'.

Definition 3.1   The national route

The national route refers to pressure group attempts to influence European Union decisions by persuading their national administrations to pursue their cause at the Council of Ministers or to amend or delay EU laws.

Pursuit of the *European route* to influencing decisions in the European Community/Union has become more important to groups since the SEA and TEU. As already noted, these Acts shifted power from national governments to EU institutions by giving the EU new competencies, enhancing the role of the EU Commission in policy initiation, removing the national veto on the Council of Ministers, strengthening the European Parliament and conferring increased powers on the 'social partners', EU-level employers' and workers' organisations. As a supranational organisation, the European Union is less than a state in that it relies for enforcement and implementation of its decisions on its members. But as a confederation in which member states have pooled elements of their sovereignty, it has the power to make authoritative decisions and this makes it into a kind of state. As a 'quasi-state', therefore, the EU represents to a considerable and increasing degree 'where the power is' and hence rewards the effort and expense of direct lobbying. Specific benefits acquired by a group with a Brussels office or representation on a transnational 'Euro-group' include advance or early stage intelligence of measures about to be considered by the Commission and an opportunity to shape measures through contacts with EU officials and/or influence them at an early stage. Because the structure of decision-making in the EU is highly complex and the actual process of decision-making highly unpredictable, this puts a premium for groups on getting early warning of planned measures or about the latest developments on measures already in the pipeline: '. . . in many ways the real benefits of lobbying are to minimise one's surprises' (Mazey and Richardson, 1993, p. 21). In the world of lobbying groups, forewarned is forearmed and may enable a group to react early enough to a proposal to influence its outcome. Secondly, a presence in Brussels allows a group to build relationships with EU officials and as a consequence permits 'continuous trading' to take place between groups and Brussels policy-makers. Such constant to-ing and fro-ing between groups and Commission officials makes EU policies 'as much peace treaties between competing interests and nations as they are "rational" decisions' (Mazey and Richardson, 1993, p. 21). Having an input into policy at the pre-publication stage is particularly important for groups simply because such a high proportion of a proposal – about 80 per cent according to one Brussels bureacrat – is retained in the final Commission directive. As a lobbying strategy, influencing policy at its formative stages is more likely to be effective than fighting a last ditch 'fire brigade campaign' aimed at persuading European ministers to reverse or abandon a policy already announced (see Box 3.1). One feature facilitating use of the European route is ease of access to leading EU institutions such as the Brussels Commission and the European Parliament (although not to the Council of Ministers). As Justin Greenwood points out: '. . . in most cases it is possible to simply pick up the phone and dial in order to speak to an official or parliamentarian, or even to call by on a passing visit to Brussels' (Greenwood, 1997, p. 52). To sum up, the European route became of increasing importance to groups in the 1990s and the remainder of this chapter is accordingly devoted to explaining the various ways in which groups organise to lobby the EU, how they select their targets among EU institutions and their overall impact on Europe.

Definition 3.2   **The European route**

The European route, or 'Brussels strategy', refers to pressure group attempts to influence European Union decisions by lobbying the European Union institutions themselves, either directly or through membership of a Euro-group.

Organising to lobby the European Union

Groups can lobby the European Union either *directly* or through membership of a *Euro-group. Direct lobbying* can be done from the home country by phone or written communication, but increasingly for British groups is done by establishing a presence on the European mainland – from offices in (or near to) Brussels itself. In a survey of over 100 British pressure groups conducted in the early 1990s, not only did two-thirds of groups report increased contacts over the previous decade, but also 12 per cent of groups had established a Brussels office (Baggott, 1992, p. 21). Direct lobbying has always been important for business and farming groups but since the late 1980s has become increasingly important for trade union, consumer and environmental groups too. The reasons that these particular interests have established direct representation at EU level are not far to seek. They relate first to the extent and nature of matters that are now decided by the European Union or for which responsibility is shared between the EU and member states. Thus, the EU has extensive policy involvement in matters relating to trade, agriculture, fishing and the internal market whilst responsibility for policies including competition, industry, energy, transport, equal opportunities, working conditions, consumer protection and the environment is shared with member states (Nugent, 1994, p. 293). Second, Brussels has been called an 'insider's town' in which wealthy insider groups enjoy considerable advantages over those without a Brussels presence (Greenwood, 1997, p. 37). British pressure groups with Brussels offices in the late 1990s include the Confederation of British Industry, at least 25 companies, the Trades Union Congress, the General, Municipal and Boilermakers Union, the Law Society, Amnesty International, Greenpeace and Friends of the Earth. The role of the Brussels office of the CBI is to maintain contacts with the European Commission and the European Parliament; to advise the CBI and its members on lobbying European institutions; on occasion to engage in direct lobbying of EU institutions (about 20 per cent of CBI representations to European institutions are made by the Brussels office); and to forge links with the Euro-group, UNICE (see below) (Grant, 1993, pp. 169–74). The cost of setting up a Brussels office is one of the

BOX 3.2

The TUC adopts a strongly pro-European line

After years of coolness towards the European Community, the TUC adopted a strongly pro-European line in 1988 for two main reasons. First, throughout the 1980s it had been consistently cold-shouldered and the union movement deprived of rights and privileges by Conservative governments at home. Second, at the 1988 TUC annual conference, the French socialist and former Commission president Jacques Delors held out the prospect of a 'social dimension' within the European Union, involving enhanced concern for workers' rights and industrial democracy to offset the free market pro-business orientation of the EU's industrial and commercial policies. He wanted the trade unions to be written into Europe's social and economic decision-making and he was keen for new social policy initiatives in Europe to come about as a result of social dialogue between unions and employers, the new 'social partners'. For British labour, this gave the only prospect of advancing worker rights available. As Ron Todd, the then general secretary of the Transport and General Workers Union, stated at the 1988 TUC conference: 'The only card game in town at the moment is in a town called Brussels, and it is a game of poker where we have got to learn the rules and learn them fast'. The TUC now maintains two representatives in Brussels and the General, Municipal, Boilermakers and Allied Trades Union (GMBATU) has a one-person office. Since the late 1980s, British trade unionism has participated at two levels in Europe. First, together with the German DGB, the TUC works through ETUC, the European Trade Union Confederation, which enjoys insider status with DG V of the Commission (Employment, Industrial Relations and Social Affairs), gained prestige following its institution as a 'social partner' alongside UNICE at the Treaty of European Union (1992), with leading business groups co-wrote the Social Charter in 1992, and post-1995 called for a full employment strategy to restore 'balance' to economic and monetary union. The Social Charter seeks to improve the rights of European workers by establishing a shorter working week, the right to belong or not to belong to a union; the right to strike; the right of unions to engage in collective bargaining; the right of workers to receive information and be consulted about the operation of companies; and greater protection for part-time, temporary, young, disabled and retired workers. Second, the TUC and the large unions kept up the pressure on British governments to implement pro-worker European legislation such as the Social Charter (finally implemented by Britain, 1997) and other European social policy initiatives such as the Works Councils Directive and on the European Union to deliver employment-creating and employment-protecting policies across Europe.

(Sources: Greenwood (1997); Mazey and Richardson (1997); *The Guardian*, 12 September 1995, 9 September 1996)

Questions

1. Why did the TUC adopt 'a strongly pro-European' line in the late 1980s?

2. Find out and briefly explain why British trade unionism was generally unsympathetic towards the European Community and British membership of it before the late 1980s.

3. Why has gaining benefits for labour been an uphill struggle for trade unionists even at European level in the 1980s and 1990s?

4. What is the Social Charter?

main reasons that over two-thirds of all groups based in Brussels are business groups (Greenwood, 1997, p. 10). The expansion of the range of areas affected by EU policy-making helps explain why a widening range of groups, especially labour, environmental and consumer groups, are prepared to support the financial cost of a Brussels office in the 1990s.

The other main way in which a British pressure group or major interest can lobby the EU is by *working through a Euro-group*. The 1992 survey of over 100 British business, labour and preference groups (i.e. charities, cause and ideological groups) already mentioned found that a large majority of them (75 per cent) were members of a Euro-group (Baggott, 1992, p. 21). Perhaps it is not so surprising that working through a Euro-group is so popular since the European Commission retains its original preference for dealing through Euro-groups where possible as these are often (although not always) compre-hensive groupings able to speak authoritatively for interests and sectors across the whole European Union. For example, UNICE represents European business, ETUC seeks to advance the interests of European labour whilst CEFIC (European Chemical Industry Council) is a powerful organisation able to draw on large resources (it has a headquarters staff of 80 and can spend millions of ECUs per year) to represent the European chemical industry. The Commission allocates places on its advisory committees to Euro-groups before giving any to single interests, often gives drafts of directives to European business sector associations for comment and provides significant sums of money to encourage non-business groups to operate at European level. For example, the trade union Euro-group, ETUC, and its related associations were estimated to be in receipt of about £4 million ECUs per annum from the Commission in the early 1990s whilst the environmental Euro-group (EEB) got about half its total funding from European institutions, including a grant of over 400 000 ECU in 1995 (Greenwood, 1997, pp. 3–4, 168, 186). The breakdown of formal European-level groups is as follows: business, 67 per cent; public interest, including environmental, consumer and civil/social groupings, 21 per cent; professions, 10 per cent; and trade union, 3 per cent. Two-thirds of Euro-groups are federations of national associations and the remainder are direct membership organisations or hybrid groupings made up of national associations and individual firms. UNICE and ETUC are both federations of national associations whilst ERT (European Round Table) is a direct membership association consisting of 40 executives of some of the largest multinational firms in the world (see Table 3.1).

How effective are Euro-groups? A certain division of opinion exists between academic observers. Some academics have argued that many European confederations (two-thirds of all Euro-groups) find it difficult to be really effective European-level lobbyists (Grant, 1995, p. 105). Typical difficulties include inadequate resources and problems in developing common platforms among their diverse national memberships. Some federations have collapsed because of an inability to develop a policy consensus among the diverse national interests they represent, as the Committee of Common Market

Table 3.1 The main Euro-groups

Name	Founded	HQ staff	Membership	Comments
Business				
UNICE (Union of Industries in the European Community)	1958	30	32	Main employers group
ERT (European Round Table)	1983		46	'Rich club' consisting of chief executives of top multinational companies
AM-CHAM-EU (EU Committee of the American Chamber of Commerce)	1985	17	150	Voice of US business in Europe
EUROCHAMBRES	1958		32	Confederation of national associations of chambers of commerce
Agriculture				
COPA (Committee of Agricultural Organisations in the EC)	1958	approx. 50	22	Confederation of national and regional farmers' unions
Trade union				
ETUC (European Trade Union Confederation)	1972	49	48	Main EU trade union group
Environmental				
EEB (European Environmental Bureau)	1974	11	136	Main EU environmental group
Consumer				
BEUC (European Bureau of Consumer Unions)	1962	13	25	Main voice consumer of interests

Automobile Constructors did in 1990, and even apparently successful Euro-groups such as UNICE and ETUC face continuing difficulties in achieving coherent positions on issues. Some groups such as the farmers' lobbyist COPA have declined in influence as the agricultural budget has fallen and as EU concerns have diversified. However, against this, it has been pointed out that a number of European federations are both well-resourced and effective lobbyists: such groups include the European Confederation of Iron and Steel Industries (EUROFER) and the European Federation of Pharmaceutical Industry Associations (EFPIA). It should also be remembered that group confederations possess the great advantage in dealings with the Commission of being inclusive of all major interests in their domains. Direct membership organisations, which include in associations such as AM-CHAM-EU and ERT some of the most effective lobbying organisations in the European Union, lack this 'one-stop shop' characteristic, a considerable drawback so far as the Commission is concerned (Greenwood, 1997, pp. 61–71, 110–17).

Targets for group influence in the European Union

Decision-making in the European Union is a complex, multi-level process and groups must be prepared to pursue influence at more than one level. None-theless, the main targets for groups reflect their assessment of where power mainly lies in Europe and they therefore tend to focus on the European Commission and the Council of Ministers without neglecting the Euro-pean Parliament and the European Court of Justice.

The European Commission

Although both the Council and European Parliament can prompt proposals from it, the European Commission is formally responsible for the initiation and implementation of all EU policies. It is the only EU institution which is involved in each of the different stages of the policy cycle, from agenda-setting to the formulation and implementation of a policy. This central role in EU policy-making makes the Commission the primary target for most interests and groups for whom the administrative structure of the Commission there-fore becomes of considerable importance. It is headed by 17 Commissioners (two each from the major countries, one each from the rest) who are expected by both groups and member states to defend their interests in EU policy-making (Mazey and Richardson, 1993, p. 200). Commission decisions are taken by the College of Commissioners, if necessary by majority vote. Leading national groups such as the CBI and leading Euro-groups such as COPA enjoy regular meetings with individual Commissioners, thus possessing, in view of the 'considerable amount of horsetrading' that takes place between Commissioners, 'a real opportunity' to exercise influence, albeit a 'fairly unreliable' one (Hull, cited in Mazey and Richardson, 1993, p. 84). Com-missioners are supported by small *cabinets*, whose heads prepare the agenda for weekly meetings of Commissioners. However, legislative proposals originate at a lower level of the Commission and most groups therefore target their efforts at one or more of the 23 Directorates-General into which the Commission is divided. Directorates-General (DGs) are the basic units of organisation of the Commission; each specialises in a particular policy area and has a staff of between 120 and 850. The main focus for lobbyists is the permanent staff within a DG who prepare the initial drafts of proposals: thus, for example, business groups will be in regular contact with the DGs dealing with Economic and Financial affairs, the Internal Market and Industrial Affairs and Competition (DGs II–IV), labour groups with the DG handling Employment, Industrial Relations and Social affairs (DG V), the farming lobby with the DG responsible for Agriculture (DG VI) and environmental groups with the DG in charge of Environment, Nuclear Safety and Civil Protection (DG XI).

Certain features of the Commission encourage and facilitate group contacts. First, the Commission, with a mere 12 000 personnel, is seriously understaffed for the range of functions it undertakes, is therefore dependent for specialist advice on outside interests and hence is accessible to them in a way not invariably the case with national administrations. Second, after 1992, following criticisms, the Commission has sought to achieve greater openness to interests by such steps as making greater use of Green Papers, earlier publication of its legislative programme and other measures aimed at ensuring the relevant groups are consulted during the policy initiation stage. Finally, in the gift of the Commission are places on its numerous advisory committees, which are divided into the more powerful expert committees of national officials and experts and the consultative committees consisting of full-time representatives of associations and groups (Nugent, 1994, pp. 101–3). As already noted, lobbying at the first stage of policy initiation before proposals are drafted offers groups the greatest chance of significant influence and in practice drafts may change several times as a result of group inputs.

The Council of Ministers

The Council of Ministers is the most powerful decision-making body in the European Union, its main role being to accept or reject Commission proposals. Groups do not have direct access to the Council, which is an inter-governmental body, but can attempt to influence it, first, as already noted, by using domestic policy networks to persuade ministers to adopt their cause. The advent of Qualified Majority Voting on the Council (62 out of 87 votes required for a qualified majority, 26 for a blocking minority) puts a premium on compromise and opens a second channel for group influence by means of Euro-group pressure on other national governments. Grant argues that business associations 'put some effort into persuading like-minded sister federations in other European countries (particularly the Danish, Dutch and Germans) to lobby their ministers in order to create a blocking minority under qualified majority voting arrangements' (Grant, 1993, p. 185).

Strategies of lobbying towards the Council of Ministers

With qualified majority voting, a *European* lobbying strategy becomes essential for groups *in addition* to the maintenance and strengthening of links with national officials.

(Mazey and Richardson (1993), p. 15)

A final route to possible influence is through the various committees of officials which prepare policy proposals for final decision by ministers. Proposals are examined first by working parties of national officials from the relevant departments of national administrations and then by the Committee of Permanent Representatives (COREPER), which is made up of high-ranking civil servants from the member states. For pressure groups and interests, contact with national permanent delegations at COREPER forms a third avenue of potential influence on the Council of Ministers.

The European Parliament

Draft proposals of the European Commission go to the Commission's Economic and Social Committee (ESC) (an assembly of 189 representatives of employers, workers and other interests, with consultative status and little influence) and to the European Parliament for consideration. Although the powers of the European Parliament were increased – in an effort to remedy the 'democratic deficit' – by the Single European Act and Treaty of European Union, they remain limited: its legislative powers relate only to limited areas specified by these two Acts and it has only limited powers to initiate legislation. Nonetheless, its greater powers have increased its attractiveness to lobbyists. Under the cooperation procedure introduced by the SEA, the European Parliament was given the right to a second reading of legislation relating to the single market and the power to propose amendments to it. Where the Parliament produced an absolute majority to amend or reject the 'common position' adopted by the Council of Ministers, the Council could overrule it only by a unanimous vote, a situation that forced the Commission and Council to take the Parliament's views seriously and to engage in bargaining with it. Between mid-1987 and the end of 1993, the Commission accepted 44 per cent and the Council 24 per cent of the European Parliament's second reading amendments to all legal instruments under the cooperation procedure (Nugent, 1994, p. 178). Under the co-decision procedure intro-duced by the TEU, the powers of the European Parliament were extended even further by giving it a veto in policy areas relating to the internal market, the free movement of workers, the treatment of foreign nationals, consumer protection, public health, transport, research and development and the environment. Under the co-decision procedure, if the Council cannot accept the Parliament's amendment achieved by a majority vote, the matter goes to a conciliation committee (whose membership is evenly divided between Council and European Parliament), and if then unresolved, the Parliament can, by a majority vote, prevent the legislation going ahead. These changes have persuaded groups – especially the consumer, environmental and animal welfare lobbies but also including business interests – to make increasing use of the European Parliament. The most powerful of its 19 standing committees is the Environment, Public Health and Consumer Protection Committee, whose claimed 'successes' include the disposal of batteries, initiatives on lead-free and ozone-depleting substances and the rejection of an industry-inspired Commission draft to allow the patenting of genetic modifications (the Bio-Patenting Directive) (Greenwood, 1997, pp. 48, 191–2). There is also evidence that the growing importance of the European Parliament in modifying proposals for regulations and other matters has made it an increasing target for business associations (Bennett, 1997, p. 71). A 1994 estimate of the number of lobbyists of MEPs in Brussels (EP standing committees) and Strasbourg (EP plenary sessions) were 140 public affairs consultancies, 160 law firms, 572 trade and professional associations and 58 regional and local authorities (*Financial Times*, 26 May 1994, cited in Grant, 1995, p. 113). Concern about certain aspects of this intensified lobbying led the European Parliament to adopt a code of conduct for MEPs (July 1996), with a code for lobbyists to follow soon (Greenwood, 1997, pp. 96–7). However, it was reported in early 1998 that under half of MEPs had returned the form detailing their financial interests for 1997 (*The Guardian*, 11 January 1998).

The European Court of Justice

The European Court of Justice (ECJ) can be of importance for groups because of its key role in interpreting and enforcing EU legislation. Thus, it has been used by women's groups to implement equal pay and treatment of men and women workers and by environmental lobbyists to implement quality of drinking water legislation. Cases can be brought before it by the European Commission, member states, groups and individuals. More recently, it has ruled against the British Government on the Working Time Directive, thereby ensuring almost 4 million British workers gain extra holiday rights; ruled that national governments were responsible for ensuring the free movement of goods during strikes (a blow to the French Government which failed to guarantee free movement during a series of lorry drivers' strikes); ruled against the denial of job perks to same sex partners; and its rulings in 1998 provided the basis for equal pay claims by tens of thousands of NHS women workers in 1998 (*The Guardian*, 13 November 1996, 10 December 1997, 1 October 1997, 11 March 1998). As well as bringing cases directly, groups and companies can act as 'whistleblowers' on infringements of EU laws by their national governments, thereby bringing pressure on the Commission as the guardian of the EU legal framework to pursue the matter with the European Court of Justice. Large companies that feel they have been adversely affected by European regulations may take the case to the ECJ, as has happened in the car, airline and steel industries (Bennett, 1997, p. 67).

Policy networks in the European Union

Whilst just as valuable as in member states for organising the policy process, policy networks are, for a number of reasons, more difficult to achieve at European Union level. As Martin Smith points out, there is a paradox in European policy-making in that the characteristics that make policy networks desirable also make them hard to achieve. Thus, policy networks are desirable because of the extremely complex, multi-level, intensely conflict-ridden nature of the EU decision-making process. However, factors differentiating EU politics from UK politics and making policy networks more difficult to attain include:

- the much greater range of conflicting interests in the EU
- the fact that the range of conflicting interests includes those of member states who may on occasion refuse or fail to implement EU policy as well as a wide range of groups
- the difficulty of organising representation of interests across national frontiers
- the relative smallness of the Brussels bureaucracy in relation to the size of its tasks compared with the UK civil service (and indeed most other national bureaucracies)
- the variegated nature of the Brussels bureaucracy for which there is neither a common selection process, common training nor common culture
- the greater openness of European institutions, especially the Brussels Commission to lobbyists.

As a result of these factors, although policy networks exist at EU level, they are much more likely to be issue networks, i.e. open, unstable sets of relationships with large, fluctuating memberships, than policy communities. Policy communities can certainly be found in Brussels. Agricultural policy, for example, has always been made in a relatively closed policy community, dominated by DG VI of the Commission, member states' ministers of agriculture and farmers' groups, based on a consensual desire to increase both production and farm incomes, and with consumer and environmental groups excluded. Similarly, the entrenched institutional power of producer groups dominates sub-sectors of policy-making such as chemicals and technology

(Peterson, cited in Marsh and Rhodes, 1992, p. 244). However, these are the exception rather than the rule. Other policy areas – the environment, for instance – are more likely to be issue networks, characterised by large numbers of participants, constantly fluctuating memberships, conflictual relationships, and lack of consensus or at best weak consensus.

The impact of organised interests on EU policy-making

Three conclusions emerge from contemporary research on the impact of organised interests within the European Union. First, organised groups and interests play a key and increasingly important role both in driving forward European integration and in EU policy-making; second, the policy networks approach is the best method of understanding the role they play in everyday policy-making; and third, although groups representing business interests remain the most powerful, public interest groups – notably the environmental, consumer and trade union lobbies – have achieved increasing influence in the 1990s. The underlying reasons for these three points are discussed in turn.

First, the last decade has seen a revival of the theory that, as well as influencing policy-making on a day-to-day basis, groups play an important part in driving forward the project of European integration itself. Thus, much recent work suggests that European business groups played a leading role in creating the agenda for the Single European Act (1986) and the Treaty of European Union (1992). As one respondent commented to Mazey and Richardson: 'there was a very effective business "Mafia" at work, which "captured" leading European politicians and convinced them that something like the SEA and 1992 (i.e. the TEU) were needed' (Mazey and Richardson, 1997, p. 120). Further, in their study of groups in the lead-up to the 1996 Inter-Governmental Conference, these two academics found that the success of the business lobby in framing the agenda for Maastricht had been noted and business groups were lobbying to establish the 'competitiveness' of the European economy as the major theme for that Conference (Mazey and Richardson, 1997, pp. 120, 122). Second, the crucial and increasing role of groups in day-to-day EU policy-making was the consequence both of the intrinsic nature of the EU as a supranational organisation but also of post-1986 changes in its decision-making structure. First, not only at Commission level but even at Council of Ministers level, 'much of the power is wielded, in practice, by civil servants' (Peterson, 1997, p. 4). About 70 per cent of all EU decisions are taken in 'technocratic working groups', where 'most lobbying takes place' (Hayes-Renshaw and Wallace, 1997, p. 284, cited in Peterson, 1997, p. 4). A small bureaucracy, often itself deficient both in technical knowledge and in understanding of the potential social impact of its decisions, depends on groups for such information. Second, following the SEA and TEU,

EU policy-making has become to a considerable extent 'inter-institutional' in nature and this means that, in policy areas within the EU's competence, groups must lobby and find allies across the EU institutions and across the national capitals, Brussels, Strasbourg and Luxembourg. Finally, the segmentation of EU policy-making into sectoral arenas, each with 'its own "sector-dedicated" Council, Commissioner, Directorate-General and EP committee', favours specialised inputs, thereby enhancing the role of groups with such information.

Second, *policy networks* are the most useful model available for the understanding of the EU policy-making system. In particular, it sheds light on two key aspects – that in order to influence policy across such a large, complex system, groups must be able first, to form stable relationships with European institutions, especially the Commission and second, be capable of making and maintaining alliances with other groups. The significance of policy networks became more pronounced in the 1990s. As John Peterson has observed: '. . . as the European Union has become a more important tier of governance in Europe, EU policy networks have become a more important link between states and societies. A considerable amount of EU decision-making now occurs within policy networks' (Peterson, 1997, p. 17). During the 1990s, in particular, such factors as the vagueness of certain inter-governmental bargains (over the single market, for instance) gave the Commission and its associated policy networks greater potential to 'fill in' key policy details.

Third, and finally, business groups are by far the most powerful actors at European level, their most recent success from the mid-1990s onwards being to help persuade European political leaders first to adopt monetary union and then to retain their allegiance to the introduction of a single currency. The Chairman of the European Round Table, for example, argued before the 1996 Inter-Governmental Conference that a single currency was critical because it would 'simplify industrialists' operations and raise their profitability. The cost of changing money alone amounts to Ecu £15 billion a year' (cited in Mazey and Richardson, 1997, p. 124). However, it should be remembered that business is not invariably successful; nor is it a monolithic bloc; nor is it always at one with European policy-makers. Thus, the failure of the French car manufacturer Peugeot to persuade the Commission to drop its plans to fit catalytic converters on small cars illustrates not only that big business does not always get its way but also that building alliances, acting in concert and being prepared to compromise are conditions of success at this level (Mazey and Richardson, 1993, pp. 210–11). Second, sometimes firms are at loggerheads with other firms: thus, British Airways has encouraged DG IV to take action against state aids for Air France whilst Renault has complained about regional aid to its rival car manufacturers Ford and Volkswagen (Greenwood, 1997, p. 131). Equally, companies are often in conflict with the Commission, which has imposed fines on producers of cement, steel beams and cardboard cartons for breaking its rules on competition and in 1998 was reported to be planning action against Mercedes and Opel for discouraging non-German distributors from selling cars more cheaply to German customers who travel in search of bargains (Greenwood, 1997, p. 131; *The Guardian*, 2 February 1998). Finally, although producer interests generally are predominant, the 1990s have seen many non-producers achieve a measure of influence at European level. To some extent, they have done this by 'lobbying with the grain' – that is, trying to secure concession or side-payments as the price for their support for further European integration along the general lines determined by business. Evidence from the 1990s suggests that taking on board rival agendas from environmentalists ('sustainable development'), trade unions ('social Europe'), consumer groups (food safety) and all public interest groups (greater citizen participation and remedying the 'democratic deficit' in the EU) may be the price that business and the Commission are prepared to pay in order to achieve further European integration (Mazey and Richardson, 1997, pp. 122–31; Peterson, 1997, pp. 17–18).

Summary

- Interest groups have always played a key role in the European Union (European Community before 1993). Agricultural interests were especially influential in the early years but since the early 1980s business interests have played a particularly important part in furthering European integration; during the 1990s, as the competencies of the European Union have broadened to include new policy areas, environmental, consumer and trade union influences have increased.

- Lobbying at European level intensified from the mid-1980s as a consequence of the Single European Act (1986) and Treaty of European Union (1992) which extended the range of EU policy-making and changed the EU decision-making process in ways that enhanced the importance and inter-relationships of EU institutions and weakened the influence of national governments.

- Groups lobby EU institutions by means of the *national route* or the *European route*, or by a combination of the two routes. The national route involves a British pressure group in lobbying the British government to press its case at the Council of Ministers or in seeking exemption from and/ or delay in or modification of EU policies at the implementation stage. The European route involves lobbying European institutions directly or seeking to influence them through a Europe-wide association.

- The main targets of groups at European level are the European Commission, the Council of Ministers, the European Parliament and the European Court of Justice, broadly in that order of priority. But it should be remembered that the most effective lobbyists are prepared to focus on whichever institution is the most appropriate for their present purposes and, in a complex, multi-level system this can involve them in lobbying two or more institutions at the same time. Also, whereas insider interests such as business and agriculture possess well-established relations with the Brussels Commission, outsider public interest groups often concentrate more on developing contacts with the European Parliament or, in the case of environmentalists, for example, in simply drawing the attention of the Brussels Commission to national infringements of EU directives.

- Policy networks exist at EU level in most policy areas. These vary from policy communities in agriculture to issue networks in institutions dealing with environmental policy. Overall, for various reasons, including the vagueness of inter-governmental agreements which left the Commission in interaction with groups to fill in key policy details, policy networks became more significant in the 1990s.

Further reading

Sonia Mazey and Jeremy Richardson write clearly and perceptively on pressure groups in the European Union. See in particular, Mazey, S. and Richardson, J. (eds) (1993) *Lobbying in the European Community* (Oxford: Oxford University Press); Mazey, S. and Richardson, J. (1993a) 'Pressure groups and the EC', *Politics Review*, 3, 1, September; Mazey, S. and Richardson, J. (1993) 'Interest groups in the European Community' in J.J. Richardson (ed.) (1993) *Pressure Groups* (Oxford: Oxford University Press); and Mazey, S. and Richardson, J. (1997) 'Policy framing: interest groups and the lead up to 1996 Inter-Governmental Conference', *West European Politics*, 20, 3, July. There is a useful chapter on 'Business interests and the European Community' in Grant, W. (1993) *Business and Politics in Britain*, 2nd edn (London: Macmillan). Greenwood, J. (1997) *Representing Interests in the European Union* (London: Macmillan) is a mine of information on groups in the EU, their modes of operation and influence whilst 1990s developments are dealt with illuminatingly by Peterson, J. (1997) 'States, societies and the European Union', *West European Politics*, 20, 3, July.

CHAPTER 4

Pressure groups and government

Earlier chapters have explored key concepts in the understanding of pressure group relations with government, e.g. insider and outsider groups, policy networks (Chapter 1) together with the main postwar phases in these relations (Chapter 2). The previous chapter examined the emergence of an important new target area for group lobbying activity: the European Union. This chapter focuses exclusively on the relationships between groups and government. It asks: 'Why is government the primary target for pressure groups in Britain?' 'What benefits do groups and government derive from the process of close consultation that has developed?' 'How do policy communities form and become de-stabilised?' 'Why have think-tanks become such important influences on government?' 'How can the rise of a massive multi-million pound lobbying industry intermediating between the interests and government be explained?'

The influence of the political system on pressure group activity

The pattern of pressure group activity in a country is powerfully shaped by its constitutional and institutional arrangements. Compare, for example, the United Kingdom with the United States. Britain is a unitary state in which power lies principally with the central government whereas the United States is a federal system where power is divided between the federal government and the state governments. Britain has an executive-dominated parliamentary system whilst the United States has a system in which power is shared between the executive (Presidency) and legislature (both Houses of Congress). Britain has a largely written but uncodified constitution in which the paramount rule is the sovereignty of parliament and the courts have no significant role in constitutional interpretation; in the United States, which has a written codified constitution, the paramount constitutional arbiter is the Supreme Court. The contrasts could be continued but the main point of the comparison is already clear: that Britain is a centralised political system with power concentrated in a single institution or set of institutions, the core executive, whereas in the United States, despite the twentieth-century tendency for power to flow towards the Presidency, power is dispersed among a variety of co-decision-making centres. This situation is almost certainly changing at the moment with power gravitating towards the European Union and, within the UK, towards new devolved assemblies in Scotland, Wales and Northern Ireland, developments that make the British state more federalistic and lessen the sharpness of the contrast with the United States. Nonetheless, the contrast in essentials remains. Pressure groups possess multiple powerful access points in the USA – the Presidency, federal bureaucracy, both Houses of Congress, influential congressional committees, the judiciary, state governments and local governments. In Britain, with its well-disciplined executive-dominated parliament and weak local government, groups have far fewer powerful points of access.

The realities of the distribution of political power and influence embodied in British constitutional arrangements are well recognised by British pressure groups. The concentration of power in the 'core executive' (Prime Minister, ministers, civil servants) makes it the primary, if not the only, focus of their lobbying efforts.

> The overwhelming majority of outside organisations are clear in their perception that ministers and civil servants are the key actors in the policy process.
>
> (Michael Rush, 1990, for the Study of Parliament Group, pp. 271–2)

Research shows that pressure groups broadly agree on where power lies in the political system – with the Prime Minister, Cabinet ministers, junior ministers, senior civil servants and junior civil servants (Table 4.1). Thus, the 253 organisations surveyed by the Study of Parliament Group placed influences on public policy in the following rank order: 1, civil servants/government departments; 2, ministers; 3, the media; 4, Parliament; 5, particular sections of public opinion; 6, public opinion generally; 7, other pressure or interest groups; 8, political parties generally; 9, one political party in particular (Rush, 1990, p. 272). Another survey of over 100 groups, which differentiated more precisely between institutions in the hierarchy of government, showed groups ranking power-holders as follows: 1, Prime Minister; 2, Cabinet ministers; 3, senior civil servants; 4, junior ministers; 5; the media; 6, junior civil sevants; 7, backbench MPs; 8, political parties; 9, the House of Lords (Baggott, 1992, p. 19). Finally, a lobbying consultant, grading British governing institutions on a scale from least influence (0) to most influence (10), allocated the following scores to institutions: the Prime Minister 10, civil servants 8, ministers 7, backbench committees 6, House of Lords EU Select Committees 6, MPs/Peers collectively 4, House of Commons Select Committees 3, House of Lords

Table 4.1 Frequency of contacts between pressure groups and decision-makers in Britain

Institution/Office	Percentage of groups in contact at least		
	Once a week	Once a month	Once a year
Prime Minister/PM's Office	1	11	53
Cabinet ministers	8	37	81
Junior ministers	11	49	86
Senior civil servants	19	50	82
Junior civil servants	34	67	85
MPs	31	61	89
Peers	18	50	84
Media	81	94	98

Note: Senior civil servant: Permanent Secretary, Deputy Secretary, Under Secretary grades. Junior civil servant: Assistant Secretary and Principal.
Source: Baggott (1992), p. 19.

chamber 3, House of Commons chamber 2 (Miller, 1990, pp. 53–6). The major omission here is the importance of the EU, which would surely receive a high ranking in any late 1990s survey. Even in 1990, Miller could write: 'The work of the European Commission, Council of Ministers, European Parliament and European Court of Justice, and their influence on UK legislation should be learnt and understood by any serious lobbyist ... In many areas, an organisation's attention should now be turned at least as often to Brussels as to Whitehall and Parliament' (Miller, 1990, p. viii). However, apart from this omission, which would be corrected in any late 1990s survey, these early 1990s surveys and views show that groups and political lobbyists have a clear understanding of where power lies in the British political system.

But this does not mean that groups actually *target* institutions from the top down. The Prime Minister may possess overall control but in practice only a very limited number of the most powerful organisations would have any chance of direct access. Examples might be the head of ICI or Formula One motor racing (see Box 4.2). Most government decisions are taken within departments and again, as most pressure groups and political consultants realise, often at a relatively low level within the departmental hierarchy. As Baggott's survey shows (Table 4.1), although rather surprisingly over half the groups surveyed claimed to be in contact with the Prime Minister at least once a year, higher percentages of pressure groups have regular contacts with junior ministers than with Cabinet ministers and with junior civil servants than with senior civil servants. The survey bears out groups' awareness that, in the words of one lobbyist, 'far less policy is initiated from the top down' and 'real power rests further down the Civil Service hierarchy' than is often believed (Miller, 1990, p. 51). The main target of pressure groups in Britain, then, is Whitehall, and within Whitehall, the highest levels of contacts are with junior ministers and the lower ranks of the higher civil service (assistant secretary and principal grades). Research offers a picture of a high level of frequent, routine contacts between pressure groups and government, especially at levels just below the highest ranks of the ministerial and civil service hierarchies.

Pressure groups and government

The great majority of contacts between groups and government are of an *informal* nature, for example, telephone conversations, face-to-face meetings, and social contact including lunches. But *formal* links are also extensive, and are institutionalised in a number of ways, including government committees, pre-legislative consultative documents and statutory instruments.

- *Government committees.* These include *executive bodies* which are established to carry out executive, administrative, regulatory and commercial functions on behalf of government. Examples are the Commission for Racial Equality and the Medical Research Council. There were 358 executive bodies with over 4000 appointees in 1995. Also included are *advisory committees* set up to advise ministers and departments on specific areas. Examples are the Spongiform Encephalopathy Advisory Committee and the Nuclear Weapons Safety Committee. There were 829 advisory bodies with over 10 000 appointees in 1995. In addition, there are also Committees of Inquiry (over 2000 since 1900) and Royal Commissions (35 between 1944 and 1995) such as the Royal Commission on Criminal Justice (1991). A wide range of groups and organisations are invited to serve on or present evidence to such bodies.

- *Pre-legislative consultative documents.* Before legislating on a particular issue, governments often circulate details of their proposals to those interested in the matter. Each year between 200 and 300 documents are issued, most of them with a limited circulation but also including Green Papers (about 30 per year in the early 1990s), which achieve more publicity and invite comments from a wider range of groups. Groups convey their views either in writing or sometimes directly to ministers or officials, normally within a consultation period lasting about two months.

- *Statutory instruments.* Government is often under statutory obligation to consult interested groups over statutory instruments (sometimes called delegated or subordinate legislation), that is, further legislation which ministers are empowered to make by a parent Act. Approximately 2500 statutory instruments are laid before parliament every year. Mandatory consultation with affected interests is required in a significant proportion of these instruments but often takes place anyway even where it is not mandatory. Most departments maintain lists of bodies to be consulted and these groups and organisations are circularised routinely when legislations or decisions affecting their interests are under consideration.

Government–group consultation: a matter of mutual advantage

The policy-making process in Britain gives groups a key role and it has become a well-established custom that policies are formulated only after consultation with affected interests. Three important features of the British political system and political culture underpin this practice of routine consultation with groups. First, civil servants are generalists rather than specialists; consequently, they depend on groups to supply the specialised information required for sound decision-making and legislation. There is thus a *functional* need for governments to consult with affected interests. Second, whilst elected governments claim democratic legitimacy, groups too are representative of a particular (functional or preference) constituency and can claim a certain legitimacy. In addition, in the British system of 'first past the post' elections in which no postwar government has achieved the support of as much as half the voters, groups can often claim broader support in public opinion than governments. Third, it is an important norm of a consensual political culture that, rather than ride roughshod over affected interests, policy-makers should try to gain their agreement, which usually means seeking the views of groups and taking account of them in forming policies. As has been remarked, one test of a 'good' policy has has often been its *acceptability* to affected interests, a perspective that sees final policies as analogous to 'peace treaties' between government and groups (Richardson, 1993, pp. 86–9). Thus, there is a *cultural* bias emphasising the need to legitimate decisions through consultation (Jordan and Richardson, 1987a, p. 171).

The system of routine government–group consultation has great benefits for both sides. Governments receive up-to-date, often technical and highly specialised advice; 'market' information about how various sectors of the economy are performing or about how policy proposals are likely to affect particular interests; compliance with decisions and policies by the main interests in each field; and assistance from organisations – where required – in the administration of projects. For their part, groups gain a hearing for their points of view; a chance to influence decisions and gain concessions for their members; and the possibility of an executive role alongside government in the implementation of policy and even of the receipt of funds from the executive to assist such a role. Groups therefore regularly participate at all three main stages of policy-making by governments: agenda-setting; policy formation – what might be termed the Green Paper to White Paper stage; and policy implementation.

As has already been noted (Chapter 1), not all pressure groups gain regular access to government, a point recognised in the commonly employed distinction between 'insider' groups which do possess regular access, and 'outsider' groups, which do not, either because they do not wish it or because government is unwilling to confer such status on them. The insider/outsider classification has two sides, referring both to the *strategy* groups employ and the *status* they achieve. Achieved status, of course, depends on government, and it is useful to examine at this point what qualities of a group are likely to persuade government to confer legitimate status upon it and draw it into a regular consultative relationship. Broadly speaking, the following characteristics are likely to make a group acceptable to government.

- *Representativeness.* A group is able to speak for a large proportion of its sphere of interest, for example, all or a majority of doctors, engineers, motor manufacturers or poultry producers; in an industrial relations context, it has been suggested that a group with much below half its potential membership would be suspect to government (Jordan and Richardson, 1987a, p. 190).

- *Reasonableness of its demands.* A group's objectives should be compatible with the aims of government and specifically with the overall framework of government policy; excessive or unrealistic demands seriously prejudice a group's acceptability to government, '...their shopping list is so enormous that they have lost credibility' (a civil servant on the road lobby in the mid-1980s, cited in Jordan and Richardson, 1987a, p. 190).

- *Ability to 'talk the same language'.* A group should understand government procedures, i.e. 'know its way around Whitehall' or, at least, the relevant part of it and, above all, should be willing to compromise. Rather than drawing up a 'wish list' of demands and expecting to get all or most of them, it should develop the ability to recognise and accept 'the best deal going'.

- *Reliability and quality of its advice.* A group needs to 'get things right' on a consistent basis – track record is important and errors or exaggeration may lead to a group's exclusion by government.

- *Economic leverage and veto power.* Groups with economic clout such as business groups or with veto power such as trade unions can impede a government's capacity to implement its policies and can expect to be consulted.

Groups may fail to gain recognition from government for a variety of reasons, of which two key ones are:

- *incompatibility*: groups possessing aims incompatible with government policy such as the Campaign for Nuclear Disarmament (CND) which calls for the renunciation of nuclear weapons or the Animal Liberation Front (ALF) which practises extremist tactics of freeing animals from fur farms and laboratories are classic outsider groups regarded as illegitimate by government

- *contentiousness*: groups whose aims are controversial, bringing them into conflict with other groups such as the Abortion Law Reform Association whose goals are opposed by the Society for the Protection of Unborn Children, are generally unacceptable to government.

It would be wrong, however, to make a simple distinction between regularly consulted 'insider' groups and totally excluded 'outsider' groups. In fact, the position is more complex. Civil servants generally consider that it is better to over-consult than to under-consult: they prefer 'to shoot widely' and risk over-consulting rather than leave any significant interest out of the process. Thus, departmental consultation lists are long and the consultation process is lengthy and extends beyond insider groups with well-established legitimacy to include a large number of outsider groups (see Box 4.1). For example, Friends of the

---

BOX 4.1

Insiders, outsiders and government

| | Percentage of groups in contact | | | |
| | Weekly | | Monthly | |
	Insider	Outsider	Insider	Outsider
Prime Minister	2	–	14	10
Cabinet ministers	12	5	45	37
Junior ministers	14	10	67	38
Senior civil servants	25	12	49	45
Junior civil servants	55	12	76	62

Based on survey of over 100 pressure groups divided into three main types: business, labour and preference.
Adapted from Baggott (1992), p. 20.

Questions

1. To what extent does the above table suggest that outsider as well as insider groups are in frequent contact with government? In so far as this is the case, how do you account for it?

2. Why do you think larger percentages of groups are in regular contact with junior civil servants and ministers than with senior civil servants and Cabinet ministers?

Earth, a classic campaigning outsider group, is consulted both formally and informally on policies affecting the environment and has accepted invitations to sit on departmental advisory committees. Some writers get round this more complex situation by coining a term such as *thresholder group* to describe a group that moves between insider and outsider strategies, as the TUC did for much of the 1980s (May and Nugent, 1982). Other writers, noting that 'groups must work pretty hard at ruling themselves out of consultative status', prefer to conclude that, whilst many groups have access to governmental decision-makers, what matters is that far fewer have influence (Jordan and Richardson, 1987a, p. 192). The truth is that a wide range of groups are normally consulted by government departments – sectional and cause, insider and outsider – but that the bulk of routinised contacts and the greatest possibility of group influence are likely to involve sectional insiders.

Policy networks

It was suggested in Chapter 1 that the bulk of governmental decisions took place in routinised relationships involving ministers/officials and group representatives known as *policy networks*. The term policy networks covers a broad spectrum of relationships from small, stable, close-knit sets of government–group relations known as *policy communities* to larger, less stable and more discontinuous linkages termed *issue networks*. Although the precise nature of the government–group relationships existing in any particular policy area can be discovered only by empirical research, the policy network concept does underline several more general features of governmental decision-making. First, policy is *compartmentalised* in vertical segments with each segment inhabited by a different set of organised groups (Figure 4.1). Second, departments develop *patron–client* relationships with the main interests they deal with, often identifying closely with these interests and pressing their demands within government. Thus, MAFF has traditionally sided with the interests of food producers against consumers whilst the Department of Transport has often been perceived as pro-roads rather than other forms of transport. Third, the existence of policy communities strongly influences policy *outcomes*, in large part by restricting the policy options under consideration and biasing them in favour of the dominant group or groups, usually producer or professional. Thus, policy-making in Britain takes place within policy networks which are more or less exclusive, i.e. containing a restricted range of interests within a policy area and excluding or marginalising others (Rhodes and Marsh, 1996, p. 220). The existence of policy communities/networks has traditionally been seen as resulting in considerable policy continuity within British government. The remainder of this section tests this common perception by considering how existing networks can

Figure 4.1   Successful groups know the geography of power and target appropriate access points.

be threatened and how far both networks and policies may change as a consequence.

The 1980s and 1990s have seen considerable pressure upon existing policy networks, largely from two sources. Changes of government have brought political pressure from the top whilst developments in knowledge have threatened the stability of policy communities from below. The result has been a period of major policy change. The main *political* spur was the change of government in 1979 which brought the Conservatives to power. The upshot was an ideologically inspired change of policy away from state interventionism and in favour of free markets, and a change in policy style away from the incorporation of major interests in policy-making and in favour of increasing the distance between government and the major producer and professional groups. These developments underlined the potentially dynamic role of ministers within policy networks. Compared with the other two key elements – civil servants and pressure group bureaucrats – ministers were members of policy communities for a short term, had political reputations to make and could – and in this case did – possess new solutions to problems (privatisation, market reforms) which they were keen to apply. Many Conservative ministers were determined to shake up dormant policy areas and to assert their supremacy over the leading interest groups. They were no respecters of existing policy community arrangements. This phase of policy-making under-lined ministerial potential for disruption of policy communities and networks by a range of actions, including ignoring all established interests within a network, favouring some against others and admitting new groups to a network to the detriment of its existing members – sometimes by changing the 'rules of the game' (Dudley and Richardson, 1996, pp. 568–70).

Examples of this process include the exclusion of trade unions from high-level consultation (see Chapter 2) and the planning of health and education reforms without the full involvement of representatives of doctors and teachers in the 1980s. Thus, in 1983, rather than develop reforms of the National Health Service from within the health policy community, the Thatcher Government appointed a group of outsiders – four businessmen under the chairmanship of Sir Roy Griffiths – to inquire into the effective use of resources within the organisation. The consequence was an increase in the power of managers and a reduction in the power of doctors to decide priorities for the distribution of NHS resources. When the Griffiths report proved unable to solve deep-rooted problems, Thatcher announced a review of the NHS but again, rather than involving the British Medical Association and the Royal Colleges, the usual policy community participants, the review was made up of ministers, civil servants and special advisers mainly drawn from right-wing think-tanks. The government had radical reform in mind and realising that doctors might prove obstacles to this objective it excluded them from the review committee, inviting their representatives merely to submit proposals to the Secretary of State for Health. This confrontational style was continued by the Health Minister, Kenneth Clark, who imposed a new GP contract on the medical profession in 1990 (Smith, 1995, pp. 97–8). A similar situation occurred in the making of the 1988 Education Reform Act, with teachers' organisations, normally part of the education policy community, largely excluded from pre-legislative consultation.

> ...the attempts by the post-1979 Conservative government to reform health and education ... were very high risk policies, introduced in the face of much public concern and often against deeply entrenched interests. Ministers, backed particularly by Mrs Thatcher, 'went it alone' against the combined weight of the well-organised clients of their departments and a hostile public opinion.
>
> (Dudley and Richardson, 1996, pp. 569–70)

A second source of pressure upon policy communities and networks arises from the growth of new *knowledge* leading in turn to the emergence of new pressure groups. One political scientist has well explained the emergence of new issues and groups in the agricultural policy-making arena as follows:

> Scientific development has led both to new problems and to the rediscovery of old ones. The development of factory farming has meant that a large number of animals are kept in confined areas. As a result, disease spreads quickly through stock. Consequently, a high death rate is expected and large doses of antibiotics have to be used in the production of pigs and chickens. Intensive techniques have also resulted in the spread of disease through the food chain. As cattle have been fed parts of sheep, herds have developed BSE. Likewise, chickens have been fed chicken remains thereby reproducing salmonella in the chicken population. New technology has introduced food preservation techniques, such as irradiation. This technology has produced high levels of opposition from retailers, consumer groups and trade unions and has helped to politicise the issue of food. Increased use of additives, pesticides, and hormones in food production has prompted NSMs (New Social Movements) and established groups to provide more information on the impact that these chemicals have on humans.
>
> (Smith, 1995, p. 89)

As a result, the dominant food-producing and food-processing interests in the previously stable agricultural policy community have faced competition from new environmental, animal welfare and consumer groups. Other examples relating to transport and health may be cited of the destabilising consequences for policy communities of new knowledge. Scientific discoveries about the environmental impact of the burning of carbon fuels and the emission of waste gases, and about the consequences of smoking for the incidence of cancer, bronchitis, heart disease and other illnesses have destabilised these policy communities, undermining the authority of key groups and introducing new participants pressing the interests of consumers and the environment (Box 4.2).

BOX 4.2

The tobacco industry, smoking and health: the weakening of a producer network

The formation of a producer network

Until the 1970s a producer network dominated by the tobacco industry managed government relations with the industry. At the core of the network were the multinational tobacco corporations, British–American Tobacco Industries, Imperial, Gallahers and Rothmans International which conducted relations with government through their trade association, the Tobacco Advisory Council (TAC). The tobacco industry had relations with several government departments including the Department of Health and Social Security and the Department of the Environment but the main ones were the Department of Trade and Industry, its sponsoring department down to the late 1980s, and the Treasury. These two departments and the tobacco manufacturers had close relationships and formed the core of the tobacco producer network. TAC represented the tobacco manufacturers in discussions with government over taxation and over voluntary agreements on the control of advertising, sponsorship and the promotion of cigarettes and tobacco. Its overall aim was to keep tobacco taxation low (or, preferably, eliminate it altogether) and to prevent intervention which might harm the interests of the industry. Formal links between the industry and government were cemented in the usual ways: corporate entertainment (e.g. at Wimbledon) and former civil servants retiring to take up posts in the industry. Inter-departmental committees on the tobacco industry (unpublished but leaked to *The Guardian* in 1980) argued that the government could not afford to do without tobacco revenue (1951) and, that whilst a fall in tobacco consumption would significantly reduce loss of life through smoking-related diseases, a fall of 20 per cent in tobacco consumption would add another £12 million to the pensions bill by the year 2001 (1971).

The rise of the anti-smoking lobby

From the 1970s, the tobacco industry has been increasingly threatened by the publicity given to scientific evidence linking smoking, cancer and heart disease and by the rise of an anti-smoking lobby led by the British Medical Association and the single issue pressure group Action on Smoking and Health (ASH). From the early 1980s, the BMA and ASH called for a ban on tobacco advertising and budgetary increases in tobacco tax. In order to combat the anti-smoking lobby, the tobacco industry sought support from other interests, notably advertising and sport and entertainment. Strong commercial links now bind the tobacco industry to the advertising industry, which derives considerable revenue from tobacco advertising, and the sport and entertainments industries, which enjoy massive sponsorship from the tobacco companies. The tobacco industry also receives major backing from the large wholesalers and retailers dealing with tobacco products. The policy network thus expanded but tobacco remained at its core, with the other interests occupying subordinate positions. In order to compete publicly with its opponents, the industry also promoted itself through the Freedom Organisation for the Right to Enjoy Smoking Tobacco (FOREST) and the Tobacco Alliance. Overall, tobacco manufacturers were forced to accept health warnings on cigarette packets, the phasing out of high tar cigarettes and certain limitations on

BOX 4.2 (CONTINUED)

sports sponsorship spending but successfully resisted the threat of anti-smoking legislation in the 1980s.

New Labour and the tobacco industry

Pressure on the tobacco industry intensified in the late 1990s. First, Labour came to power in May 1997 on a manifesto promise to ban tobacco advertising since 'smoking is the greatest single cause of preventable illness and premature death in the UK'. However, six months later the government surprisingly announced that it wanted to exempt Formula One motor racing from the proposed EU directive banning tobacco advertising. The phased EU ban on tobacco advertising and sponsorship announced in December 1997 exempted Formula One until 2006. The episode caused a furore in Britain largely because of the simultaneous announcement that Labour had received a pre-election gift of £1 million from the Formula One chief, Bernie Ecclestone. Ecclestone had talks with the Prime Minister, Tony Blair, on 16 October to put the F1 case: that if tobacco sponsorship were banned, the sport might move to the Far East, leading to the loss to Britain of 50 000 full-time jobs, 150 000 part-time jobs and exports worth £900 000 a year. The anti-smoking lobby countered that the association of smoking with a glamorous sport such as motor racing helped make it attractive to young people. Embarrassed by the public suspicion of party favours in return for funding, Labour gave the £1 million gift to a cancer charity. But it seemed that once again the industry had been able to defer damaging regulations by means of the access to government gained by its commercial and financial muscle.

Second, controversy was further fuelled in March 1998 by the report of a government-appointed committee of medical experts which was expected to form the basis of a White Paper on smoking later in 1998. The Scientific Committee on Tobacco and Health definitively linked passive smoking and killer diseases and called for smoking to be banned in public buildings and all but a few areas of public transport. It found that living with a smoker increased a non-smoker's chance of getting lung cancer by 25 per cent and of getting ischaemic heart disease by 23 per cent. It called for government to take effective action to limit the 'preventable epidemic' of 120 000 deaths a year from smoking. It suggested that the industry was targeting the young and vulnerable to recruit the 300 new smokers a day it needed to replace those who died from smoking-related diseases. In July 1997 came the news that the four leading tobacco companies were to seek a court injunction banning the government from taking this report into account in formulating its White Paper on smoking. The companies claimed that they had always been fully consulted by the committee's predecessor, the Independent Committee on Smoking and Health, but that the new committee had sought their views on one issue only (passive smoking and lung cancer) and had failed to give them the chance to comment before publishing its report.

(Sources: Read (1992); *The Guardian*, 5, 6 November 1997, 12 March, 7 July 1998; *The Observer*, 9 November 1997)

Questions

1. Describe the main participants in the tobacco producer network down to the 1980s. What features of the industry enabled it to develop such close relationships with government?

> BOX 4.2 (CONTINUED)

2. Which groups are major participants in the anti-smoking lobby? How was their emergence related to the discoveries of scientific research?

3. State the main arguments of the tobacco lobby and its opponents. Which side's arguments do you find most convincing, and why?

4. What evidence is there that the tobacco producer network had been severely disrupted by the 1990s and has developed into an issue network?

5. To what extent does the Formula One affair reflect tensions in the Labour Party between Old Labour and New Labour? How far do this affair and subsequent developments in the relationship between government, the tobacco industry and anti-smoking groups exemplify the point that changes of government can produce changes in policy networks?

Changes of government, advances in scientific knowledge and other changes have certainly disrupted policy communities and networks in recent decades, but how far have they changed them for good? A general observation might be that *policy* challenges shook the positions of entrenched groups in a wide variety of policy areas in the 1980s, in some cases displacing them with other interests (e.g. doctors lost out to managers in the NHS) or marginalising them completely (e.g. trade unions in economic and industrial policy-making). A large number of professional lobbies failed to prevent legislation seen as detrimental to their interests: these included teachers, lawyers and local authorities as well as doctors and trade unionists. However, it may be doubted whether policy networks involving these interests experienced lasting alteration. First, even though out of favour with ministers, many of these groups retained good contacts with civil servants during this period (Baggott, 1995, p. 119). Second, often after phases of resistance to changes – for example, the doctors opposed the NHS reforms in the late 1980s, teachers boycotted the Standard Assessment Tests introduced by the 1988 Education Act – affected groups often moved back into closer relations with government at the policy implementation stage. As one close observer has contended:

> The destabilisation of policy communities – evident in such diverse areas as health, education, law reform and the structure of the legal profession, and water policy – was almost invariably followed ... by a return to the accepted values and norms of the policy process. Thus, once a sector had been 'shaken and stirred', the affected interests were then soothed by being invited back into the inner circle of negotiations with government. The new policy style was to address reform deficits by challenging entrenched groups, to insist that the principles underlying the reforms should be maintained (e.g. that there should be a national curriculum in education and that there should be regular testing of pupils), but literally to negotiate the implementation stage with the affected interests and to make significant changes in the process.

(Richardson, 1993, pp. 97–8)

However, policy communities/networks that were destabilised by new *knowledge*, often reinforced in its impact by pressure from new groups and social movements, seem to have been more difficult to reconstitute. The evidence in policy areas such as agriculture, food, transport and smoking is clearly that the dominant producer groups have acted as powerful constraints on policy change. For example, over food safety issues such as BSE, food irradiation, listeria, and use of the hormone BST and over the health risks of smoking, the speed and effectiveness of government response are extremely questionable (Smith, 1995, p. 91; Baggott, 1996, pp. 2, 8). The suspected underlying reason is an unwillingness to confront the major producer interests concerned, thereby risking damage to their industries. A student of the animal rights movement concludes: 'It is questionable ... how far elected politicians can alter the direction of long-standing and insulated policy communities within which those with vested interests in the use of animals are influential' (Garner, 1998, p. 465). However, the animal protection movement has enjoyed a certain measure of success in recent times including reform of the law on animal experimentation (1986) and the abolition of veal crates and sow stalls and tethers and, whilst these may certainly be seen as 'managed concessions' involving no serious damage to agribusiness or research interests, it is equally clear that this part of the agricultural policy area has been politicised. Moreover, in this, and in other areas such as the food, transport and smoking policy communities, politicisation has brought various new consumer, environmental and health groups into the circle of policy-making. These groups may be on the outer circle of the policy communities but it is extremely likely that they are there to stay and that their influence is more likely to increase than diminish. Thus, disruption to policy communities and networks by new knowledge, especially when linked to new social movements, has the capacity to bring about permanent change. Symptomatic of the way policy-making can move against producer groups is the exclusion of the tobacco interests from full-scale consultation by the government advisory committee on secondary smoking mentioned in Box 4.2.

Think-tanks and government policy

Since the 1970s, independent private sector research organisations known as 'think-tanks' have become increasingly influential on government policy. Thus, important influences on Conservative governments in the 1980s and 1990s were the Institute of Economic Affairs (IEA), the Adam Smith Institute (ASI) and the Centre for Policy Studies (CPS), whilst Demos and the Institute for Public Policy Research (IPPR) are seeking to perform a similar role for the Labour Government elected in 1997. Themselves a kind of intellectual pressure group, think-tanks on occasion have displaced other pressure groups within policy networks. By no means a new phenomenon – Labour's Fabian Society dates back to 1884 – their recent growth of influence is a novel development. No analysis of contemporary British government would be complete without reference to their role. What exactly do they do and how may their rise be explained?

> ...think-tanks have become an indispensable part of our system of government. If we had a constitution, they would get an honourable mention in it.
>
> (Gerald Holtham, Director of the IPPR, *Daily Telegraph*, 13 July 1998)

The role of think-tanks is mainly twofold – feeding ideas into government and expressing radical ideas to which government may wish to test the public reaction but with which it does not currently wish to be associated. First, in terms of policy influence, think-tanks such as the IEA, ASI and CPS propagated some of the key ideas informing Conservative policies in the 1980s, including privatisation, contracting out of government services and trade union reform. They injected ideas into the health and education policy networks which inspired reforms such as GP fundholding, internal markets and trust hospitals in the NHS, and opting out of schools and the national curriculum in education. Thus, think-tanks were 'pulled' into the policy process in the 1980s, often becoming linked to government through policy networks (Stone, 1996, p. 215). Second, they became useful for government only after first creating the 'political space' for their new ideas away from Westminster and Whitehall. Think-tanks have played an important role in placing ideas previously seen as too radical on the political agenda. One example is privatisation of prisons: widely discounted when first mooted in the mid-1980s, this policy was adopted in 1993 when the first privatised prison was established and, although generally derided in opposition, was extended by Labour in government, with the result that the population of contracted out prisons rose to over 3700 in 1998.

One reason for the growing influence of think-tanks is the declining usefulness – as perceived by contemporary politicians – of traditional sources of policy such as the civil service, the universities and the parties' own research departments. Thus, key influences behind the growth of the postwar welfare state and managed economy were academic intellectuals working as temporary civil servants in wartime, and a key role in the Conservative response to these developments was played by its research department. Similarly, in the 1960s the Labour governments sought policy advice from leading left-wing university academics. Meanwhile, the civil service proved well-adapted to 'steady-state' administration of a going concern, but less valuable for radical reforms. A party seeking to break with the postwar social and economic policy consensus such as the Conservatives in the late 1970s, therefore, had to look for ideas in other areas than the consensus-dominated civil service and universities. Starved of resources, neither major party's research departments any longer seemed fit for the task of generating new ideas or developing detailed policies. Hence, the Conservatives from the 1970s and Labour in the 1990s turned to think-tanks to fill the void (Table 4.2).

Table 4.2   The main think-tanks

Institute of Economic Affairs (1955)
Established to improve public understanding of the principles of economics.
  Oldest organisation advocating free market ideas but remains less geared to immediate political influence and the service of governments than the newer free market institutes.

Centre for Policy Studies (1974)
Established by Margaret Thatcher and Keith Joseph to convert the Conservative Party to free market ideas.
  Strong lobbyist for privatisation in the 1980s; also influenced the introduction of vouchers for nursery education, the poll tax and curriculum reform and kept up pressure on Thatcher administrations for trade union reform.

Adam Smith Institute (1977)
Free market think-tank which concentrated on the detailed application of free market ideas in the spheres of local government, the NHS and privatisation of industry in the 1980s and 1990s.
  Claims special influence on rail privatisation. 'Britain has led the way in privatisation supported by the work of the Adam Smith Institute' (John Major, 1992).
  The most advocacy and media-orientated think-tank with a strong emphasis on the practical application of theory (Stone, 1996, p. 230).

Social Market Foundation (1989)
Founded as a think-tank for the Social Democratic Party.
  After the party's demise has sought to stimulate debate, particularly on the organisation of the public services in a free market economy.
  A recent publication is *Is Conservatism Dead?* by John Gray and David Willetts.

Institute for Public Policy Research (1988)
Launched by people close to the then Labour leader Neil Kinnock to stimulate left-wing thinking and performed detailed policy work for Labour in opposition.
  A strong modernising influence, it became to the Labour Party what the CPS had been to the Conservatives in the 1970s.
  Claims influence on Labour's ideas on competition policy, the University of Industry and welfare to work.
  Proposed legally binding child commitment ceremony as alternative to marriage in 1998.

Demos (1993)
Established by Martin Jaques, a former editor of *Marxism Today*, and Geoff Mulgan, a former research assistant to Gordon Brown, with the aim of mapping out the post-Thatcherite agenda in the same way that the IEA helped to shift the boundaries of economic thinking in the 1960s and 1970s.
  Claims to have introduced communitarianism into the language of political debate but main claim to practical influence is the setting up of a Social Exclusion Unit by Tony Blair.

The professional lobbying industry

Professional political consultancy firms have existed for a long time but their numbers expanded rapidly in the 1980s in part due to the favourable de-regulated pro-business climate created by Conservative governments. By the 1990s there were over 50 consultancy firms with names like Westminster Strategy, the Public Policy Unit, Politics International and Shandwick Public Affairs in a multi-million pound industry. These commercial lobbyists function as intermediaries between their clients and government. Their clients include not only a wide range of outside interests – business and cause groups – but also public bodies. Thus, business groups such as Alvis, Racal and Siemens (arms manufacturers); Novartis and Zeneca (genetic engineering firms); BP, Virgin Rail and the Chemical Industries Association; cause groups such as the International Fund for Animal Welfare and the League Against Cruel Sports; and public bodies such as the BBC, the British Council, the Commission for Racial Equality and the Millennium Commission all employed commercial lobbying firms in the 1990s (*The Independent*, 21 March 1998; *The Guardian*, 14 August 1998). Commercial consultancy firms provide a range of services such as relevant information on political and parliamentary developments and more specialised advice on lobbying campaigns. The latter may include, for example, how to launch a 'fire brigade campaign', advice on which ideas will fit in with government programmes and therefore stand the most chance of success, and the finding of allies, i.e. other groups with similar interests in order to add weight to a particular lobbying effort. Much of the work of lobbying consultancies is unexceptionable and indeed valuable in 'oiling the wheels' of a democratic society. The increased specialisation of lobbying, with companies, for example, creating their own in-house lobbying expertise as well as employing specialised political consultants, has developed alongside the postwar 'consultation culture' (Jordan, 1991). However, by the late 1990s, some disquieting issues had arisen around the commercial lobbying industry (Box 4.3).

BOX 4.3

The commercial lobbyists

During the 1990s, several important issues emerged around the activities of the multi-client consultancy industry.

The 'revolving door' syndrome: innocent or flawed?

The services of former civil servants are much valued by consultancy companies and evidence from the early 1990s suggested that one in two civil servants leaving Whitehall joined consultancy firms or went into consultancy work in 1993 compared with one in eight in 1989. Former Ministry of Defence and DTI officials were in the greatest

---

BOX 4.3 (CONTINUED)

demand. Strict rules are supposed to apply to the movement of civil servants into private sector appointments relating amongst other matters to waiting periods (up to two years). In 1983, the Commons Treasury and Civil Service Select Committee felt that the extent of this movement was in danger of undermining traditional civil service independence and impartiality. Supporters insist that this practice is of benefit not only to the firms and individuals concerned but to the public too because it enables private business to present a better-informed case to government. But critics suggest that unless very stringently controlled it places consultancy firms, their clients and private business in the position to gain large contracts from inside knowledge.

The 'cash for access' affair – privileged information for the well-heeled?

The 'cash for access' affair embarrassed the Labour Government in July 1998 when *The Observer* newspaper revealed that key Labour advisers when the party was in opposition were now working for lobbying companies and at the very least were promising to use their contacts with government to obtain benefits for their clients. These included advance knowledge of confidential information (e.g. the Chancellor's speeches), help in securing a place on business policy-formulating task-forces, meetings with ministers and special advisers, and lunch at No. 10 Downing Street. The revelations prompted the Opposition leader to attack Labour's 'culture of cronyism' and Prime Minister Blair to respond by tightening government regulations on contacts with lobbyists. Civil servants and special advisers were told that they must not leak confidential and especially market sensitive information to a lobbyist and must not help a lobbyist attract business by arranging for clients to have privileged access to ministers or undue influence over policy. They could accept modest hospitality from a lobbyist but should pull back if they found it happening a lot. The guidelines suggested that where the clients of lobbying companies were given access to state their case, civil servants should seek out opposing groups to present the counter arguments, thereby blunting the advantages lobbyists have in contacting and influencing government.

Lobbying consultancy services: always useful or often a waste of money?

Information released during the 'cash for access' affair revealed that large numbers of public bodies were spending large sums of taxpayers' money on consultancy services whose real necessity was not always apparent. For example, the British Council pays Westminster Strategy £1600 a month to monitor parliament and activity affecting it by the Foreign Office and two other departments; the Commission for Racial Equality pays Rowland Public Affairs £30 000 a year for similar political monitoring whilst the Audit Commission pays four lobbying companies a total sum of £311 000 a year, mainly for running its press office but also for parliamentary monitoring and handling its presentations at party conferences. Critics allege that much of the information acquired so expensively could be discovered in-house from the Internet at a tiny fraction of the cost. The public bodies reply that it is more effective to employ a consultancy company for political monitoring than their own staff. Where such firms have been required to lobby government, moreover, concessions have been gained – for example, Newham Borough used lobbyists to press John Prescott not to cancel the Channel Tunnel link whilst Luton Borough Council used the same lobbying company to assist it in gaining additional public money for its municipal airport.

BOX 4.3 (CONTINUED)

Reverse lobbying: parties use lobbyists to contact business

Material published by the press in 1998 also revealed not only the large number of former Labour Party staff working for lobbying companies (over 30) but also that the party's fundraisers were using lobbying companies to seek sponsorship from their clients. Thus, the party informed political lobbying firms of sponsorship opportunities available to their clients at its annual conference: a table for ten at the conference gala dinner at a cost of £2000 would give corporate clients the opportunity to meet a junior minister, select committee member or MP.

(Sources: Miller (1990); Jordan (1991); *The Independent*, 21 March 1998; *Daily Telegraph*, 9 July 1998; *The Guardian*, 13 February 1995, 28 July, 14 August 1998; *The Observer*, 5, 12, 19 and 26 July 1998)

Questions

1. Are professional lobbying firms an essential or expendable part of the democratic process?

2. How far is it acceptable that government departments and/or public bodies should use taxpayers' money to employ lobbying firms to discover information about government which they could discover less expensively or free for themselves?

3. How far will the tightening of the internal government regulations on contacts between civil servants and lobbyists make commercial lobbying acceptable? Should there also be a statutory register of lobbyists to make lobbying more open and accountable?

Summary

- The concentration of power in the core executive in Britain makes it the primary, if not the only, target for pressure groups.

- Although group–government contacts take place at all levels of government, the bulk of such contacts take place at the junior ministerial and junior civil servant levels.

- Insider groups are involved in a high level of regular, routinised contacts with government but research shows outsider groups to be in frequent contact also.

- Most pressure group–government contacts are informal but there are also extensive formal links through group representation on executive bodies and advisory committees and systematic consultation before legislation, including statutory instruments.

- There are advantages both to groups and government in the consultative process, with government gaining up-to-date, specialised information and groups receiving the capacity to influence government policy-making.

- The qualities of a group that persuade government to confer legitimacy upon it by drawing it into a regular, consultative relationship include its representativeness, willingness to compromise, the reliability and quality of its advice, and its economic leverage and veto power. Groups with extreme and/or controversial demands are almost invariably unacceptable to government.

- The bulk of government decisions are made within routinised sets of relationships involving ministers, officials and groups known as policy networks. This concept usefully suggests how government decision-making is compartmentalised in vertical segments, how officials often identify closely with the main groups in their network and how the existence of policy networks influences policy decisions by biasing outcomes in a particular direction.

- Recent decades have demonstrated how policy networks can change as a consequence both of changes of government and ministerial style and of the growth of new knowledge and social movements.

- The policy influence of intellectual pressure groups known as think-tanks has grown in recent decades, largely because of the major parties' diminished confidence in the civil service, the universities and their own research departments as sources of new ideas.

- A multi-million pound lobbying industry developed in the 1980s and 1990s to mediate between government and its clients who are drawn from all parts of the group spectrum. Whilst this largely fulfils a useful purpose and operates within acceptable bounds, public concern has arisen about some of its activities, including whether the former government 'insiders' it employs (civil servants, party advisers) enable it on occasion to exploit their close relationships with government unfairly on behalf of particular clients.

Further reading

Classic works on the relations between pressure groups and government are: Richardson, J.J. and Jordan, A.G. (1979) *Governing Under Pressure* (Oxford: Blackwell); Jordan, A.G. and Richardson, J.J. (1987a) *Government and Pressure Groups in Britain* (Oxford: Clarendon Press) and Jordan, A.G. and Richardson, J.J. (1987b) *British Politics and the Policy Process* (London: Allen and Unwin). A very useful brief essay is Richardson, J.J. (1993) 'Interest group behaviour in Britain: continuity and change' in Richardson, J.J. (ed.) *Pressure Groups* (Oxford: Oxford University Press). An overview of policy networks theory is provided by Rhodes, R.A.W. and Marsh, D. (1996) 'The concept of policy networks in British political science: its development and utility', *Talking Politics*, 8, 3, Spring whilst Marsh, D. and Rhodes, R.A.W. (eds) (1992) *Policy Networks in British Government* (Oxford: Clarendon Press) contains some interesting case studies. Another useful case study is

Dudley, G. and Richardson, J.J. (1996) 'Promiscuous and celibate ministerial styles: policy change, policy networks and British roads policy', *Parliamentary Affairs*, 49, 4, October. On the influence of think-tanks, there are Cockett, R. (1995) *Thinking the Unthinkable: Think-Tanks and the Economic Counter-Revolution, 1931–1983* (London: Fontana) and Stone, D. (1996) *Capturing the Political Imagination: Think Tanks and the Policy Process* (London: Cass).

CHAPTER 5

Pressure groups and parliament

This book so far has focused on British politics as a constant process of bargaining and negotiation between *government* and groups and has had little to say about *parliament* and groups. Indeed for some accounts, which depict Britain as 'a post-parliamentary democracy', the analysis to this point would need to go little further as the central executive territory remains the primary focus of pressure group activity and there is little opportunity for parliamentary participation in the group–government world (see for example, Richardson and Jordan, 1979; Smith, 1993a, 1995; Marsh and Rhodes, 1992; Richardson, 1993). Without denying the validity of the policy networks analysis advanced by this school of political science, however, other writers have made a persuasive case for the continuing importance of parliament – and therefore of group lobbying of parliament – in the British political system (see especially Judge, 1993; Rush, 1990; Norton, 1990, 1993). According to this argument, parliament retains a vital role in British democracy for two main reasons. First, parliament remains crucial because it legitimates the outcomes of group–bureaucracy negotiations. The authority of government in negotiating with groups is delegated from representative institutions, and public policy decisions emanating from government are legitimised by a presumption of the ultimate authority of parliament. The practical implication of this is that when civil servants negotiate with groups they are constrained in their dealings by the knowledge that their ministers will ultimately be held accountable to parliament. Second, in practice decisions may be significantly influenced by parliament and hence, as will be seen throughout this chapter, groups may seek to use parliament over a wide range of issues and political circumstances. This chapter explores how groups attempt to exploit the lobbying opportunities available in parliament. Judged from the all-embracing perspective of government, groups may occupy only the 'nooks and crannies' of political influence, but from the perspective of the groups themselves, these avenues may loom large. The chapter first examines group perceptions of parliament as a target for influence; second, looks in detail at precisely how groups use parliament to further their purposes; and finally, considers how groups are represented in parliament and in particular the problems that certain types of financial relationship between groups and MPs have generated in the 1990s.

The continuing significance of parliament

The best evidence for the continuing importance of parliament as a target for groups is contained in a survey of a wide range of sectional and promotional organisations by the Study of Parliament Group (SPG) in 1986 (Rush, 1990). The research showed that 'organisational contacts with parliament are extensive' (Table 5.1).

Lobbying of parliament may even have increased in the 1980s: 45 per cent of groups in a survey by Baggott reported an increase in contacts with MPs and 37 per cent, increasing contacts with peers (Baggott, 1992, p. 21). Possible reasons for this increase include the rise in back-bench independence from the 1970s; the establishment of the new system of departmental select committees in 1979, which provided another channel of potential influence; the growth of specialist political influence; the expansion of the professional lobbying industry in the 1980s; the distancing of government from the major producer groups after 1979; and Conservative domination of the House of Commons, 1979–97, which had the effect of directing pressure group attention to Conservative back-benchers and the House of Lords as the main obstacles to government legislation.

An increase in parliamentary lobbying by groups is quite compatible with groups' realistic understanding of the location of power in the British system. In the SPG survey, groups ranked parliament fourth – below government departments, ministers and the media but ahead of public opinion and parties – as influences on public policy (Rush, 1990, p. 272). Groups' lobbying of parliament, despite their clear perception that the bulk of decisions in the

Table 5.1 Pressure groups contacts with parliament

Type of contact	%
Regular or frequent contact with MPs	74.7
Presented written evidence to a select committee	65.6
Regular or frequent contact with peers	58.7
Presented oral evidence to a select committee	49.0
Contacts with all-party groups	47.6
Contacts with party subject groups or committees	40.9

Source: Rush (1990), p. 14.

British system are taken in Whitehall, leads to an apparent contradiction to be explained. Does this mean that groups are misguided, wasting their time and their clients' money in efforts at political influence which are doomed to fail?

The answer is that groups are not misdirecting their efforts and in fact validly and effectively target parliament in a wide range of particular circumstances:

- *Destabilisation of policy communities, for instance by the emergence of new interests.* For example, the breakdown of the agricultural policy community over food safety and environmental issues in the late 1980s leading to the politicisation of an issue and its entry into the wider public arena (e.g. salmonella in eggs).

- *The emergence of new issues* often after a change of government, e.g. privatisation and regulation of utilities in the 1980s and 1990s. For example, the Water Authorities Association was assured by already-privatised utilities that 'their best bargaining time had been when their bills had been on the parliamentary timetable' (cited in Judge, 1993, p. 127); other groups such as British Shipbuilders and British Gas used parliament to publicise their rearguard action against privatisation.

- *Pursuit of a dual – 'belt and braces' – strategy.* Even where established policy communities and networks have not broken down or been disrupted, many groups follow a strategy of establishing contacts with parliament as well as with the executive, even if they do accord parliamentary lobbying lower priority. Thus, lobbying parliament often complements lobbying Whitehall – a 1985 survey of 180 large companies found that 61 per cent saw a need for monitoring parliament. 'Through MPs, interest groups hope to reach ministers and officials, and often do so' (Adonis, 1993, p. 119).

- *Second chance attempts to retrieve situations lost at the policy formation stage.* If groups fail to influence legislation affecting their interests in its formative stages, lobbying parliament during the passing of a bill provides them with another opportunity to gain concessions: most groups are interested in 'relatively narrow, often very narrow, aspects of policy' and often require quite small, rather technical, amendments in order to achieve their goals. This is obtainable through parliamentary lobbying because 'parliament affects the full range of policy only on very rare occasions. On matters of detail, however, Parliament can and does have an impact and many outside organisations are well aware of it' (Rush, 1990, p. 276).

- *'Climate-setting', i.e. shaping the future policy agenda and establishing their own credibility in a field*, even where no legislative change is in sight by, for example, inspiring questions or giving evidence on the working of existing policies to departmental select committees, thereby making policy implementation into 'the next round of policy development' (Pross, 1986, cited in Judge, 1993, p. 130). In this way, parliament forms part of 'a continuing background briefing' (Rush, 1990, p. 276).

- *Sponsoring legislation on social and moral reform issues* through private members' bills or, in the case of local authorities and business groups, using parliament to promote private bills.

An earlier explanation that groups lobbied parliament because they lacked access in Whitehall is no longer valid in view of the evidence that groups with good access to civil servants and ministers lobby parliament on a regular basis. Earlier studies which suggested that groups with well-established insider relationships with government departments had few contacts with parliament while outsiders lacking such executive contacts focused mainly on parliament were borne out only 'to a degree' by the SPG survey. There were differences between the two types of group but these were mainly of emphasis, with outsider and promotional according greater priority to parliament and insider and sectional groups prioritising the executive. But all types of group ultimately accorded some attention to parliament, whilst perfectly aware that policy is largely formed 'outside the parliamentary arena' (Rush, 1990, p. 273).

The SPG research thus demonstrated 'beyond doubt that Parliament is a significant focal point for pressure group politics'. By a considerable margin, groups regarded MPs as the most important form of parliamentary contact, the overall rank order being: 1, back-bench MPs; 2, select committees; 3, back-bench peers; 4, all-party groups; 5, party committees (Rush, 1990, p. 254).

Groups' use of parliament

There are three main ways in which groups seek policy influence within parliament: by seeking amendments to government bills; by sponsoring bills themselves; and by trying to create a climate of opinion favourable to their goals.

Amending government legislation

Although parliament is an increasingly useful channel for pressure group influence, it is very much a last resort. In terms of influencing legislation, the pre-legislative stage is by far the greatest opportunity for influence. At the legislative stage, major successes such as the 1986 Shops Bill – during which pressure group lobbying triggered a back-bench revolt which forced the government to withdraw the Bill – are very rare (see Box 5.1). More usually, groups seek amendments: 53.6 per cent of respondents in the SPG survey stated that they expressed their concern about legislation by asking MPs to propose an amendment at the committee or report stages of a bill. Because most successful amendments are government amendments, the groups' main target is usually the junior minister charged with piloting legislation through the Commons. Groups can operate either through back-benchers of the governing party or through the opposition.

With the opposition lacking relevant briefings on a bill, pressure groups often function as a kind of 'civil service' to it by providing much-needed information and advice. As J.A.G. Griffith has remarked: 'On important bills the affected interests outside parliament will be anxious to help (the Opposition) in the hope of bringing further pressure to bear on the Government to accept amendments. And if they are powerful they will be well and expertly staffed and will have or will engage lawyers to draft amendments so that all Opposition members need to do, if they are so minded, is to sign the amendment provided and hand it in to the Public Bill Office. At times, this servicing by professionals comes close in its drafting and in its briefing to the service provided for the Minister by his department' (Walkland and Ryle, 1981, pp. 124–5). Griffith continues: 'Sometimes those leading for the Opposition set up working parties of their own drawn from outside, affected interests and also draw on teams of lawyers from outside Parliament. These groups may meet regularly to prepare the Opposition case in detail against the bill when it is in committee ... So also those leading for the Opposition may regularly meet with their supporters, on a standing committee, or specially selected group if the bill is committed to the whole House, and may seek to divide amongst them the task of moving amendments' (Walkland and Ryle, 1981, p. 125). Examples of cooperation between the opposition and outside interests are numerous. Within the poverty lobby, for example, groups such as Age Concern and the Disablement Income Group are 'heavily involved in parliamentary lobbying on a continuing basis ... DIG has three parliamentary vice-chairmen, one from each of the major parties, and also a number of sympathetic MPs upon whom it draws to ask parliamentary questions and *to raise amendments to legislation in committee*' (Whiteley and Winyard, 1987, p. 95, italics mine). Also, the Child Poverty Action Group engaged in 'damage limitation' against the 1986 Social Security Act although it had to admit that 'only two concessions were wrung from the government during the Bill's passage through parliament' (cited in Whiteley and Winyard, 1987, p. 124).

How effective is group lobbying at the legislative stage? One commentator has argued persuasively that groups are 'modestly effective' in their attempts to influence legislation. They are most effective on 'those measures which are not at the heart of the partisan battle between Government and opposition'. Indeed, 'the more partisan the debate carried over into committee from second reading, the more group representations are subordinated to, or squeezed out by, party considerations' (Norton, cited in Rush, 1990, pp. 190–1). However, the fact that only a minority of bills each session falls into an 'exclusively partisan' category gives scope for group influence, as is evident from the SPG survey in which well over half of respondents claimed success in influencing legislation (Table 5.2). Box 5.1 provides an interesting example of how group lobbying first blocked and then assisted government reform of the Sunday

Table 5.2 Pressure group perceptions of success in influencing legislation

Response	%
Very successful	7.2
Quite successful	48.3
Not very successful	38.6
Unsuccessful	5.8
Total	99.9

Source: Rush (1990), p. 193.

BOX 5.1

Reform of the law on Sunday shopping (1994)

The background

Reform of the Sunday shopping law became a parliamentary issue in 1986, when the Thatcher Government failed with a measure introducing total deregulation, and once again in 1994, when the Major Government succeeded in introducing partial deregulation of Sunday shopping. At stake was the right of shops to open on Sundays and sell a full range of goods. The Shops Act (1950) prohibited Sunday trading except for a limited number of exceptions. However, the Act was full of anomalies – for example, shops could sell fresh but not frozen vegetables, a car battery but not a torch battery, fish and chips from a Chinese takeaway but not from a fish and chip shop, and so on – and was increasingly ignored by shops. By the early 1990s, almost 150 000 shops were thought to be opening on Sundays. The first bill attempting reform of the outdated legislation in 1986 was defeated narrowly on second reading by 296 votes to 282 as 72 rebel Conservatives combined with the Labour opposition with the backing of a vociferous campaign from the churches and main shopworkers' union.

The Sunday Trading Act (1994)

In 1986, the Conservative Government imposed a three-line whip on second reading but in 1994 it gave the Commons a free vote on three options: total deregulation; partial deregulation, allowing all shops under a certain size (280 square metres) to open all day and larger ones for six hours; and limited opening, allowing certain types of shop to open throughout the year and all shops to open only on the four Sundays before Christmas. The partial deregulation option eventually won the day by 333 votes to 258 in December 1993, but only after another fierce lobbying campaign by the groups concerned. These were:

- *For partial or complete deregulation*. The main lobbyist for reform was the Shopping Hours Reform Council (SHRC), a coalition of retailers established in 1988 to campaign for abolition of the Sunday trading law. It included several supermarkets and DIY stores such as B&Q, which was already trading illegally on Sundays. Its case was that

BOX 5.1 (CONTINUED)

consumers wanted to shop on Sundays and that the existing law was anomalous and widely flouted. Whilst keen for total deregulation, if that proved politically unobtainable, it was prepared to settle for the compromise 'six hour' proposal with safeguards for workers who agreed to work on Sundays. It ran an effective campaign targeted on MPs, advising retailers to invite MPs to visit their stores on Sundays to meet staff and customers.

- *For restricted trading/limited opening.* Keep Sunday Special (KSS) was an independent campaigning body (established in 1985) which had the support of trade associations, small and medium-sized companies, the main churches and the trade unions. It supported restricted trading, i.e. allowing certain shops such as convenience stores, corner shops, DIY stores, garden centres, motor spares shops, newsagents and video shops to open on Sundays but not large food supermarkets or clothes shops (Figure 5.1). Its case against full or partial deregulation of Sunday trading was that it would increase competition in the retailing sector which could lead to a significant deterioration in pay, conditions of work and quality of employment in retailing and jeopardise the rights of retail workers not to work on Sundays and to receive a wage premium for Sunday working. The Retailers for Shops Act Reform (RSAR), a coalition of large and small retailers established in 1992 which included Marks & Spencer and other high street stores such as the Burton Group, Kwik Save and Littlewoods, also opposed total and partial deregulation and wanted to restrict Sunday opening. But whilst backing the KSS position, it would go slightly further and permit Sunday trading on the four Sundays before Christmas. The Union of Shop, Allied and Distributive Workers (USDAW) opposed reform based on total deregulation in 1986, fearing downward pressure on wages as a result of increased competition in retailing. But the union changed its position as a result of experience between 1992 and 1994 when, with widespread illegal opening unchecked by the authorities, thousands of its members volunteered to work on Sundays for double-time rates and a consultation exercise revealed that a majority did not object to Sunday trading provided working was voluntary and paid for at double-time rates. Finally, the Lord's Day Observance Society (LDS, 1831) worked closely with KSS. Its campaign stressed mitigating the impact of change and protecting the rights of employees who did not want to work on Sundays.

Why reform succeeded in 1994, having failed in 1986

- As in 1986, there was only minority support for total deregulation but, with some diehard opponents having left the House, there was more support amongst MPs for partial deregulation.

- The lobby against change was weaker, despite substantial spending estimated at £5–7 million by the KSS campaign.

- The lobby for change was stronger, mainly because the larger retailers were now openly campaigning for reform through the SHRC, having kept a low profile in 1986. There was increasing support from the public, because of favourable experiences of Sunday shopping; the Labour Party, now more of a consumers' and less of a producers' party; and the unions, with the main one, USDAW, now supporting partial deregulation.

BOX 5.1 (CONTINUED)

Figure 5.1 Happy Sunday shoppers.

The outcome

Having been forced to accept the 'six hour' Sunday opening proposal, USDAW worked hard at the committee stage in cooperation with Labour's Front Bench and its nine sponsored MPs to ensure the final legislation enshrined the best deal available for workers. In general, the union was satisfied with the employee protection written into the Act of 'no dismissal or detriment' (i.e. workers could not be dismissed or suffer detriment for refusing to work on Sundays). But it failed to get the government to accept amendments that would have introduced legally enforceable double-time 'premium' payments, forced employers to make up hours lost when workers opted-out of Sunday working by offering alternative weekday work, limited the working day to eight hours and reduced the notice period for opting out from three months to one

BOX 5.1 (CONTINUED)

month. In the Lords, the union worked with Brenda Dean, formerly SOGAT (Society of Graphical and Allied Trades), and Margaret Jay, spokesperson for the SHRC. Through the SHRC, USDAW signed an agreement improving employment conditions for Sunday workers with eight major retailers employing approximately half a million workers. (Source: Watts (1995))

Questions

1. Why did the SHRC encourage retailers to invite MPs to visit their stores on Sundays? How effective was this as a campaigning tactic?

2. How and why did USDAW change its position on reform of the Sunday trading law between 1986 and 1994?

3. Why did the Lord's Day Observance Society advocate mitigating the impact of change rather than opposing it?

4. How far is this case study an example of successful cooperation between the opposition and outside interests?

5. 'Effective lobbying depends on the willingness to compromise. The goal of pressure groups is not the optimum deal but the best deal available in the circumstances.' Comment on this statement from the perspective of one or more groups involved in this case study.

shopping law on which, when it was introduced for the second time in 1994, MPs had a free vote. The issue involved not only matters of conscience but also powerful commercial interests.

However, groups often achieved their goals or some of their goals despite the faulty techniques they employed, being guilty of badly timed, poorly targeted efforts and of using poor quality material. Too many of them failed to suggest amendments. In general, groups were too addicted to blanket coverage of MPs rather than the selective pin-pointing of sympathisers; of moving too late after a bill had received its second reading; and of petitioning and organising lobbies, all of which made success less likely (Rush, 1990, pp. 194–6).

Groups may also try to influence statutory instruments (secondary or delegated legislation). Statutory instruments are new government regulations that are merely laid before parliament. They frequently cover matters of sectional interest and are generally laid only after consultation with affected groups. Indeed, to a greater extent than primary legislation, secondary legislation is the product of negotiations – often technical in nature – between civil servants and affected groups within small policy communities. Having numbered a mere 543 in 1979 and averaged an annual 1900 in the early 1980s, statutory instruments rose sharply in the 1990s to 3334 in 1994. Of the groups participating in the SPG survey, 36 per cent had attempted to influence or change the contents of a statutory instrument once laid before parliament. However, the ineffectiveness of seeking influence at this stage – rather than at the formulation stage – is apparent from the evidence: only 11 out of over 2500 statutory instruments were withdrawn in the three sessions 1980/1–1982/3 (Rush, 1990, p. 208).

Sponsoring legislation

(1) Private Member's Bills

Pressure groups sponsor a relatively small proportion of Private Member's Bills: between 1979–80 and 1985–86, their share was 25 bills in the seven sessions, 23 per cent of the total – in historical terms, a low percentage. Moreover, once introduced, group-sponsored bills have less chance of becoming Acts than Private Member's Bills which originate in government departments and the reports of official committees (altogether, 41 per cent of the total between 1979–80 and 1985–86). This is because, whereas measures deriving from government departments and official reports are 'narrow, technical and non-contentious', pressure group-sponsored bills are often 'broad, non-technical and contentious', and as such likely to encounter opposition not only from government but also from rival groups who can persuade sympathetic MPs to 'talk out' a measure. Between 1979 and 1986, a mere five bills – 8 per cent of all balloted bills – originated in pressure groups (Marsh and Read, 1988, pp. 45–8). In order to succeed, Private Member's legislation needs government consent; legislation opposed by government has little chance of success. Government can block Private Member's Bills it dislikes either by refusing to allow them sufficient time or by getting its own back-benchers to table damaging amendments, which was the reason the Civil Rights (Disabled) Bill fell in 1994. Private Member's legislation thus constitutes 'a relatively hazardous route for pressure group influence' (Grant, 1995, p. 76).

Nonetheless, Private Member's legislation offers a rare opportunity to groups to promote desired change rather than simply respond to initiatives from elsewhere. Of the three-quarters of respondents to the SPG survey who had regular or frequent contact with one or more MPs, over one-third (37 per cent) had asked an MP to sponsor a Private Member's Bill (Rush, 1990, pp. 201–2). Outsider groups, promotional groups, consumer, socio-cultural and labour organisations were the bodies most likely to sponsor Private Member's Bills. In the 1960s – the most successful period for pressure group sponsorship of Private Member's legislation – cause groups promoted bills liberalising the law on abortion, divorce, homosexuality and capital punishment. Even if it fails to become law, a Private Member's Bill at least provides a mechanism for 'tension release': subjects of public concern such as abortion, video nasties, obscene publications, foreign trips for paedophiles, ageism in job advertisements, noisy neighbours, pyramid selling and fox-hunting have received a parliamentary airing in this way. Moreover, Private Member's Bills can get a topic onto the political agenda, sometimes encouraging government to introduce measures of its own. Few of the 20 measures topping the annual ballot for Private Member's legislation in 1995–96 had the necessary ingredients for success: government backing and all-party support. Moreover, the Wild Mammals Protection Bill which did reach the statute book in 1996 did so only at the price of excluding contentious plans to outlaw fox-hunting. Among Private Member's Bills that failed, however, were those to conserve water, protect whistle-blowers and switch to Central European Time: these measures were typical of Private Member's Bills in their contentiousness, high degree of public concern and failure because of lack of government support (see Box 5.2).

BOX 5.2

The 1997–98 Private Member's Bill to ban fox-hunting

The background

The Labour Party's 1997 manifesto promised a free vote in parliament on a ban on hunting with dogs.

The Wild Mammals (Hunting With Dogs) Bill: the main stages

- May 1997 – Animal rightists, their opponents and other lobbying groups were present at the back-benchers' ballot for the right to introduce a Private Member's Bill; realistically, only the first six in the ballot have any chance of their bill succeeding. New Labour MP Michael Foster came first and immediately declared an interest in introducing a bill banning hunting with dogs.

- October 1997 – Foster announced his bill.

- November 1997 – The bill received a huge Commons majority of over 250 (411 votes to 151) at second reading.

- December 1997 – The bill entered its committee stage, i.e. line-by-line scrutiny by 20 back-bench MPs chosen to reflect the second reading vote. Supporters of the bill were anxious to debate every issue in order to prevent further debate when the bill returned to the full House whilst opponents were keen to slow progress down to make sure there was plenty to discuss later. The government was technically neutral but its business managers did not want the bill to leave the Commons for fear that the Lords would use the bill to delay the rest of its legislative programme, which included key constitutional and other measures. In any case, it knew the bill was likely to be defeated in the Lords since Lord Cranborne, the opposition leader in the upper house and a keen fox-hunter himself, had predicted that the 'green welly brigade' – pro-hunting hereditary peers who seldom turned up except on the few issues that interest them – would turn out in force to vote the measure down.

- 6 March 1998 – Having been amended in committee, the bill returned to the full House for report stage and third reading. Time was scarce (in effect, two Fridays) because other Private Member's Bills were also ready for third reading and under the Commons rules had precedence. At this stage, pro-hunting MPs, marshalled by a

BOX 5.2 (CONTINUED)

former Conservative Home Office minister, sought to delay the bill (filibuster) as much as possible by tabling hundreds of amendments. Foster could stop a filibuster by calling a vote but needed 100 of his supporters available at all times while his opponents needed a series of amendments and new clauses raising issues not covered by committee discussion. Conservative MPs' time-wasting tactics succeeded: it was reported that 'in colourful but aggravating scenes, they filibustered, threw top hats around the chamber, made numerous points of order, and were even warned against using up time by walking slowly through the voting lobbies ... as part of the time-wasting, (they) debated the definition of "a dog", with one insisting that if the bill went through, "dogs" would be banned from fox-hunting but not bitches'.

- 11–13 March – Foster made a last-minute attempt to ban hunting, first tabling amendments to kill his own bill, then attempting to add a clause to the Wild Mammals Act which would outlaw hunting with dogs, but his opponents discovered the plan and once again drafted sufficient amendments to kill the attempt.

The lobbyists

The parliamentary progress of the bill was accompanied by fierce lobbying by animal rightists and their pro-hunting opponents. The key groups were the Campaign for the Protection of Hunted Animals, an umbrella group of anti-hunting organisations which included the RSPCA, the League against Cruel Sports and the International Fund for Animal Welfare, and the Countryside Alliance, the main pro-hunting lobby in which the British Field Sports Society was prominent. Anti-hunting groups argued that hunting with dogs was a cruel practice which demeaned a civilised society whilst their opponents contended that banning it would involve the suppression of a legitimate minority pastime by a tyrannous majority. Each side sought to appeal to public opinion, the former by commissioning opinion polls which showed a majority in favour of a hunt ban, the latter by organising two large demonstrations in the capital in July 1997 and March 1998.

(Sources: *The Guardian*, 13 and 29 November 1997; 6, 7, 13 and 14 March 1998)

Questions

1. How far does the failure of the bill to ban fox-hunting exemplify the statement that 'no Private Member's Bill has any serious chance of becoming law unless it is politically uncontroversial and/or enjoys at least tacit government support' (Adonis, 1993, p. 109)?

2. 'The reason that the Labour Government would not promise the Foster bill more time was politics – its unwillingness to offend powerful rural interests combined with its calculation that the bill would become stuck and defeated in the Lords, thereby delaying its whole legislative programme.' How far can its position be justified?

3. Examine the lessons of this episode for pressure group use of the Private Member's Bill procedure to change the law.

4. Should bills that enjoy majority support on free votes always become law?

(2) Private bills

Private bills often prove a useful form of legislation for sectional groups. They are largely promoted by local authorities or nationalised industries to acquire land or promote a new activity and may amount to as many as 70 in a single session (Grant, 1995, p. 70).

Creating a favourable climate of opinion

In addition to requesting the tabling of an amendment or the sponsoring of a Private Member's Bill, groups make a variety of other demands on MPs. These include arranging a meeting in the House of Commons, arranging a meeting with a minister, arranging a dinner or reception, putting down a parliamentary question, giving oral or written evidence to a select committee, and establishing contacts with party subject groups and all-party groups (Table 5.3).

Groups may seek to raise their profile by contacting MPs on an individual basis or as a member of a committee or group, e.g. party subject committee, all-party committee and select committee. Contacts by groups with MPs on an individual basis include requests to MPs to table questions; support Early Day Motions (a way of publicising an issue); initiate debates (e.g. short adjournment debates at the end of each day); or raise a point in a departmental select committee (Baggott, 1995, p. 144). Groups can also try to influence on an individual basis by organising mass letter-writing campaigns and by wining and dining MPs whom they consider sympathetic (Grant, 1995, pp. 67–8). According to the SPG survey, business groups were more likely to ask an MP to arrange a dinner whilst consumer groups were more likely to ask a Member to table a motion or sponsor a Private Member's Bill. Around one-third (34.4 per cent) of the SPG sample sent information or briefings to MPs regularly (14.3 per cent) or often (20.1 per cent) and about three-fifths

Table 5.3 Requests to MPs by groups

Request	%
To put down a parliamentary question	83.1
To arrange a meeting at the House of Commons	78.3
To table an amendment to a bill	61.9
To table a motion	51.3
To arrange a meeting with a minister	49.7
To arrange a reception, dinner or similar function at the House of Commons	41.3
To introduce or sponsor a Private Member's Bill	37.0

Source: Rush (1990), p. 109.

(59.3 per cent) did so occasionally. Much of this is probably binned unread. Nonetheless, most of the SPG sample (92.5 per cent) found their contacts with MPs useful (46.8 per cent) or very useful (45.7 per cent). Because of the priority MPs accord to their local roles as spokespersons for constituency interests, constituency welfare officers and local ombudsmen, groups often try to lobby through constituency links (Rush, 1990, pp. 107–13).

Party subject committees can be a useful channel of influence for pressure groups: they have links with the whips' offices and party headquarters and can raise issues at the weekly meetings of the Parliamentary Labour Party and 1922 Committee. The Conservative Education Secretary Sir Keith Joseph withdrew his proposals on parental contributions towards student grants after opposition in the Conservative Education Committee (1984) and, according to Nigel Lawson, the introduction of cash accounting for small businesses in the 1987 budget 'stemmed directly' from views expressed at meetings of the 1922 Committee and back-bench Finance Committee (Grant, 1995, p. 73). Back-bench subject committees also played a role in watering down government proposals for the brewing industry in 1989 (Baggott, 1995, p. 147). A leading commercial lobbyist has summed up their role in the 1979–92 period as follows: 'At a time of large Government majorities they are a powerful focus for back-bench opinion on the Government side, with privileged access to Ministers and a representative role enhanced by their regular meetings, at which business, industry and other interest groups are given the opportunity to voice their concerns or be questioned by MPs' (Miller, 1990, p. 40).

Two-fifths of the SPG sample (40.9 per cent) had made contact with party committees and nearly three-quarters of these rated their contacts with the committees useful (61.2 per cent) or very useful (12.6 per cent) (Rush, 1990, p. 130). For their part, the subject committees 'look to the interest groups to provide specialised information, invite their spokesmen to speak at the weekly meetings (although two-thirds of the presentations were unsolicited), make fact-finding visits, organise full morning seminars on important topics to which various pressure groups will be invited to contribute, and hold joint meetings with other subject committees should the issue of concern cross committee boundaries' (J. Barry Jones in Rush, 1990, p. 122). Whilst approaching pressure group submissions with a degree of scepticism, committee members felt able to use group resources without compromising their integrity. Indeed, committee members from both sides of the House 'felt strongly that they needed information provided by organised interests to perform their back-bench functions': such material helped to 'cut out the work' in formulating parliamentary speeches and generally assisted MPs in performing their duties in a more professional manner (Rush, 1990, p. 123).

Unlike subject committees, *all-party groups* operate largely outside the party power structures and form a 'natural focus' for pressure groups. They enable groups to stimulate parliamentary interest in an issue, raise its political salience and eventually place it on the political and parliamentary agenda. In 1988, 25 of the 103 all-party subject committees were serviced administratively by pressure groups – for example, the Animal Welfare Parliamentary Group by the RSPCA and the Chemical Industry Group by the Chemical Industries Association. The provision of administrative services gives pressure groups many opportunities to emphasise their viewpoints, for example, in the drafting of agenda papers, information packs and policy statements, and in the summarising of official reports. All-party groups can serve as vehicles for 'short, sharp, single-issue, high profile campaigns' such as that waged by the Wing Airport Resistance Association (WARA) in 1970–71 against an inland site for London's third airport or for 'low-key, long-term background campaigns' such as that mounted by the Parliamentary Information Technology Committee (PITCOM) after 1981 to promote the corporate image of information technology. Almost half the groups (47.6 per cent) in the SPG sample had had contacts with all-party groups and over two-thirds of them found such links useful (47.9 per cent) or very useful (21 per cent) (Rush, 1990, pp. 123–33).

The system of Commons *departmental select committees* (DSCs) expanded after 1945, especially after 1979. Despite the overall limitations on their impact, the DSCs can send for 'persons, papers and records' and it is this power to take evidence that makes them attractive to pressure groups as channels of influence. Pressure groups figure prominently on the circulation lists of DSCs and submit a significant proportion of the oral and written evidence received by these committees: in 1985–86, according to the SPG survey, over two-fifths (43.6 per cent) of the evidence submitted to DSCs came from outside organisations, mainly pressure groups, and for certain committees – agriculture, energy, education, social services, trade and industry – the proportion coming from outside bodies was over 50 per cent. Thus 'outside interests are a major source for the committees of non-governmental information' (Rush, 1990, pp. 144–5). Nearly half (49.0 per cent) of the organisations responding to the SPG survey had appeared before a select committee and nearly two-thirds (65.6 per cent) had submitted written evidence. Insider groups were more likely than outsider groups to be invited to provide oral and written evidence to the DSCs. The great majority in the SPG survey believed that their evidence had made an impact on the DSCs and their reports, 16.3 per cent of respondents rating their impact as significant and 69 per cent considering that they had had some impact. The value of this channel to pressure groups is twofold. First, presenting evidence to the DSCs affords the groups a useful publicity outlet in an increasingly significant forum for debate (Giddings, cited in Drewry, 1989, p. 378). Second, 'in so far as select committees can make recommendations, a significant proportion of which are accepted by government, it is likely that pressure groups do have some effect from time to time ... Many of the recommendations made in committee report concern the details of policy, rather than the principle, and the details of policy are what many organisations are interested in influencing' (Rush, 1990, p. 148). In terms of the broader consequences for the democratic system, it seems that the expansion of the select committee system in recent decades has extended the opportunities for groups to seek to influence public policy through parliament.

The House of Lords

The House of Lords became an increasing target for pressure groups in the 1980s and 1990s, mainly because of its growing assertiveness in amending government legislation. Although some defeats were subsequently reversed, the House of Lords defeated the government on 241 occasions between 1979 and 1997. This assertiveness continued under Labour with the Lords defeating the Labour Government on no fewer than 31 occasions between May 1997 and 22 July 1998. Resistance to the government included the blocking of the move to lower the age of consent for gay sex from 18 to 16 in July 1998, thereby frustrating the wishes of gay rights pressure groups such as Stonewall and OutRage. The upper house also became more attractive to groups because of its increased activity: the number of sitting days, average daily attendance, the number of sitting hours and the average length of sittings all rose dramatically between the 1950s and the 1980s. The looser party ties in the Lords further contributed to its appeal to groups. The SPG survey showed that well over two-thirds of organisations (70.2 per cent) had used the House of Lords to make representations or influence policy, and of this group, 83.6 per cent had regular or frequent contact with one or more peers (Rush, 1990, pp. 159–60). Groups use the Lords as they use the Commons, first, to influence legislation and second, to achieve greater publicity for their views. With regard to the former, groups may ask peers either to move amendments to govern-ment bills or introduce a Private Member's Bill. With reference to the latter, groups might request peers to ask a starred question (to elicit information), ask a question for a written answer, ask an unstarred question (leading to debate on an issue) or speak in debate raising points on their behalf. Over four-fifths (81.8 per cent) of respondents in the SPG survey found their contacts with the Lords useful (58.5 per cent) or very useful (23.3 per cent). More surprisingly, perhaps, when questioned about the usefulness of both Houses of Parliament, nearly half (47.7 per cent) of all respondents in the SPG survey rated the two Houses about equal when seeking to make representations or influence policy, with 26.1 per cent of the rest regarding the Commons as more useful and 23.9 per cent considering the Lords more useful (Rush, 1990, p. 164).

The representation of outside interests in the House of Commons

The House of Commons as a representative institution is primarily represent-ative of voters organised in constituencies. But it is also representative of party and of groups. These three kinds of representation combine in an MP, who is always a representative of constituency, normally a representative of party and frequently although not invariably the representative of an interest or interests. The representation of interests in parliament – financial, landowning, commercial – is not new and has a long history. Lobbyists may gain access to the House of Commons in a variety of ways.

Sponsorship of parliamentary candidates

One important way for groups to gain representation in the Commons has traditionally been by sponsoring parliamentary candidates, but this practice declined after 1995 when direct sponsorship of Labour Party candidates by trade unions was severely curtailed. Between 1945 and 1992 the trade unions had normally sponsored between about a third and a half of all Labour MPs. In general, small sums were involved and went towards the candidate's election expenses rather than directly to the candidate. Unions could not instruct sponsored MPs how to speak or vote since that would have constituted a breach of parliamentary privilege but they did expect the MPs to watch over their interests. Some unions lobbied for particular causes through their sponsored MPs and union-sponsored MPs were prominent in helping to defeat Labour's Industrial Relations Bill in 1969. However, beginning in the 1980s Labour sought to distance itself from the unions, a trend reinforced by the controversy over parliamentary sleaze and the subsequent Nolan Report in the 1990s (see below). Instead of union sponsorship of individual MPs, Labour introduced 'constituency plan agreements' between unions and selected constituency Labour parties (CLPs) with the unions gaining representation on CLP general committees in return for their financial support (Butler and Kavanagh, 1997, p. 206). However, union sponsorship did not end completely in 1995 as was revealed by the 1997 Register of Members' Interests in which several Labour MPs declared that they had received union help with their election expenses in the traditional manner (*Register of Members' Interests*, October 1997 edition).

MPs as advisers, consultants and directors

The Nolan Committee (1995) found that 168 MPs – 145 Conservatives, 15 Labour, six Liberal Democrat and two others – shared 356 consultancies. Thus, about 45 per cent of the entire Conservative Party but a much larger proportion – 66 per cent – of Conservative back-benchers received fees from outside interests. Of the 168 MPs, 26 held multi-client consultancies with public relations firms working for many clients whilst 142 possessed consultancies with specific companies and trade associations. Overall, nearly one-third of the non-ministerial House of Commons worked as paid advisers, consultants or directors. The fees involved could be considerable, with some MPs more than doubling their parliamentary salaries in this way. Interests involved in fee-paying relationships included finance, food manufacturing, pharmaceuticals, hotels, tourism and leisure, electronic instruments, retail clothing, tobacco, brewing, British wine, cable television and waste disposal.

Lobbyists' access through aides and research assistants to MPs

During the 1980s, it became apparent that professional lobbyists for commercial groups were gaining privileged access to the House of Commons by infiltrating their staff as aides and research assistants to MPs. The House of Commons Service Committee reported in 1987–88 that it had received 'disturbing evidence' of direct approaches to MPs from lobbying organisations which in some cases blatantly sought 'the issue of a House of Commons photo-identity pass as a cover for commercial lobbying activities in return for services to the Member concerned' (2nd Report, cited in Adonis, 1993, p. 116). In 1995, the House of Commons Register of Interests of Members' Secretaries and Research Assistants showed 18 individuals working for ministers and MPs who declared 'other gainful occupations' with lobbyists and political consultancies, ten working as in-house consultants with companies such as BP and BAe, and a further nine working as freelance consultants (*The Observer*, 22 January 1995).

Lobbying of MPs by professional consultancy firms

Lobbying of MPs by professional consultancy firms on behalf of commercial clients developed into a multi-million pound industry in the 1980s, with total fees earned by 50 consultancy firms reported to be over £50 million in 1991. Most of the clients of the consultancy firms are businesses: a 1985 survey of 180 large companies found that 41 per cent employed government affairs consultants and 28 per cent employed PR companies for work involving government; 61 per cent of firms saw a need for monitoring parliament (Adonis, 1993, p. 117). The 1996 Register of Interests revealed that MPs were being paid up to £2 million in consultancy fees (*The Observer*, 12 May 1996).

Direct lobbying of parliament by all types of group

Direct lobbying of parliament by a wide range of outside groups increased in the 1980s. Three-quarters of groups in the Study of Parliament Group (SPG) survey had regular or frequent contacts with one or more MPs. Over one-third of groups (34.4 per cent) sent information or briefings to all or a large number of MPs regularly or frequently whilst nearly three-fifths (59.1 per cent) did so occasionally (Rush, 1990, pp. 14, 109). The extent of the relationship between all-party groups and outside interests was revealed in 1995: of the 129 all-party parliamentary groups in 1992 specialising in subjects rather than international ties, 38 were financed by individual businesses, groups of companies and trade associations, with 18 of these staffed by consultants from lobbying firms; a further three all-party groups had connections with lobbying companies whilst most of the rest were staffed or financed by charities (*The Observer*, 17 September 1995).

MPs' pursuit of outside occupations

Many MPs, especially those in business but also lawyers, those with media interests and others, continue to pursue or build up outside occupations on a part-time basis. An *Observer* investigation in 1995 found that 130 MPs, mostly Conservatives, earned over £3 million a year from 275 directorships. Of the 100 MPs with directorships for whom financial information was available, 88 were Conservatives, ten were Labour and two, Liberal Democrat. In addition, other MPs continued to augment their parliamentary salaries by outside interests, one of the most lucrative pursuits being broadcasting and journalism (*The Observer*, 15 October 1995).

Outside interests in the House of Lords

Former careers and interests

The former careers of life peers in the House of Lords enable it to represent a wide range of interests. As Nicholas Baldwin has written: 'Since the passage of the Life Peerages Act in 1958 the House of Lords has acquired newly ennobled bankers, engineers, diplomats, lawyers, businessmen, trade unionists, military commanders, politicians, academics, educationalists, scientists, administrators, and senior civil servants...' (Rush, 1990, p. 156). Former officials of trade unions and business groups such as the CBI are found in the Lords as well as numerous members of promotional groups such as Amnesty International and the Howard League for Penal Reform.

The institutional representation of propertied and monied interests

The life peerage may permit the representation of a variety of professional interests but the essence of the upper house has been its embodiment of hereditary landownership and ecclesiastical privilege. Nearly one-fifth (38) of *Money Magazine*'s 1988 list of Britain's 200 wealthiest people were peers, with members of the Lords estimated to own five and a half million acres between them. With its large landowning, City and professional contingents, concludes Andrew Adonis, 'the Lords is naturally a staunch defender of the free market and employers' and the professions' vested interests'. When these interests conflict with lobbies for the disabled, pensioners and the countryside, 'it is usually the interests, not the lobbies, which win the day' (Adonis, 1993, p. 238).

Peers as paid consultants

The extent to which peers held paid consultancies and received fees for representing outside interests emerged in the 1990s. Peers had been traditionally regarded as speaking for themselves in debate and not on behalf of outside interests and hence, if they took part in a debate in which they had a direct outside interest, they were required by custom to declare it. Peers also developed the habit of indicating that an outside body agrees with the views they are expressing or that they are specifically acting for an outside body. However, in the absence of a register of interests such as had existed in the Commons from the 1970s and with many peers often speaking without declaring an interest, concern grew in the 1990s about the prevalence of paid consultancies in the Lords. A register of interests for the Lords was rejected in 1990 but re-considered by an all-party committee chaired by Lord Griffiths in 1995. Giving evidence to the Griffiths Committee, a Liberal Democrat peer, Lord Lester, stated that one of his commercial clients at the Bar had 'paid substantial sums and given indirect financial benefits to four peers to ask questions and take other action on behalf of him and his company'. At the same time, Lord McIntosh, the Labour deputy leader in the Lords, drawing attention to the extensiveness of paid consultancies, cited the example of Lord Lucas of Chilworth, a Conservative peer, who had the previous week moved 100 amendments in the committee stage of the Environment Bill while being paid as the parliamentary consultant to the National Association of Waste Contractors. He had disclosed his interest and therefore broken no rules but Lord McIntosh believed his fellow-peer's action should be against the rules, and it soon afterwards became so. Following the recommendations of the Griffiths Committee, a Register of Interests was established in the House of Lords (1996) which required peers to publish their outside consultancies but not their fees. The new rules also barred them from speaking, voting or lobbying on behalf of their clients. The new Register of Interests (1996) showed that 22 peers acted as paid parliamentary advisers to outside interests and a further five acted as paid lobbyists for outside companies, including lobbying firms (*The Guardian*, 16 February 1996).

MPs and outside interests

Public concern about the outside financial interests of MPs mounted in the 1990s and was one of the issues leading to the appointment of a committee on standards in public life under the chairmanship of Lord Nolan in October

1994 (see further on 'sleaze', Doig, 1995, 1997). According to the general theory of representative democracy prevailing in Britain, Members of Parliament are expected to exercise their independent judgement on public affairs free of any intervention or interference by outside interests. During the 1990s, however, three instances of MPs' behaviour came to light which appeared to breach this principle. MPs were found to be accepting payments first, for advocating the causes of clients in parliament; second, for tabling amendments to bills in standing committee; and third, for asking questions of ministers in parliament, the going rate for asking a parliamentary question being about one thousand pounds. As well as interfering with the integrity of an MP's judgement, these activities are generally considered wrong because they give those prepared to pay privileged access to influence and because they impose an additional and arbitrary burden on public resources (the cost – often considerable – of answering a parliamentary question). The Nolan Committee was appointed in the immediate aftermath of the 'cash for questions' affair, in which it was alleged by the *Sunday Times* that two Conservative MPs had each accepted £1000 for tabling a parliamentary question. Investigation of the affair by the House of Commons Committee of Privileges led to each being reprimanded, suspended – the one for twenty, the other for ten sitting days – and their salaries withheld for the duration of their suspension. But this decision – in April 1995 – related to individuals. A few weeks later came the broader judgement of the Nolan Committee on the outside interests of MPs in general (May 1995).

The Nolan Committee found that 'the activities of MPs, particularly in the fields of lobbying, advocacy and consultancy, had undermined respect for the House of Commons, its authority and the ability of MPs to discharge their functions, as they should, free from conflicts of interest, according to their own judgement and in the interests of their own constituents and the general public. It was clear from the evidence that arrangements were being entered into by some MPs which seemed to negate the duties of MPs to put public interests first...' (Oliver, cited in Ridley and Doig, 1995, p. 43). Of particular concern to the Nolan Committee was 'the enormous growth in paid consultancy'. Its most severe criticisms were directed at the multi-client consultancy which involved MPs in advocacy on behalf of, or advice to, lobbying or PR firms serving many separate and frequently changing companies. The main objections to paid consultancies were threefold: they arose solely out of the consultants' membership of the House of Commons and enabled wealthy outside interests to 'buy' influence; they operated in secret, with MPs required neither to state all their clients nor list their fees; and they raised acute questions of conflict of interest in MPs, who had to draw the line between a legitimate right to raise concerns on behalf of their clients and succumbing to improper pressure involving bribery.

The main recommendations of the Nolan Commitee are set out in Box 5.3, together with the extent to which they had been implemented by 1998. The rules relating to MPs' relationships with outside interests have now been

BOX 5.3

The Nolan Report and its implementation

Nolan recommendations	Implementation
1. MPs should be free to have outside employment unrelated to their role as MPs	Endorsement of existing practice
2. MPs should be banned from holding consultancies with lobbying companies	Not accepted
3. The House of Commons should institute its own inquiry into the merits of other types of consultancy	Paid advocacy banned, including tabling questions, motions and amendments for fees on behalf of outside interests. Ban on acting in any delegation on behalf of a paid outside interest. Restrictions on MPs' right to speak in debates on behalf of a paid outside interest
4. House of Commons should restate 1947 Resolution barring MPs from entering into contracts or agreements that restrict their freedom to act and speak as they wish, or which require them to act in parliament as representatives of outside bodies	House accepted need for re-commitment to the objectives of the 1947 Resolution, but its wording to to be reviewed in context of draft Code
5. The nature of MPs' interests should be more clearly described in the Register of Members' Interests, with remuneration listed in bands and estimates made of the monetary value of benefits in kind. Contracts relating to provision of services for outside interests should be deposited with the Register	MPs required to disclose earnings from all consultancies derived from parliament from 31 March 1996 and to register all contracts with the Parliamentary Commissioner
6. House of Commons should draw up a new Code of Conduct for MPs, with more detailed rules and guidance on avoiding conflicts of interest	New Code of Conduct published 16 July 1996. Includes ban on using confidential information received in course of parliamentary duties for personal gain
7. An independent Parliamentary Commissioner for Standards should be appointed, with responsibility for maintaining the Register, giving advice and guidance to MPs on matters of conduct and investigating allegations of misconduct	New Parliamentary Commissioner for Standards, Sir Gordon Downey, began work on 15 November 1995. Reports to new Committee on Standards and Privileges

tightened up. In its resolution of 6 November 1995 relating to the conduct of Members, the House of Commons stipulated that it is wrong for any Member to enter into any 'contractual agreement with an outside body, controlling or limiting the Member's complete independence or freedom of action in parliament ... the duty of a Member being to his constituency and the country as a whole, rather than to any particular section thereof ...'. Paid advocacy by MPs is now prohibited in formal matters as is the purchase of access to ministers and civil servants via an MP. Where contracts with outside interests are made, they must be deposited with the Parliamentary Commissioner for Standards (Oliver, 1997, p. 552). The new Parliamentary Commissioner for Standards, Sir Gordon Downey, cleared 15 MPs of any impropriety in accepting election expenses from the lobbyist Ian Greer but found that former Conservative ministers Neil Hamilton and Tim Smith had received payments from Mohammed Al-Fayed for lobbying services and criticised them along with four other MPs for failing to declare or register their interests (Downey Reports, March and July 1997). Hamilton was supported by his constituency party but lost his seat in the 1997 General Election to an anti-sleaze candidate, Martin Bell. The Commons Standards and Privileges Committee upheld the Downey report on Hamilton, criticising him for behaviour that fell 'seriously and persistently short' of the standards expected of MPs.

Nolan's recommendation to ban MPs from holding consultancies with multi-client lobbying companies was not accepted and, whilst paid advocacy on behalf of an outside interest was prohibited, it remained permissible for MPs to continue to receive fees for *advising* outside interests. However, the second Register of Members' Interests (October 1997) published under the new rules of fuller dislosure showed a 66 per cent drop in consultancies from 240 to 80. This fall was largely the result of the new composition of parliament following Labour's landslide victory in May 1997 together with the Nolan reforms and embarrassment over parliamentary sleaze. Nonetheless, corporate culture continued to make an impact on the new Labour-dominated House of Commons, with MPs declaring a large amount of free travel and junkets with free air tickets to all parts of the globe and corporate entertainment at a wide variety of sporting and cultural events including the British Grand Prix at Silverstone, Wimbledon, Lord's, the English National Ballet and the Globe Theatre. Tony Blair's failure to register a visit to Silverstone in July 1996 when leader of the opposition by himself, his wife and children as the guests of the governing body of Formula One earned him a rebuke by the Commons Standards and Privileges Committee in 1998. Also early in 1998, the Committee ruled that Lord Steel had broken parliamentary rules when, as an MP before the 1997 General Election, he had failed to register his employment agreement worth £93 752 as chairman of the Countryside Movement. He had disclosed his appointment in the 1996 Register but had failed to deposit the agreement which is required if an MP undertakes any parliamentary activity for an organisation. He had also failed to declare an interest when tabling three Commons motions which included attacks on the International Fund for Animal Welfare's donation to the Labour Party, which he linked to the party's plans to ban hunting.

The rules relating to disclosure of interests, therefore, are still unclear and are being clarified on a case-by-case basis. MPs are required to register any financial interest or material benefit that might reasonably be thought to influence their actions, speeches or votes in parliament or actions taken in their capacity as MPs. But MPs may still not register certain payments for a variety of reasons including genuine uncertainty about what should be registered or because, in their view, the payments are not for services provided in their capacity as MPs or because they consider registration an invasion of their privacy. Many doubt whether the rules are tight enough. Defiance of the disclosure rules is still possible because the Commons resolution adopted on 6 November 1995 did not have the force of statute law. Penalties for refusal to comply, if proven, range from a rebuke to suspension, but the latter punishment can be ordered only by the whole House of Commons.

Even after the post-Nolan tightening of procedures, self-regulation of its own affairs by the House of Commons remained the rule. This system remains on trial and there are grounds for anxiety as to whether it will prove sufficiently stringent to allay public concern that MPs can make a lot of money by using office improperly. In the past, self-regulation had given grounds to doubt whether self-regulation was sufficiently impartial or strict to control misconduct by MPs. Legitimate questions remain to be answered. Has the new Parliamentary Commissioner adequate powers to investigate charges of corruption and misconduct? Or should MPs be made subject to the ordinary criminal law in bribery cases? Under existing law it is not an offence to bribe or offer a bribe to an MP or for an MP to accept a bribe. Thus, Mohammed Al-Fayed could not be prosecuted for giving a bribe nor could Neil Hamilton and Tim Smith be prosecuted for accepting bribes. The lifting of parliamentary privilege to permit prosecution of MPs for bribery is currently being considered by the Home Secretary Jack Straw. Finally, should the Commons have 'grasped the nettle' and banned paid consultancies, as Nolan wanted? The decision to prohibit paid advocacy rather than paid consultancies appears the weaker of the two alternatives. In that sense, it resembled the situation in 1969 when, following a select committee recommendation to ban paid advocacy, the Commons opted for the easier option of establishing a Register of Members' Interests (1974), which encouraged rather than discouraged paid consultancies, and underlay their proliferation over the following two decades.

BOX 5.4

The debate on MPs and outside interests

The controversy over political sleaze in the 1990s raises serious questions about what is appropriate in the relations between parliamentarians and outside interests. Two important questions are as follows.

Should MPs be full-time professionals or part-time politicians with outside interests?

Many people would follow the Nolan Committee in accepting that MPs should be permitted to have a money-making outside occupation in business, the law, journalism, or whatever, but, like Nolan, draw the line at the representation of outside interests for a fee, a practice generally regarded by Nolan as dubious and some of which (multiple consultancies) he wanted banned. However, those who believe parliamentary representatives should be full-time professionals would wish to prevent Members from retaining any remunerated occupation too. Many of the arguments on either side of the issue apply to both types of outside interest – retention of a profession and the take up of a fee-paying consultancy. The main arguments in favour of MPs being prevented from possessing outside interests are:

- to ensure they devote all their time to the pursuit of their constituents' and the public interest
- to remove allegations of hidden, behind-the-scenes influence together with all suspicions that influence can be bought by wealthy groups
- to eliminate conflicts of interest for MPs
- to ensure the merits of a case, not money, are what count in parliamentary debate.

Against this, it is argued that the retention of outside interests by MPs:

- improves the quality of debate by extending the range of information and experience available to parliament
- prevents parliament becoming an inward-looking assembly staffed by full-time career politicians lacking experience of the world outside the narrow parliamentary sphere
- helps MPs insure against the inevitable insecurities of an MP's life
- through links with trade unions, improves working-class representation – otherwise minimal – in the House of Commons.

What perquisites of office are permissible to MPs?

As already noted in the text, MPs declare a large number of consultancies as well as a wide variety of free trips and entertainments in the Register of Interests. An *Observer* poll (11 May 1997) after the 1997 General Election revealed that MPs themselves held the following views when asked: Should MPs be banned from all consultancies and outside interests?

BOX 5.4 (CONTINUED)

	Lab MPs	Con MPs	LD MPs (%)
Agree	69	7	54
Disagree	31	93	46

And MPs themselves hold the following views on the questions: Is it right or wrong for an MP to accept from an outside lobbyist...

	Lab MPs	Con MPs	LD MPs (%)
...a free lunch?			
Right	68	96	70
Wrong	22	0	7
...wine or whisky at Christmas?			
Right	27	60	31
Wrong	66	34	55
...payment for giving advice on parliamentary matters?			
Right	9	54	17
Wrong	87	44	72

Questions

1. Should MPs be allowed: (a) to possess paid occupations outside parliament; (b) enter into paid contracts to represent outside interests; and (c) enter into paid contracts with outside lobbying organisations? Assess the strength of the arguments in each case.

2. Account for the differences between MPs of different parties in their answers to the *Observer* poll. State your views, giving reasons, on the receipt of gifts, free lunches, travel tickets and entertainment from outside interests by MPs and on their receipt of payment for being outside lobbyists.

Summary

- Although of less importance than the executive as a target for pressure groups, parliament remains a significant focus for influence by a wide range of groups including both sectional and cause groups, insiders as well as outsiders. The importance of parliament for groups has even increased in recent decades with three-quarters of groups telling a major study that they had regular or frequent contacts with MPs.

- Parliament can be important to groups in a wide variety of circumstances, including the breakdown of policy communities, the emergence of new issues, the pursuit of a dual strategy embracing both the executive and legislature, a late 'second chance' possibility to influence legislation, agenda-setting and enhancing credibility, and sponsoring legislation on social and moral issues.

- Pressure groups may ask MPs to table an amendment, sponsor a bill, or help to publicise an issue by, for example, putting down a parliamentary question or supporting an Early Day Motion. They may ask an MP to arrange a meeting with a minister. They also frequently contact MPs as members of committees – party subject committees, all-party committees, and departmental select committees. The utility of such contacts is not one-sided: MPs value groups as sources of useful information and expertise.

- The relative freedom from party ties, increased activity, and greater assertiveness against governments of the House of Lords combined to enhance its usefulness to pressure groups in the 1980s and 1990s. Groups use the upper house as they use the Commons – to influence legislation and to achieve publicity for their views.

- In the mid-1990s, the outside interests of MPs became a matter of intense public concern as it became apparent that MPs had been accepting cash for asking parliamentary questions, tabling amendments to legislation and advocating clients' cases in parliament. Following the Nolan Report, the Commons banned paid advocacy and introduced other more stringent regulations governing the relations between MPs and outside interests. MPs must now deposit their contracts with outside bodies with the new Parliamentary Commissioner for Standards and make more specific declarations of the remuneration they receive in the Register of Interests. But despite the tightening of the rules, parliamentary self-regulation remains on trial.

Further reading

A key work on the relationship between parliament and pressure groups remains Rush, M. (ed.) (1990) *Parliament and Pressure Politics* (Oxford: Clarendon Press). This relationship is considered briefly in Adonis, A. (1993) *Parliament Today*, 2nd edn (Manchester: Manchester University Press) and at greater length in Judge, D. (1993) *The Parliamentary State* (London: Sage). The perspective of the lobbyists themselves is well stated in Miller, C. (1990) *Lobbying Government: Understanding and Influencing the Corridors of Power*, 2nd edn (Oxford: Blackwell) and Jordan, A.G. (ed.) (1991) *The Commercial Lobbyists: Politics for Profit in Britain* (Aberdeen: Aberdeen University Press). The issues surrounding political sleaze and the Nolan Report are well covered in Ridley, F.F. and Doig, A. (eds) (1995) *Sleaze: Politicians,*

Private Interests and Public Reaction (Oxford: Oxford University Press); Berrington, H. (1995) 'Political ethics: the Nolan Report', *Government and Opposition*, 30, 4, Autumn; Norris, P. (1996a) 'The Nolan Committee: financial interests and constituency service', *Government and Opposition*, 31, 4, Autumn; Doig, A. (1997) '"Cash for questions": Parliament's response', *Parliamentary Affairs*, 51, 1, January; Woodhouse, D. (1997) 'Cash for questions: Commissioner's Inquiry', *Parliamentary Affairs*, 51, 1, January; and Vandermark, A. (1994) 'Lobbying and registration: biting the bullet or shifting the focus?', *Talking Politics*, 7, 1, Autumn. Oliver, D. (1997) 'Regulating the conduct of MPs. The British experience of combating corruption', *Political Studies*, XLV, 539–58 offers an incisive overview.

CHAPTER 6

Pressure groups and public campaigns

The pressure groups and campaigns forming the primary concern of this chapter offer a broad contrast to the groups at the centre of the previous three chapters. First, they do not generally aim *directly* at the central institutions of the established political system – at government, civil service and parliament – but rather they seek to exert pressure *indirectly* by means of public campaigns. In other words, they are for the most part outsider groups involved in a wide variety of public campaigning and protest activity on behalf of a large number of causes. The campaigns vary from the small-scale localised protest (e.g. against hospital closures) to the big London-centred demonstration involving hundreds of thousands (e.g. those against the poll tax or the Child Support Agency); they range from the short-term 'fire-brigade' campaign alerting the public to an immediate threat (e.g. miners against pit closures) to the long-term educational campaigns (e.g. those aimed at improving the welfare of wild and farm animals) (see Table 6.1). However, although they take place outside conventional insider channels, the ultimate target of such campaigns is still influence over political decision-makers. Just like insiders, outsider groups seek – indeed, in view of the importance of sustaining and increasing their memberships, some would say, they *need* – political successes. Second, public campaigns often – although not invariably – involve different kinds of groups to those involved in more conventional political lobbying. Thus, some outsider groups, run bureaucratically and hierarchically from London or a major city with minimal public participation, are quite similar in organisational terms to sectional and insider groups. However, a feature of many of the groups engaged in protest in the 1990s has been their *dissimilarity* from traditional top-down organisations; protest against new motorways, for instance, or the export of veal calves has typically involved loose coalitions of local action groups and more experienced eco-warriors or animal rightists from outside. Protesters and campaigners have engaged in a variety of activities outside the normal political process, from peaceful legal methods, to the peaceful illegal and, at the other extreme, the violent and illegal.

Table 6.1 Some leading single-issue campaigns and protests in the 1990s

Aims	Main groups	Outcome
Ban handguns	Snowdrop Campaign	1997 and 1998 Acts banning handguns
Abolish poll tax	Anti-Poll Tax Federation	Replacement of poll tax with council tax
Reform of Child Support Act	Network against the Child Support Act	Resignation of Child Support Agency head; some reforms
Opposition to Criminal Justice and Public Order Act (1994)	Freedom Network Justice	Postponement of certain powers and qualified police implementation of some other powers
Abandon deep-sea dumping of Brent Spar oil rig	Greenpeace	Shell (oil company) shelved plan in favour of recycling rig near Stavanger, Norway
Ban live export of veal calves	Compassion in World Farming Brightlingsea Against Live Exports	EU decision to end veal crate system in 2008; possible earlier action by British government
Ban hunting with hounds	League Against Cruel Sports Hunt Saboteurs	Failure of Private Member's Bill to ban fox-hunting (1998) National Trust ban on stag-hunting on its land
Reduce large road-building programme	Alarm UK (coordinating over 300 local groups) Earth First!	Sharp scaling back of new road-building after 1996; cancellation of some projects, e.g. Oxleas Wood
Abandon plan for second runway at Manchester Airport	Campaign Against Runway Two – a coalition of local groups and green activists	Public Inquiry endorsed construction of runway two, which went ahead
Curb traffic in urban areas	Reclaim the Streets	Ongoing creation of pedestrian precincts and bypasses
Abandon use of organophosphate chemicals in sheep dips	Self-help groups, e.g. Pesticides Exposure Group of Sufferers Friends of the Earth	No reduction in availability of OP products but increasingly stringent regulations on their use
Ban genetically modified (GM) crops	Genetic Engineering Network GenetiX Snowball Wide spectrum of environmental groups	EU support but under study by government working party; House of Lords report (1998)

Table 6.1 (cont.)

Aims	Main groups	Outcome
Ban arms exports	Ploughshares movement	Four women cleared (1996) of causing £1.5 million damage to Hawk jet bound for East Timor
Ban landmines	International Campaign to Ban Landmines	Oslo Agreement (1998) by 90 countries to work for total ban but it faces many obstacles
Remove *fatwa* (death sentence) on Salman Rushdie for *Satanic Verses*	Article 19 (anti-censorship group)	Iranian government dissociated itself from *fatwa* (1998)
Reduce age of consent for gays to 16 and repeal section 28 Local Government Act (1988)	OutRage Stonewall	Legislation reducing gay age of consent to 18 (1994)
Enhance disabled welfare and rights	Disablement Income Group Disability Benefits Consortium	Disability Discrimination Act (1995) but even after being extended by Labour, still excluded 320 000 disabled (92.5%)
Repeal 1967 Abortion Act	Society for the Protection of the Unborn Child Pro-Life Alliance	Small change to 1967 Act, reducing 28 week limit to 24 weeks
Increase women's representation at highest levels of politics and public life	300 Group; Emily's List Labour Women's Network Labour Women's Action Committee	120 women MPs after 1997 General Election, 18 women ministers and five women in Cabinet
Constitutional reform	Charter 88 Liberty	Devolution to Scotland and Wales (1997); abolition of hereditary peers, electoral reform and Freedom of Information Act

This chapter examines the character, tactics and targets of public campaigning groups. It focuses in particular on delineating the wide range of the single-issue groups themselves, on relating them to the changes in contemporary political culture, and on describing their use of the media and their targeting of political parties, the courts and local government. Analysis of the overall significance of choice of an outsider/public campaigning strategy and its role in groups' success and failure is reserved to the next chapter.

Public campaigning in the 1990s

Table 6.1 gives some indication of the extent and variety of public campaigns by single-issue groups in the 1990s. It shows public concern over a wide range of local and national issues embracing the environment, animal rights, civil liberties, health, international morality, and the welfare of minorities. Many of these campaigns have been extraordinarily successful, a key factor in the widespread impression that public protest has increased in recent years. For example, the Anti-Poll Tax Federation forced the government to replace the tax, the Snowdrop Campaign speedily achieved a total ban on handguns, the Greenpeace campaign against the deep-sea dumping of toxic waste persuaded the oil company Shell to retract its plan and recycle the Brent Spar oil rig instead, and the wave of direct action protest against new motorways was an important factor in a sharp reduction in the government's road-building programme in the mid-1990s. Joining a single-issue pressure group, it is clear, has become 'a more rewarding type of political participation for many people than membership of a political party' (Seyd and Whiteley, 1992, p. 204). It is rewarding in the two senses of enabling people to express their individual political identities and in offering them a greater opportunity than do increasingly centralised political parties for personal achievement, the chance 'to make a difference', to have an impact on public life. As the organisers of the Countryside March argued: 'One of the things governments hate is big numbers of single issue voters because you can't buy them off with anything else' (cited in Jordan, 1998, p. 316).

Whilst public campaigning is the leading strategy of outsider groups, and the main focus of this chapter is hence on outsider public campaigns, public campaigning is increasingly used by insider groups too. Sometimes, sectional insiders employ public campaigning alongside their traditional insider strategies. Equally they may be forced into public campaigning when access to the usual channels of insider influence is denied them. For example, when the government refused to consult doctors' representatives over the terms of a new GPs' contract in the late 1980s, the British Medical Association launched a national newspaper campaign based on advertisements which, under a large photograph of the Secretary of State for Health, asked: 'What do you call a man who will not consult the doctor? Answer: Mr Clarke'. Similarly, many normally insider groups such as farmers and country landowners who felt that their concerns were not being heeded by New Labour as they previously were by Conservative governments joined forces with other rural interests to demonstrate their concern in the Countryside March in 1998.

The extent of public involvement in protest and single-issue campaigns in the 1990s needs to be kept in proportion. Thus, some high-profile protests in the 1990s have been based on 'very small numbers of individuals' (Jordan, 1998, p. 319). Moreover, most of the very large numbers belonging to a cause – for example, the majority of the 5 million members of the environmental movement – are fairly passive, their support rarely going beyond payment of their dues or signing a petition. In other words, the intensity of commitment to a cause needs to be considered. Broadly speaking, signing a petition ranks as a relatively low cost political action for an individual; giving financial support to a cause ranks rather higher, especially if the contributions are regular, whilst, in ascending order, taking part in strikes, lobbying politicians, demonstrating peacefully, being active in a cause or group, and taking direct action for a cause are high cost activities. In general terms, and for obvious reasons, the higher the cost of the action in money and/or time, the lower the degree of public involvement. For example, most of those involved in the Snowdrop Campaign were involved mainly in the relatively low cost action of petitioning (over 700 000 signed the petition calling for a ban on handguns) and the campaign itself was run by a handful of individuals. At the other extreme were the small number of campaigns – against motorways, for animal rights – in which a small number of activists paid a heavy price in time, money, physical discomfort (perched high in swaying trees over projected sites of new roads or in underground tunnels for days on end), physical pain (sometimes roughly handled by security guards and/or police) and even loss of liberty (prison sentences of varying lengths).

Protest, participation and political culture

All told, engaging in any kind of political activity beyond voting is very much a minority affair in Britain. The British Political Participation (BPP) study found that for slightly over half the population (51 per cent), political activity is limited to voting, another quarter of the population (25.8 per cent) is almost inactive politically, and under one quarter (23.8 per cent) are involved in political activity beyond voting. Of these, nearly 10 per cent were either *contacting activists* (7.7 per cent) whose political involvement concerned mainly phoning or writing to politicians or officials, or *party campaigners* (2.2 per cent) who were principally engaged in party activities such as fundraising, canvassing, clerical work and attending rallies. The rest were politically involved wholly or to a significant extent through pressure groups: 8.7 per cent were *collective activists* participating as members of pressure groups; 3.1 per cent were *direct activists* engaged in various forms of direct action whilst a tiny 1.5 per cent could be described as *complete activists* involved in a large variety of political activities from party campaigning to group activity and numerous kinds of protest (Figure 6.1). The authors of the BPP study suggest that 'protest has become part of the array of actions citizens might consider using to make themselves heard' (Parry *et al.*, 1992). More recent evidence, spanning the years between the mid-1980s when the BPP study was done and the mid-1990s, suggests that public willingness to become

Figure 6.1   A demonstrator in front of burning buildings at an anti-poll tax rally which turned into a riot in Trafalgar Square.

Table 6.2 Trends in propensity to undertake political action, 1984–94

	1984	1991	1994
% saying they would			
Sign a petition	58	78	68
Go on a protest or demonstration	9	14	17
Form a group of like-minded people	8	7	10
Undertake three or more actions	20	29	33

Source: extracted from Curtice and Jowell (1995), p. 154.

actively involved involved in public campaigns and protests may be on the increase. Thus, the percentage of respondents telling the British Social Attitudes survey that they would undertake such actions as signing petitions, going on demonstrations and forming a group of like-minded people all rose between 1984 and 1994, as did – even more dramatically – the number of actions they would be prepared to undertake (Table 6.2).

Willingness to engage in petitioning, to form campaigning pressure groups, even to become involved in direct action within and outside the law are of course nothing new in Britain. In the nineteenth century, one may cite the anti-slavery movement, the Chartists, the anti-Corn Law and temperance campaigns and in the twentieth century the militant suffragettes and the Jarrow and other marches of the unemployed in the 1930s. However, studies of trends in public opinion together with other evidence, some of it impressionistic, suggest not only that membership of cause groups and social movements has increased in recent decades (Chapter 2) but also that the numbers engaged in radical single-issue politics have risen too.

Direct action protest

There are gradations of direct action protest.

- *Non-violent legal protest.* Most contemporary outsider groups engage in law-abiding protest on traditional lines: they campaign for their cause by organising mass petitions, demonstrations and marches; they distribute literature promoting their cause; sometimes they manage to enlist celebrity supporters. Consumer boycotts, for example, anti-apartheid boycotts of South African goods in the 1980s, fall into this category.

- *Non-violent illegal protest.* One step up 'the ladder of protest' are those direct actions such as obstruction and disruption of road-building which are also peaceful but involve breaking the law and also contain a risk of physical confrontation. The road protests built on a strong tradition of non-violent protest in Britain engaged in by earlier social movements. Members of 1990s eco-groups such as Earth First! and Alarm UK learnt from the civil disobedience campaigns of the peace movement in the 1980s. They used ingenious techniques to make eviction more difficult, thereby prolonging their protest and escalating the cost to construction companies and governments through lengthy delays to their programmes. The obstructive repertoire included 'embedding tubes in concrete which could be used to lock the protester to almost anything; digging tunnels to make it dangerous to move heavy machinery, or walkways and tree-houses above ground level which required specialist teams of climbers to make eviction possible' (Doherty, 1998, p. 382). Whilst the protesters were prepared to expose themselves to danger, they knew that any move towards violence by them risked damaging their cause in public opinion. Other groups using non-violent, illegal methods include the non-payment tactics of the Anti-Poll Tax Federation; the blockage of the waste pipe of the Sellafield nuclear reprocessing plant by Greenpeace; the disruption of hunts by the hunt saboteurs; and even the damage to property caused by break-ins and release of animals from laboratories and fur farms by animal rightists.

- *Violent, illegal direct action.* An extreme fringe of the animal rights movement has been prepared to use violence to achieve its ends, including letter bombs and car bombs against scientists using animals in their research and incendiary devices against stores selling furs.

In August 1996, two journalists announced that 'Britain is believed now to have more grass-roots direct action environmental and social justice groups than ever before' (John Vidal and Alex Bellos, *The Guardian*, 27 August 1996). They based this belief on a *Guardian* survey conducted with a dozen campaigning groups which showed that there had been over 500 separate 'actions' against authorities in the past year. The actions included: demonstrations against Shell over the death of the Nigerian human rights and environmental activist Ken Saro Wiwa as well as against the Brent Spar; over 200 anti-hunting events per week; shareholder action at the headquarters or regional offices of McDonald's, Nestlé, Lloyds and Midland banks, Costain and other large firms; 'critical mass' bike rides protesting against traffic congestion and pollution; Reclaim the Streets 'parties' in which protesters blocked a section of main road; and a wide variety of other demonstrations and protest actions against atmospheric, land and water pollution, violation of the green belt by developers, noise, quarries, and motorways. The writers noted some interesting trends: that the fastest growth in grass-roots protest was in city-based groups with neither formal membership lists nor constitutions; and that groups were increasingly combining their resources with other groups in partnerships and coalitions. There was increasing public support for direct action even involving law-breaking. Thus, respondents to British Social Attitudes surveys showed a decline in those saying that people should obey the law without exception from 53 per cent in 1983 to 41 per cent in 1996 whilst those saying that on exceptional occasions people should follow their conscience even if it means breaking the law increased over the same period from 46 per cent to 55 per cent (Curtice and Jowell, 1995, p. 95). Two years later, seemingly little affected by the change of government from Conservative to Labour, protest and public campaigning carried on unabated, and may even have intensified (Box 6.1).

BOX 6.1

The summer of discontent: direct action protests in 1998

The Guardian columnist John Vidal found an explosion of grass-roots protest in the summer of 1998. He commented:

> The modern phenomenon of 'direct action' started with anti-nuclear protests and moved, via Greenpeace and Friends of the Earth, to environmental, animal welfare and road protesting. Today it is spreading into almost every area of life and becoming the ultimate expression of political, environmental, corporate or social disquiet.

Direct action protests carried out during the summer of 1998 included:

- action aimed at disarming a nuclear submarine at the Faslane Trident base outside Glasgow by members of the Ploughshares group
- a mass trespass on the South Downs in favour of open access
- the release of thousands of mink from mink farms by the Animal Liberation Front
- demonstrations by hundreds of pig farmers against supermarkets and food companies importing cheap foreign bacon
- disruption of the picnics of opera-goers at Glyndebourne by activists, revolutionaries and social deviants complaining about inequality and land rights
- destruction of 25 of the 325 test fields of genetically modified crops by Earth First! and other activists
- continuing disruption of hunts and grouse shoots by the hunt saboteurs
- defence of the last green space in Southampton against development by the Church of England by the Arboreal Activists Reinforce Decent Values Against Redevelopment Killing group.

The article contained several reasons for the spread of protest. First, after the honeymoon period, there was a widespread feeling of disillusionment with the Labour Government, with increasing numbers prepared to act rather than talk. Second, people were learning quickly that protest was an effective way of getting their concerns on the local and national political agenda, and, in addition, they were being trained in non-violent direct action by groups like Friends of the Earth. Third, following the example

BOX 6.1 (CONTINUED)

set by the Ploughshares women acquitted of damaging a Hawk jet in 1996, people were increasingly willing to be arrested so that juries could judge their actions. Underlying the contemporary protest movement was 'the theme of accountability'. People felt that decision-makers in business and politics were not properly accountable to them. Many activists were angry about the secrecy and the corruption of the way in which major developments are decided and about the arrogance of scientists who think they know best.

Questions

1. Would you agree that direct action protest is 'spreading into almost every area of life'? Cite evidence from this passage to justify your view.

2. Do you agree with the proposition that single-issue pressure groups are more popular than political parties as a way of influencing political decisions? If so, why do you think this has occurred?

3. Are all the actions describable as being carried out by cause groups or can any of the actions be described as sectional? If so, which?

4. Briefly describe a recent protest action carried out in your locality or region. Was it entirely carried out by local groups or did it involve outsiders? If so, which group/s? Evaluate the motives of participants in the protest: how far was it a 'nimby' (not in my backyard) action, how far did it involve more altruistic motives? (See below for discussion of nimby campaigns.) Give reasons for its success or failure.

Groups' use of the media in public campaigns

In the Study of Parliament Group survey, groups ranked the media third overall (behind ministers and civil servants) as an influence on public policy and one-fifth of the groups surveyed placed the media first as a public policy influence (Rush, 1990, p. 272). Groups' behaviour bears out their perception of the crucial importance of gaining media attention to their respective causes. According to one survey, three-quarters (74 per cent) of outsider groups and over four-fifths (86 per cent) of insiders claimed to be in contact with the media *at least once a week*; half the groups were in *daily* contact with the media (Baggott, 1992, p. 20; Baggott, 1995, p. 183). This emphasis by groups on achieving good media contacts is demonstrated by their frequent employment of media-experienced people as their directors or as heads of their public relations departments.

Few promotional or protest groups possess the resources necessary to run extended media campaigns. Yet media exposure is usually, if not invariably, vital to their success. In Grant Jordan's phrase: 'Protest without media coverage is like a mime performance in the dark: possible but fairly pointless'

(Jordan, 1998, p. 327). How then can groups persuade the media to give coverage to their causes?

Sometimes groups are 'knocking at an open door' in the sense that the cause they advocate is inherently newsworthy. This was the case with the Snowdrop Campaign to ban handguns. The sense of public outrage generated by the horror of the shooting of 16 children and their teacher not only prompted continuous coverage in all the media but also persuaded several newspapers such as the *Sunday Times*, *Sunday Mail*, *Sun* and *Scotland on Sunday* to adopt the Campaign. This 'concerted campaign' by a significant section of the press 'ensured the subject became a political issue' and played an important part in Snowdrop's success (Thomson *et al.*, 1998, pp. 330, 342–3).

More usually, campaigning groups are at the other extreme of newsworthiness, and although media publicity may be equally vital to them, they have to work much harder to achieve it. Coverage of the campaign against the use of organophosphate chemicals in sheep dips (and elsewhere in agriculture), for example, was initially limited to specialist journals such as the *Farmers Weekly* but gradually received greater media exposure during the 1990s as a consequence of such events as the Gulf War Syndrome (the mysterious illnesses suffered by Gulf War veterans exposed to the chemicals) and the suicide of Gordon McMaster MP who linked his tiredness, depression and mood swings to his exposure to organophosphate chemicals during his work as a gardener. During 1997 the issue was aired in various radio and television programmes including a two-part *World in Action* and episodes of *The Archers*. Local protests like the Druridge Bay Campaign, first against the siting of a nuclear power station and then against sand extraction from a Northumbrian bay, have usually to be satisfied with achieving publicity in the local and regional media. The Druridge Bay protesters ran a shrewd media campaign, building on the natural 'David versus Goliath' appeal of their situation to local journalists by issuing regular press releases and sponsoring publicity-attracting events such as a beach party, music festivals and an anthology of poetry celebrating the bay. Their nimby-type campaign displayed great tenacity over a 17-year period and eventually prevailed over the two threats to the bay (Baggott, 1998, p. 393).

Another local campaign, against the expansion of Manchester Airport, failed initially as a nimby-style protest by the local residents of affected Cheshire communities when the Environment Secretary gave the go-ahead for a second runway in January 1997. But it then took off in the national media as a result of the arrival of green activists, many of them veterans of earlier road protests at Twyford Down, Newbury and most recently the A30 dual carriageway protest at Fairmile in Devon. Whereas the initial nimby protest had struggled to gain coverage by the local papers, the establishment of camps on the airport construction site in the Bollin Valley by the eco-warriors, who included 'Swampy', 'Animal', 'Muppet Dave' and 'the Worm', elevated the protest to a new dimension, as the national and international media converged on the area. For four months, an unusual coalition of eco-warriors and traditional middle-class protesters, dubbed 'Vegans and Volvos' by *The Times*, and known officially as the Campaign Against Runway Two, was seldom out of the national news. Ultimately, with the eviction of the last green activists from the site, the protest failed so far as local residents were concerned and the construction of a second runway went ahead. But for 'Swampy' and the other eco-warriors the massive and favourable media attention had undoubtedly enhanced public perceptions of the environmental movement in the longer term (Griggs *et al.*, 1998, pp. 363–9).

Often, a group's ability to generate dramatic pictures will gain media attention, although this may not be always sympathetic. The media's normally unfavourable treatment of strikers, squatters, hunt saboteurs and campaigners against the 1994 Criminal Justice Act contrasted with its sympathetic handling of the campaign against the export of veal calves with its capacity to supply emotive portside images of helpless crated animals, police cordons and angry protesters. By 1995, when pictures from Shoreham and Brightlingsea hit the newspaper front pages and television screens, the campaign by Compassion in World Farming and other animal welfare groups had already made the export of live animals into a high profile media issue. Celebrities such as Joanna Lumley and Penelope Keith had declared their support for the campaign and nearly six million viewers had watched the Granada Television World in Action documentary *Animal Traffic* described by CIWF as a hard-hitting exposé 'which highlighted the suffering behind the trade'. A factor that contributed massively to the sympathetic reaction of both media and public to the direct action at Brightlingsea was the nature of the protesters, the majority of whom, in the words of a local reporter, far from being 'scruffy rent-a-mob traveller types intent on causing mayhem', were 'the sort of people who would normally count the police as allies – law-abiding locals, Mr and Mrs Averages, pensioners, young mums and children' (cited in McLeod, 1998, pp. 350–2).

> Those with points of view to articulate have realised the importance of 'events' in securing press and media coverage: an implicit contract exists whereby if protesters can give the media stories and pictures, then opportunities to air concerns are available.
>
> (Jordan, 1998, p. 327)

Greenpeace is one of the most successful groups at devising stunts and dramatic 'pseudo-events' to attract media attention. One example is its Atlantic Frontier campaign against the expansion of oil exploration which it launched in 1997 immediately after its successful Brent Spar action. During its summer-long campaign to disrupt oil exploration in the North Atlantic, Greenpeace campaigners occupied the island of Rockall for 48 days living in a solar survival capsule – a high-tech yellow pod; manacled themselves to furniture in the London offices of Conoco dressed in suits and carrying copies of the *Financial Times*; tied oil drums to Conoco's equipment; disrupted seismic data gathering; delivered a petition signed by over 250 000 to the Prime Minister; and tied the yellow pod containing activists to the leg of a rig chartered by BP for oil exploration (Bennie, 1998, p. 401).

However, media coverage is not always available. Anti-smoking groups struggle to achieve coverage in the press which receives large sums in advertising fees from the tobacco industry. A former director of ASH (Action on Smoking and Health) has stated: 'There are some well-documented cases of the tobacco lobby simply being able to swing the media as it wants. Just look around you. How many major British newspapers have run any kind of consistent campaign on cigarette smoking? Bearing in mind it kills 100 000 people prematurely each year and causes a loss of more than ten times as many working days as strikes, why aren't the media taking it up? ... the answer is ... because of the sheer power of tobacco advertising which is so important to them' (cited in Davies, 1985, pp. 155–6). As well as commercial factors, the partisanship of proprietors also plays an important role in a newspaper's coverage of events: lobbies propounding views judged hostile to the interests of their proprietor – on media regulation or football club ownership for example – would receive scant coverage in newspapers owned by Rupert Murdoch. However, the key determinant of media coverage remains editorial judgements of newsworthiness. Thus, the Scottish Women's Coordination Group campaigning for equal representation for women in the Scottish Parliament was disappointed in the coverage it received in the Scottish media, which seemed interested mainly when there were differences between women on the issue (Brown, 1998, p. 442). Conflict and controversy help sell newspapers and make for popular television programmes, not campaigns that eschew attention-grabbing public protests and stunts in favour of quiet networking and behind-the-scenes pressures.

Engaging media coverage and/or support is vital for campaigning groups because the media provide direct access to public opinion and such groups will normally fail unless they can gain public support. Even with public support, they are not certain of success because governments can choose to ignore polls or contest them with their own surveys or, on controversial issues like fox-hunting, for example, allow free votes in parliament where a cause may fail despite public support for it. Examples of campaigning producing large shifts or changing negative attitudes to positive ones are rare. Nonetheless, evidence suggests that public campaigns that receive significant media exposure can influence public opinion, normally by reinforcing pre-existing opinion. Thus, campaigning by the Hunt Saboteurs and other animal rights groups helped move opinion in favour of banning fox-hunting from a bare majority (52 per cent) in 1972 first to a two-thirds majority in 1987 (68 per cent) and thence to an even more sizeable majority (73 per cent) in 1998. A campaign enjoying positive support within the media – the Snowdrop anti-handgun campaign – achieved even more. Whereas the mass killing of 16 people at Hungerford in 1987 had not led to greater legislative controls, despite public outrage, a persistent campaign for gun control, backed by the media, achieved 68 per cent public support (MORI poll) in October 1997 (cited in Thomson *et al.*, 1998, p. 343). However, groups that campaign 'against the grain' of popular attitudes rarely succeed in shifting opinion their way. For example, the anti-abortion campaign by the Society for the Protection of the Unborn Child made little headway in three decades against the 1967 Abortion Act, a 1997 Gallup poll showing 89 per cent in favour of the availability of abortion (Read, 1998, p. 456).

BOX 6.2

New social movements

The two social movements generating most activity in present-day politics are the women's and environmental movements. Whilst each possesses a large variety of approaches and groupings, their more radical strands share beliefs in direct action methods, unstructured, non-hierarchical organisation and fundamentalist ideologies typifying new social movements.

The women's movement

Whilst the suffragette demand for votes for women (1900–28) was the earliest modern expression of the quest for female equality, the contemporary women's movement dates back to a series of women's liberation conferences at Ruskin College, Oxford between 1970 and 1978. Disappointed at progress since the 1920s, this 'second wave' of feminism demanded free access to abortion and contraception, childcare, equal pay and job opportunities, and protection against sexual harassment and rape. Differences soon emerged between liberal and socialist feminists, who stressed the goal of achieving equal opportunities and representation in public life for women (the socialist feminists as part of the long-term struggle against capitalism), and radical feminists, who prioritised the fight against patriarchy – literally 'rule of the father' but extended by radical feminists to mean male domination in general, in the private as well as the public sphere of life. Each strand of feminism pursued its goals through different tactics and groupings. Thus, the *300 group* (1980) is an all-party group which aims to get more women into parliament, the European Parliament, local government and public life, and *Emily's List* (1988), founded by the Labour MP Barbara Follett, provides financial help and training for women candidates. The campaign by liberal and socialist feminists has achieved its most significant successes through the Labour Party, notably its decisions to adopt a target of 40 per cent women on the party's policy-making bodies within ten years (1990) and to provide for women-only shortlists in half the party's winnable seats (1993). Although subsequently overturned by an industrial tribunal ruling as contravening the Sex Discrimination Act, the women-only shortlists policy helped in the election of a record number of 120 women MPs in 1997 (102 of them Labour). Meanwhile, radical feminists have focused on the sphere of personal relationships and women-only group activities rather than the male-dominated public arena, setting up rape crisis centres, 'well-woman' clinics and refuges for female victims of domestic violence, and campaigning against pornography and for the legal

BOX 6.2 (CONTINUED)

rights of women who kill systematically violent partners. The Women's Peace Camp at Greenham Common in the 1980s and the Women Against Pit Closures (1984–85, 1992) were both important as demonstrating women's capacity for independent collective action and as having an importance in consciousness-raising beyond their limited consequences.

The women's movement is principled rather than pragmatic, based on local groups rather than national organisation, and informal rather than hierarchical. Despite its lack of a peak organisation to organise a nationwide struggle for women's rights, it has lobbied nationally on occasion, as it did when defending the 1967 Abortion Act against attack in both the late 1970s and the 1980s. Overall, 'second wave' feminism has many achievements to its credit, including reform of the law on divorce and abortion, maternity leave, anti-sex discrimination and equal pay legislation, the Equal Opportunities Commission, greater political representation in parliament and Cabinet, and some progress in the professions. But, whilst it has placed the issue of women's equality firmly on the political agenda and in the public mind, much remains to be achieved by a movement that was showing signs of weakening in the 1990s.

The environmental movement

The main divisions within the environmental movement are between *conservationism*, which stresses preservation and protection of threatened plants, wildlife and habitats, and *ecologism*, which sees humanity as part of the natural world and stresses the need for it to respect and coexist with other life forms rather than dominate and exploit them. A similar division exists within the pro-animal movement between groups and individuals emphasising animal *welfare* and those stressing animal *rights*. Differences of tactics and approach flow from these fundamental divisions over ideology and ultimate goals, with conservationist groups seeking reform within the economic system by conventional lobbying of mainstream political institutions whilst ecologists argue for radical socio-economic change, including limits on economic growth, and employ direct action methods as well as conventional lobbying. Similarly, animal welfare groups seek improvements by conventional lobbying tactics whereas animal rightists are more prone to use direct action.

Leading conservationist groups include the National Trust (1895) and the Council for the Protection of Rural England (1926) whilst the Royal Society for the Protection of Birds (1889), the Royal Society for the Prevention of Cruelty to Animals (1824), the National Anti-Vivisection Society (1875) and the British Union for the Abolition of Vivisection (1898) are prominent in animal welfare. The foremost ecological groups are Friends of the Earth (FoE-UK, 1970), Greenpeace (1977) and Earth First! (1991) whilst the leading animal rightists include the Hunt Saboteurs Association (1964), Animal Aid (1977) and the Animal Liberation Front (1976).

Ecological groups radicalised the environmental movement in the 1970s, highlighting such issues as pollution, toxic waste and the rapid and excessive depletion of the world's natural resources. New groups such as Friends of the Earth saw the threat to the global environment as flowing from governments' pursuit of economic growth and the ecological irresponsibility of big business. FoE has promoted recycling and green consumerism, participated in public inquiries to publicise environmental dangers from

BOX 6.2 (CONTINUED)

nuclear power and road-building, lobbied the EU to tighten up standards on drinking water and beaches, and closely monitored governments' and firms' observance of EU and national standards on pollution from car exhausts and discharges into rivers. FoE has been increasingly concerned with national lobbying based on rigorous scientific research and the promotion of environmentally friendlier alternatives to government policy. However, as an organisation, FoE is decentralised and participatory (by the 1990s it had 250 local groups), and, although they are encouraged to pursue campaigning issues suggested by the national organisation, local memberships are free to adopt their own direct action initiatives. In contrast, whilst ideologically similar to FoE, Greenpeace operates through a tightly structured organisation based on a clearcut division between 'front-line troops' who engage in a series of high profile non-violent but often dangerous direct action stunts to highlight threats to the environment, and fairly passive supporters whose role is to provide the finance and moral support for these actions. It is a wealthy organisation, its 400 000 British supporters generating an annual income of £9 million and supporting a national staff of about 60, whilst International Greenpeace, with over 3 million supporters worldwide, owns about eight ships, 30 inflatables and a helicopter. Like FoE, it also engages in much conventional lobbying, advocating a precautionary approach to environmental risk, and seeking to develop the scientific expertise that will enable it to challenge and offer alternatives to the official government line. Key campaigns and concerns in the 1990s have been nuclear testing by France and others, the dumping of the Brent Spar oil rig (a 'victory' over which it subsequently apologised to Shell for overestimating the pollution risk of deep-sea dumping), the use of hormone-disrupting chemicals, industrial over-fishing, and advocacy of solar power.

Both FoE and Greenpeace have been upstaged to some extent in the 1990s by more radical direct action groups which, often in combination with middle-class nimbyism, have taken the lead in protests against new road-building and animal exports. New 'deep green' groups such as Earth First!, which had 63 local groups in 1996, are openly critical of the older environmental groups which they see as too timid and more concerned about their images than protecting the wilderness. They proudly proclaim themselves to be 'disorganisations', lacking in central offices, paid officers and formal memberships, and solely dependent upon the vigour, networking skills and convictions of volunteers. In opposing the destruction of local environments, groups like Earth First! and Reclaim the Streets have used radical tactics of tunnelling, tree-dwelling, block-ading and sabotage of equipment.

The main priorities of the pro-animal movement are opposition to hunting; the mistreatment of livestock arising out of intensive farming practices, including live animal exports; and the misuse of animals in scientific experiments. Whereas the RSPCA lobbies to ban hunting through orthodox political channels, the Hunt Saboteurs engage in non-violent direct action to disrupt hunts; and whereas the older anti-vivisection societies seek stronger controls on animal experimentation by peaceful lobbying, the ALF are prepared to use violence to end animal cruelty, including arson attacks on laboratories using animals for experimentation, bombing stores and the cars of animal researchers and releasing animals from fur farms.

(Source: Byrne (1997))

BOX 6.2 (CONTINUED)

Questions

1. How much progress has been made by the women's movement since 1970? How far has it been handicapped by: (a) internal divisions over ideology and (b) lack of formal organisation?

2. Do you consider that 'women-only shortlists' are an acceptable way of achieving the goal of increasing women's representation in parliament or was it correct to outlaw them as unfair to men?

3. What is the main difference between conservationists and ecologists in their approach to the environment? Identify the main groups following each approach.

4. Distinguish between Friends of the Earth, Greenpeace and Earth First! as organisations. Do you think the reported scorn of Reclaim the Streets' supporters for Greenpeace as a 'send-a-donation/get-the-mag/sit-in-your armchair organisation' is fair?

5. Identify a leading animal welfare group and a leading animal rights group, and state the main differences between them in tactics and overall goals.

6. What are the advantages and disadvantages of conventional lobbying, non-violent direct action and violent direct action in advancing the causes of women, the environment and animals?

Groups' use of the courts

Many pressure groups in the 1980s and 1990s resorted increasingly to the courts to politicise issues, force local and national governments and businesses to carry out their responsibilities and exert pressure for changes in the law. The League against Cruel Sports uses injunctions on behalf of landowners to keep hunts off their land whilst the campaign against organophosphate pesticides is increasingly resorting to the courts. The Transport and General Workers Union which supports a complete ban on pesticides has made a rising number of claims for compensation on behalf of agricultural workers against employers. Many cases appear to be settled out of court such as the one reported in February 1998 when a shepherd represented by Unison gained an £80 000 out-of-court settlement from Lancashire County Council (Greer, 1998, p. 416). Quite often a group will succeed merely by pointing out the illegality of a particular course of action. For example, the Council for the Protection of Rural England helped to thwart the intention of the Conservative Government in the mid-1980s to transfer pollution control to the private sector by pointing out that this step was illegal in European law (Garner, 1996, p. 164). Sometimes, the threat of legal action brings the desired result. Thus, Friends of the Earth threatened the directors of 14 major companies with private prosecutions in 1993 in order to force them to comply with limits on the discharge of pollutants into rivers set by the National Rivers Authority in 1989 (Byrne, 1997, p. 135).

Legal actions, of course, are not always successful but even where unsuccessful often bring valuable publicity. Greenpeace failed in 1997 in its legal challenge to the award of licences for oil exploration on the Atlantic Frontier by the DTI to 30 oil companies. It argued that the award of licences in this round of exploration contravened a number of European Commission directives by failing to protect sensitive cold-water coral reefs (Bennie, 1998, p. 402). But, as in the failure of its earlier court action (1994) to prevent the opening and commissioning of the Thorp reprocessing plant by British Nuclear Fuels, Greenpeace had gained valuable publicity for its case. Following the acquittal of the Ploughshares women in 1996 for damage to a Hawk jet bound for Indonesia, GenetiX Snowball, a Manchester-based group protesting against genetically modified crops, deliberately sought volunteers prepared to go to court and defend themselves for destroying genetically engineered crops.

One of the most publicised legal actions of the 1990s was that brought by the fast-food chain McDonald's against two members of a small anarchist group called London Greenpeace (no connection to Greenpeace, the international environmental group) – the so-called 'McLibel case'. Originally scheduled to last 12 weeks, the libel suit lasted 314 days, making it not just the longest libel suit but the longest case in British legal history. At the end of the case, McDonald's had silenced its critics but at very considerable costs to itself both in terms of financial expense and adverse publicity. The case began with McDonald's serving a writ for libel on five members of London Greenpeace for distributing a leaflet entitled 'What's wrong with McDonald's', accusing the company of destruction of the rain forest, cruelty to animals, exploiting children in its advertising, selling unhealthy food and paying low wages. Advised that the case would be very expensive to defend and that no legal aid was available for defamation cases, three of the five apologised, but two of them, Dave Morris, a former postman, and Helen Steel, a former gardener, chose to defend themselves in person. When, just as the trial was about to begin, McDonald's distributed 250 000 leaflets suggesting they were lying, they countersued the company. Within two months, Morris and Steel had been offered an out-of-court settlement with an undisclosed sum of money going to a charity of their choice but their condition that McDonald's stopped suing its critics was unacceptable. This condition arose out of one of their key arguments – that McDonald's used British libel laws to silence its critics; they pointed to over 50 groups, newspapers and television companies which had apologised to McDonald's over the previous two years. The outcome was a pyrrhic victory for the company. The judge concluded that McDonald's had been libelled and ordered Morris and Steel to pay £60 000 damages. But this paled into insignificance besides the costs to McDonald's – estimated at £10 million – of bringing the action and the bad publicity the company received as a result of the trial. The judge upheld some charges against the company, deciding that it was cruel to some of the animals it reared (battery hens and broiler chickens), that it exploited children in its advertising and that it paid low wages, thereby contributing to low wages in the catering trade. Throughout the trial, moreover, the unemployed 'small fries' received widespread support from the world's media in their battle against the 'burger giant'; whilst the McLibel Support Campaign regularly picketed over 500 McDonald's restaurants and distributed a further two million of the offending leaflets. A web site on the Internet with a transcript of the hearing was accessed 14 million times in the final year of the trial (*Guardian*, 20 June 1997).

Current indications are that companies and others whose lives are disrupted by campaigning groups are increasingly prepared to defend themselves in the courts. When Greenpeace, as part of its Atlantic Frontier campaign, sought to slow down the progress of BP's oil exploration west of Shetland by tying the yellow pod containing its activists to the leg of the exploration rig, BP responded by obtaining a court order freezing Greenpeace's assets, including ships, and demanding compensation of £1.4 million. This suit threatened to bankrupt Greenpeace and forced it to cease its action (Bennie, 1998, pp. 401–2). Friends of the Earth withdrew from protest activity at Twyford Down after being advised that it faced sequestration of its assets if it continued (Doherty, 1998, p. 371) whilst LYNX, the anti-fur campaign group, was forced into liquidation when it was successfully sued by a mink farm after which it faced a total bill for costs and damages of £260 000 (Grant, 1995, p. 91). In summer 1998, it was reported that protesters against genetically modified crops in Devon were facing damages of £600 000 for damaging GM crops. Governments have also pursued a tougher line against protesters. The Public Order Act (1986) gave the police additional powers to restrict and even, in certain areas, ban marches and to limit the duration and the number taking part in static demonstrations; and also created a new offence of disorderly conduct which facilitated the arrest and removal of protesters. The Criminal Justice and Public Order Act (1994) created a new offence of aggravated trespass enabling the punishment of protesters invading private land, including groups like the Hunt Saboteurs (Baggott, 1995, pp. 181–2). There were also signs not only of increased state surveillance of environmental and social justice activists in the mid-1990s with reported raids on groups' computer files, including Greenpeace's, but also of legal action against protesters with threats to sue those involved in the M11 road protests. In 1998, many groups were complaining of heavy-handed policing, the use of CS spray, intimidatory tactics and draconian 'conspiracy' charges being used against them (*The Guardian*, 20 May 1995; 15 August 1998).

Groups and campaigns targeting political parties

Groups of all kinds, both sectional and cause, insider as well as outsider, use party channels to influence MPs and ministers but they also seek to influence parties outside parliament at the political grass roots. They attempt this in the following ways.

Donations to parties

Traditionally business funded the Conservatives and the trade unions funded Labour. By the mid-1990s business was pouring large sums into Labour's coffers also while union funding of the party, although still considerable, had declined. How far do groups benefit from acting as a party's paymasters? Public suspicion has arisen that parties grant favours in return for cash but this is hard to prove. The trade unions poured money into Labour between 1979 and 1995 but got nothing or next to nothing for their money. Arguably, however, even by mid-1998, the unions had already received some recompense for their continuing donations. The Blair Government had signed the Social Chapter, removed the ban on unions at GCHQ, instituted a Low Pay Commission that had recommended a minimum wage (albeit at a level that disappointed the unions) and offered automatic union recognition by companies where over half the workforce are union members and in other cases where at least 40 per cent of the workforce vote for recognition. As for business, both the Conservative governments (1979–97) and the Labour Government after 1997 have been pro-business governments inclined to support private enterprise to the best of their ability. Nonetheless, this has not inhibited companies from making financial gifts to the major parties. However, the contention that specific businesses or individuals have gained from their financial support is more difficult to prove. But the Formula One chairman Bernie Ecclestone appeared to benefit from his £1 million pre-election gift to Labour when the Blair Government exempted Formula One from its tobacco advertising ban in November 1997. Individually, businessmen between 1979 and 1992 were estimated to be ten times more likely to receive honours if their companies made donations to the Conservative Party (Linton, 1994, p. 75). However, if implemented, the recommendations of the Standards in Public Life Committee (chairman, Lord Neill) could go far to bring an end to allegations of 'cash for favours'. In this context, three recommendations are particularly important: a cap on party election spending of £20 million; full disclosure of all donations of over £5000; and scrutiny of nominations for honours by a Political Honours Scrutiny Committee if a nominee has donated over £5000 to a party.

Sponsorship of party candidates

The classic example of sponsorship of parliamentary candidates by an outside organisation is the sponsorship of Labour parliamentary candidates by the trade unions down to 1992. Thus, between 1950 and 1979, trade union sponsored candidates constituted between one-third and two-fifths of the PLP (except in February 1974 when they made up slightly over two-fifths) whilst between 1979 and 1992, they generally constituted just over half of all Labour MPs. Typically, union sponsorship involved a grant of £2000–3000 towards a candidate's election expenses plus a further £150 per quarter paid to his or her constituency. Whilst unable to instruct the MPs they sponsored how to speak or vote in parliament, the sponsoring unions expected their MPs to support their interests. The clearest example of influence occurred in 1969 when union-sponsored MPs helped to defeat the Labour Government's Industrial Relations Bill. However, with the Labour Party seeking in the 1990s to distance itself from the unions, direct trade union sponsorship of Labour candidates was discontinued in 1995 and replaced by 'Constituency plan agreements' between the unions and selected constituency Labour parties (CLPs). By such agreements, the unions support CLPs' activities by paying money into a central pool and in return receive representation on the CLP general committees. One hundred 'Constituency plan agreements' had been made by the summer of 1997, mainly with CLPs in key marginal seats to help build up Labour strength there.

Influence on party election manifestos

Some pressure groups try to achieve their aims by persuading parties to include particular commitments in their election manifestos. Labour's 1997 manifesto, for instance, pleased animal welfare, ramblers, pro-disabled, constitutional reform and anti-landmine pressure groups and international aid charities by including commitments to greater freedom for people to explore the open countryside, a free vote in parliament on a ban on hunting with hounds, comprehensive, enforceable rights for the disabled against discrimination in society or at work, a Freedom of Information Act and the incorporation of the European Convention on Human Rights into UK law, a ban on the import, export, transfer and manufacture of all forms of anti-personnel landmines and a reversal of the decline of UK spending on international aid (Labour 1997 General Election manifesto – *Because Britain Deserves Better*, 1997, pp. 30, 35, 38, 39). Apart from gaining inclusion for their demands in a party's manifesto, pressure groups are sometimes helped by MPs and party members actually joining their groups. For example, as well as being a member of the trade union Unison, Labour MP Judy Mallaber (Amber Valley) belongs to Action for Southern Africa, Liberty, Friends of the Earth and Amnesty International (*The Times*, 'Guide to the House of Commons, May 1997', 1997, p. 58). Generally, animal welfare, environmental, civil liberties and international rights cause groups and trade unions are well represented in the PLP whilst research has shown significant support amongst Labour members for campaigning groups such as CND (18.9 per cent), Greenpeace (16 per cent), the Anti-Apartheid Movement (11.8 per cent), Friends of the Earth (8.2 per cent), Oxfam (7 per cent), Amnesty International (6.8 per cent) as well as local community action (18.8 per cent) and local tenants' or housing groups (16.5 per cent) (Seyd and Whiteley, 1992, p. 92). Some groups such as the League against Cruel Sports recognise the importance of gaining sympathisers within political parties by encouraging their members to join them. Party conferences, traditionally a haunt for lobbyists, became increasingly commercialised in the 1990s and increasingly dominated by business: at Labour's 1998 Conference, for instance, prices ranged from £117 for a floor pass to hear debates and £200 for a ticket to the Gala dinner (the prize, a quick handshake from the Prime Minister) to £1500 to sponsor a fringe meeting, £10000 for the rental of a large stand (standard size stand, £7000) and £25000 to sponsor a drinks reception before the gala dinner (*The Guardian*, 29 September 1998).

Contesting elections as a political tactic

Sometimes pressure groups contest elections as a political tactic. For example, an anti-abortion group, the Pro-Life Alliance, put up 53 candidates at the 1997 General Election but the most significant single-issue group to enter that campaign was the Referendum Party which ran 547 candidates, standing aside only where the sitting MP was definitely anti-Europe. Aiming to secure a referendum on Britain's future in Europe, the party was founded and financed – to the tune of £20 million – by the businessman Sir James Goldsmith. The party gained just over 810 000 votes, well short of its 1 million vote target, and averaged a mere 3.1 per cent of the vote in the seats it contested, with only 30 of its candidates saving their deposits. Just four of the seats lost by the Conservatives can be attributed to its intervention (Butler and Kavanagh, 1997, p. 308). It failed to broaden its appeal – as many groups do – by forging links with other like-minded groups and organisations. On the other hand, the Referendum Party certainly helped to promote Europe before and during the campaign as a political issue, helped to push as many as 317 Conservative candidates into declaring their opposition to a single currency and played its part in the pressure that persuaded all three major parties to include the promise of a referendum on British membership of European monetary union in their manifestos (Carter *et al.*, 1998, p. 479).

Local government and politics

Local government is a very important arena for pressure group activity. Participation studies show that much political participation arises out of a concern about local problems. The British Political Participation Study found that the public is twice as likely to contact local councillors as MPs and government officials (Parry *et al.*, 1992; Weir and Beetham, 1999, p. 246).

Moreover, when it asked about the major issues most affecting themselves, their families, the nation or the locality, people placed issues in the following order: 1, environment and planning; 2, economic matters; 3, unemployment; 4, transport. But when asked about the kinds of issues on which they take action, the order changed, as follows: 1, housing; 2, environment and planning; 3, transport; 4, education. Issues now at the top – 'local problems which are the responsibility of various levels of local government' – are issues that people believe they can influence, compared with issues like unemployment and economic matters such as wages and inflation which they think they have little hope of affecting (Parry and Moyser, 1993, p. 22). Problems arising out of housing, local planning, schools and traffic have the double characteristic of making an immediate impact on people's everyday lives and being matters for local decision. Hence they are more likely to spur people to take action than issues they consider as more important but also as more remote. The findings of this study are reinforced by research into the Labour Party at grass-roots level which found that significant numbers of members were involved in local organisations, including community action groups (18.8 per cent), tenants' or housing groups (16.5 per cent), charities (7.9 per cent) and women's groups (5.3 per cent) (Seyd and Whiteley, 1992, p. 92). A local community, then, contains a variegated mass of pressure groups – over 4000 were counted in one large city (Newton, 1976). What are their main characteristics and how have they been affected by recent changes in local government?

How may local pressure groups best be described? As in the case of groups targeting political parties, such groups cover a broad span, and include both sectional and cause groups, insiders as well as outsiders. The following useful fourfold typology has been suggested by Stoker (1991, pp. 107–10).

- *Producer or economic groups*, including business, trade unions and professional associations.
- *Community groups*, including local amenity societies, tenants' associations, ratepayers' associations, squatters' groups, redevelopment action groups and hospital defence committees.
- *Cause groups and social movements*, including local branches of national organisations such as Friends of the Earth and animal rights groups together with local ethnic and women's groups.
- *Voluntary organisations*, including Councils for Voluntary Service, local churches and branches of national organisations such as Age Concern and Mencap.

Many pressure groups of all types both seek and have developed close insider relations with local councils. Stoker has suggested that the political complexion of the local council is a significant influence on patterns of interest representation and this model retains a certain validity despite the severe decline of the Conservatives in local government during the 1990s (Stoker, 1991). Thus, in New Labour or Liberal Democrat councils in urban areas a broad spectrum of business, community and voluntary groups are likely to be viewed sympathetically, but tenants' and residents' associations and certain cause groups cold-shouldered as too extreme or selfish. Old Labour councils, in contrast, are more likely to look favourably on trade unions and on tenants', women's, ethnic minority and single-issue cause groups but be less receptive towards business interests. Conservative councils in general tend to favour middle-class residents' associations, the amenity lobby and the voluntary sector. But those in rural locations are sympathetic towards land-owners and farming interests and correspondingly cool towards agricultural labourers and lobbyists for those in rented housing such as Shelter, whilst Conservative councils in urban and suburban settings favour business groups and are antagonistic to left-wing cause groups, and to feminists and voluntary sector groupings regarded as 'political'. In many cases, however, statute requires local authorities to consult with particular interests before taking action. For instance, local planning authorities have a statutory requirement to consult certain amenity societies before altering or pulling down a listed building and the Department of the Environment obliges local authorities to consult local chambers of commerce over schemes to be included in their urban programmes (Grant, 1995, p. 93). Moreover, as Stoker himself argues, it is necessary to treat the typology with caution. For example, because of the central importance of business to the prosperity of any community, local as well as national, even local councils less ideologically sympathetic to business interests than the Conservatives or New Labour are likely to be drawn into close relations with their area's largest employers and property developers (Stoker, 1991, p. 128).

Indeed, local business interests together with voluntary associations and cause groups have been the undoubted gainers from the transformation of local government in the 1980s and 1990s. Between 1979 and 1997, the virtual reinvention of local government by 49 pieces of legislation had the effect of removing many services from local government, transferring them to non-elected quangos and marketising and contracting out the services that remained with local authorities. Much of the impetus for the changes came from New Right-influenced Conservative governments' desire to reduce the influence of producer and professional vested interests and increase that of employers. For instance, the Conservatives believed that the public sector unions wielded too much power in many inner-city Labour councils as did the teaching and medical professions in education and health. Their legislation removed responsibilities for such areas as urban regeneration, education and training, housing and higher education from councils, empowering in their place QGAs (Quasi Governmental Authorities) such as Urban Redevelopment Corporations (UDCs), Training and Enterprise Councils (TECs), Housing Action Trusts (HATs) and Further Education corporations. Many services remaining with local government such as refuse collection, cleaning, catering and leisure management are delivered by private and voluntary sector providers as a consequence of Compulsory Competitive Tendering (CCT). The upshot is that networks of public, semi-public and private sector organisations now run what used to be run by elected councils alone. Local government has become local governance with elected local authorities now sharing service provision with 4500 local quangos and a host of voluntary and charitable bodies. Public sector–private sector partnerships between local councils, business and voluntary organisations to provide services are common. For example, the Single Regeneration Budget (SRB), which replaced the City Challenge scheme to distribute funding for the inner cities in 1995, brings together the TECs and local authorities as partners in bidding for urban renewal funding whilst also legitimising other bodies such as voluntary organisations, community groups and private firms with an interest in urban regeneration. Key roles alongside locally elected authorities and appointed quangos in the new local governance are performed by dynamic voluntary organisations, such as community groups, stronger business organisations, including larger chambers of commerce and big firms, and regional CBIs and TUCs.

To conclude: the enabling model for local government together with the transfer of services to new public sector agencies has increased the importance in service delivery of partnerships with private business and the voluntary sector. These developments have strengthened the local interest group world. Thus, in the sphere of local government, local authorities now frequently employ voluntary agencies to provide services rather than providing them directly themselves. For example, home adaptations for the disabled in Eastbourne are provided by the local branch of Care and Repair, a Home Improvement Agency which receives an annual grant from the Eastbourne Borough Council and East Sussex County Council Social Services to assist its work. The growing practice of funding of voluntary groups by the use of grants has considerably enhanced their potential for and the likely effectiveness of their lobbying of local authorities. In addition, both in elected and non-elected local government, the 1980s and 1990s have seen great efforts to involve private companies, banks and building societies in the projects to regenerate local communities and this too has often intensified the bargaining leverage of the private sector groups concerned. Stoker cites the example of a building contractor who perhaps agrees to take part in an inner city renewal scheme in return for being granted planning permission for a suburban housing development (Stoker, 1991, p. 56). As a consequence, there has emerged a new class of local insider groups whose involvement in service delivery gives them a privileged opportunity both to influence policy decisions and lobby for additional resources for their respective areas of responsibility.

Pressure group involvement with local government has also been encouraged by the development of consultative machinery in the shape of community forums, joint committees and public meetings by local authorities.

In particular, local councils have set up consultative committees involving the ethnic minorities, women's groups and the voluntary sector. As they have extended their interests, local authorities have also worked with cause groups concerned with animal rights, crime prevention, poverty, health and dietary issues. In all these ways, participation in local decision-making by affected interests has been stimulated (Stoker, 1991, pp. 118–20; Baggott, 1995, p. 196).

Local nimby campaigns

Definition 6.1   Nimby protest/nimbyism

Nimby (not in my backyard) protests involve local residents banding together to oppose developments that adversely affect their lifestyle, homes and environments – for example, the pollution caused by new roads or the dumping of toxic waste.

Local nimby campaigns often involve local government, sometimes as a target of protest but more often as an ally. If local residents do not want a particular source of environmental pollution dumped on their doorstep, often neither does local government. Thus, local protest groups in Teesside, Humberside, Lincolnshire, Bedfordshire and Essex worked together with local authorities in the mid-1980s in a successful campaign to persuade government to abandon its plans to create low level nuclear waste sites in their areas (Baggott, 1995, pp. 199–201). Albeit unsuccessfully, local residents' groups from the affected North Cheshire villages joined forces with Macclesfield Borough Council (and initially Cheshire County Council), environmental groups and direct action eco-warriors in the early 1990s to oppose the second runway at Manchester airport (Griggs et al., 1998, pp. 360–1). At other times, the situation is more complex, with local residents either at loggerheads with their local council or bypassing it. Thus, a large group of Bromley residents campaigned against Bromley Council's decision to permit the development of a massive 20-screen, fast food and car park complex in Crystal Palace park in 1998 whilst the proposal to build an in-town Tesco superstore in Ludlow in 1998 divided the town, being supported by the local planning authority, the South Shropshire District Council and narrowly (60:40) by the town's Chamber of Trade, but opposed by the town's 500-strong Civic Society (*The Guardian*, 9 September 1998). Finally, local residents' opposition to Arsenal Football Club's proposed expansion of its stadium in Highbury Hill received newspaper publicity under the headline 'Nimby United: The one team champions Arsenal cannot beat'. Arsenal FC's plans would involve the demolition of up to 40 homes in Highbury Hill, North London, a tree-lined road of Victorian properties (*The Observer*, 10 May 1998).

BOX 6.3

Local protest: the Salisbury bypass proposal

The proposed bypass, to be funded by the Private Finance Initiative at an estimated cost of £76 million, became a controversial issue in the mid-1990s and went to a public inquiry at which the inspector found 'a strong case' for the building of the new road. However, the Conservative Government, reluctant to face another row like that over the Newbury bypass, refused to give final approval and called for further studies, thereby deferring the fate of the 11-mile road until after the 1997 General Election (*The Guardian*, 30 October 1996, 29 July 1997).

Campaigners against the bypass, who included leading environmental groups such as Friends of the Earth and the Council for Rural England, argued for its abandonment for the following reasons.

- The proposed road would destroy a Site of Special Scientific Interest – the East Hanham water meadows. These water meadows, which are part of the flood plain of the River Avon, contain rare grasses and herbs and form the location from which Constable painted a famous view of Salisbury cathedral.

- The road is unnecessary since it would divert only a small amount of traffic from the city centre: through traffic using the A36 amounts to only 6 per cent of the traffic in the city centre. Diversion of such a small amount of traffic does not justify the expense of a new road and the disturbance to people living on or close to its route.

- Traffic studies have shown that the building of new roads increases total amounts of pollution by encouraging more motorists to use their cars.

Supporters of the bypass included the Salisbury MP Robert Key, who argued the following.

- The bypass is vitally necessary to relieve the traffic congestion clogging the city centre of Salisbury. The relevant figure here is the number of vehicles entering Salisbury every day on all routes which leave without stopping (20 000, 40 per cent of the total traffic into the city), not just through traffic on the A36 (3000 a day). The bypass would keep much local traffic as well as through traffic using the A36 away from the city centre.

- The new road, chosen from three alternative routes originally proposed in 1988, has the support of the parish, district and county councils and, according to small samples of local households (300–500) polled by the MP, the support of over 75 per cent of the public too; building it would enable the council to proceed with its plans to pedestrianise the city.

- Environmental objections are serious (although Constable did *not* paint his famous view of the cathedral from the water meadow) but could be overcome by a realignment of the road, minimising impact on the SSSI and moving it further from the nearest residential area.

In July 1997 the Labour Government announced the abandonment of the proposed Salisbury bypass plan.

(Sources: *The Guardian*, 15 and 30 October 1996, 29 July 1997)

BOX 6.3 (CONTINUED)

Questions

1. Evaluate the strength of the arguments for and against the Salisbury bypass.

2. How far do you agree with Robert Key that the decision to scrap the proposed bypass represented a victory for 'the politically correct, the emotional and the fanatical' over local needs?

3. To what extent did the decision to abandon the project represent the prioritisation of the value of one aspect of the environment (the need not to destroy water meadows outside the city) over another aspect (the need to reduce pollution within the city)?

4. How would this issue appear to: (a) a non-motorist resident in Salisbury; (b) a mother of young children residing on the A36; (c) a resident on the route of the proposed bypass; (d) a local councillor; (e) a local businessman (note the chairman of the Salisbury Chamber of Commerce said that the traffic management problem in Salisbury was awful and regretted that the government had failed to address that problem); (f) a member of the Salisbury Civic Society?

Summary

- Public campaigning groups seek to affect political decisions *indirectly* by inducing changes in public opinion rather than *directly* by lobbying governing institutions. Whilst it is outsider groups that are mainly involved in public campaigns, insider groups also employ this tactic instead of or in addition to insider lobbying.

- Single-issue campaigns have been the political growth area of recent years, displacing party membership as the most popular form of political participation. High profile campaigns have been waged by groups to abolish the poll tax, ban handguns and end hunting with hounds.

- Outsider campaigning groups use a variety of protest methods from the non-violent legal (e.g. marches and demonstrations), the non-violent illegal (non-payment of tax, obstruction to road-building) and the violent illegal (bombing campaigns).

- Gaining media publicity is vital to achieving a successful campaign but although all single-issue groups seek media attention, few have the resources to run long-term media campaigns. The campaigns to ban handguns and against live animal exports and new road-building gained persistent, favourable media attention in the 1990s as did the Greenpeace campaign against the deep-sea dumping of the Brent Spar oil rig.

- The political parties, the courts and local government are frequent targets for pressure groups of all kinds, sectional as well as cause. Groups seek influence on parties through donations, persuading parties to include key demands in their manifestos, and occasionally by running against them at elections; they have also sponsored parliamentary candidates, although in the case of union sponsorship of Labour candidates, this practice ended in the mid-1990s. Donations by business brought allegations of 'cash for favours' in the 1990s and following the Neill Committee on Standards in Public Life, the law on gifts to parties will probably be tightened.

- Pressure groups have increasingly resorted to the courts in recent years to publicise issues, to force governments to carry out their legal responsibilities and to exert pressure for changes in the law. However, governments and large companies have also employed the law to fight back against groups. Governments have tightened the law of trespass, kept direct action protesters under close surveillance and sometimes used intimidatory tactics and legal action against them whilst big companies have sought sequestration of groups' assets and pursued libel actions against them. In some cases, this tactic has backfired, for example, in the McLibel case which cost McDonald's much bad publicity as well as £10 million costs and also when the government has been successfully sued for wrongful imprisonment in cases involving the Hunt Saboteurs.

- Local government is a very important arena for pressure group activity, with people often mobilising on such issues as housing, planning, schools and transport. A wide variety of public interest groups, including community groups, cause groups, social movements and voluntary organisations, are active at local level, often with insider status, alongside producer groups such as chambers of commerce, trade associations, local CBI branches and trade unions. Local pressure group activity has intensified in recent decades as a consequence of both huge structural changes in local government, including contracting out and marketisation, and the direct encouragement of greater group participation by local councils.

Further reading

Parliamentary Affairs, 51, 3, July 1998 is a very useful special issue on 'Protest Politics', with articles on a wide range of recent campaigns. Byrne, P. (1997) *Social Movements in Britain* (London: Routledge) offers a valuable discusssion of social movements together with detailed coverage of the women's, environmental and peace movements. Jordan, G. and Maloney, W. (1997) *The Protest Business? Mobilizing Campaign Groups* (Manchester: Manchester University Press) subject the nature of the support for leading cause groups and social movement literature generally to critical assessment.

Pressure groups and the policy process

CHAPTER 7

Effectiveness, influence and resources

The final two chapters provide an overview of the role of pressure groups in the political system. Chapter 8 examines the overall impact of groups in terms of democracy. It concentrates on the question of whether the operation of the system is élitist or pluralist and whether its consequences are to concentrate or diffuse power. This chapter focuses on the means deployed by pressure groups to achieve influence and the underlying reasons for their effectiveness or failure. It considers first the resources available to groups, including finances, expertise, size and quality of membership, leadership, sanctions and choice of strategy. Second, it examines the political context in which the various interests struggle to exert influence. The importance of the political framework of government ideology and institutions in shaping and setting boundaries to group effectiveness has been suggested earlier in the book (Chapters 2, 3 and 4). It is enough to cite one simple example to reaffirm the importance of this factor here. Martin Smith has pointed out that the resources available to the trade union movement were no different on 3 May 1979, the day when the Conservatives won power, than they were on 2 May 1979, when Labour still governed. But because the Conservatives took office with a programme that included the curtailment of union privileges, the power of the unions in reality had been sharply reduced (Smith, 1993a). The point brings out vividly that the impact – and potential impact – of pressure groups on policy outcomes is the product of their relationships with government in general and with different sectors of government in particular. Accordingly the concern of this chapter is as much with these interactions between groups and government – which, when sufficiently developed, become policy networks – as it is with group resources as such. But it begins with groups' resources.

Pressure group resources

Pressure group resources include finances, expertise, organisation, membership, leadership and sanctions. The nature and extent of its resources are powerful shaping factors in a group's choice of strategy.

Finances

It might generally be expected both that sectional groups are superior to cause groups in terms of financial resources and that this will give them a bargaining advantage in their dealings with government. Both these expectations are frequently true. Thus, major sectional groups such as the Confederation of British Industry, the Association of British Bankers, the motor industry, brewers and weapons manufacturers are undoubtedly more powerful organisations in terms of financial backing and economic clout than, for example, associations representing the homeless, single mothers or pensioners. In struggles for political influence, the big industrial, financial, propertied or commercial interests may be expected to prevail – enabling large supermarkets to impose their terms on small agricultural producers, big landowners to defeat demands for greater access from ramblers, and so on. The anti-nuclear lobby in the 1980s was severely handicapped by lack of resources in its protest against a Conservative nuclear energy programme backed by the major economic interests which included the Central Electricity Generating Board, the Atomic Energy Authority, large national firms such as the General Electric Company (GEC) and big multinationals such as Westinghouse and Rio Tinto Zinc. The greater resources and status of business interests and of professional groups such as doctors and engineers may be generally expected to afford them the access to government denied to the less well-resourced cause groups.

However, as it stands, this argument is too simplistic and requires qualification. Sectional groups are not invariably better resourced than promotional groups. For example, an environmental group such as Greenpeace, whose British section alone generated an income of £9 million in 1996, possesses the lobbying resources to operate effectively at all political levels – international, European Union, UK government, and local government. By contrast, some sectional groups lack adequate resources. Recent research suggests that about two-thirds of trade associations – the most common form of business representation – fall short of the basic income requirement for effectiveness proposed by the Devlin Report (1972) and reiterated by the President of the Board of Trade in 1993 (May et al., 1998, pp. 264–5). Nor do extensive resources in themselves invariably enable groups to build close insider relations with government: the trade unions, relegated to the political wilderness during the 1979–97 period of Conservative government, are a case in point. By contrast, less well-resourced cause groups such as the Howard League for Penal Reform often achieve insider status. In the two decades after 1965, groups representing single parents, the disabled, the unemployed and the elderly deployed very modest resources compared with most sectional groups but made significant gains through 'painstaking and persistent lobbying' (Whiteley and Winyard, 1987, p. 138).

In terms of effectiveness, many variables affect outcomes. Sometimes good resources of one kind can be undermined by poor resources in another area. Thus, the loyalty and sacrifice of many mineworkers and their wives in the drawn-out campaign against pit closures in 1984–85 were more than offset in the final analysis by poor leadership, inept strategy and division within the main mineworkers' union, not to mention the utter determination of the Conservative Government not to back down. Or groups with extensive resources may not succeed because they are running against the grain of government policy or public opinion. Thus, the very expensive campaigns against nationalisation run by business between 1945 and 1979 failed, largely in this case because faced by governments – especially Labour governments – who were convinced that public ownership could be the answer to industrial problems.

Expertise

A key pressure group resource is expertise. The quality of a group's expertise can make it worth consulting by government. In the case of business groups this can be market or technical information. In the case of professional groups such as lawyers, doctors or teachers, it is professional knowledge (as well as goodwill). In the case of cause groups, it is most likely to be technical and scientific knowledge. For example, governments are likely to seek the views of the RSPB on bird conservation whilst anti-roads protesters in the 1990s drew upon 'respectable scientific research into the disbenefits of building more roads'. The World Wildlife Fund for Nature has been described as 'the classic example of an insider group which uses its conservation expertise as a means of gaining access to governments throughout the world' (Garner, 1996, p. 81; 1993a, p. 203). Sometimes, cause groups also provide 'market' information but of a particular kind: for example, the reliability of the information it provides on human rights violations worldwide ensures insider access to the Foreign and Commonwealth Office for Amnesty International (Christianson and Dowding, 1994, p. 21).

Structure and organisation

To maximise their chances of success, groups need to develop internal structures that will reduce the likelihood of splits. Peak sectional organisations such as the CBI and TUC which encompass a wide variety of types of members face the problem of overcoming internal divisions in a particularly acute form. The CBI, for example, has to represent both large and small firms as well as encompassing the often conflicting interests of the manufacturing, retail and financial sectors. Concern about its failure to represent manufacturing interests effectively led to the formation of the UK Industrial Group and the British Management Data Foundation in the early 1990s. In order to satisfy the diverse interests of their memberships and to minimise the chance of splits leading to the formation of breakaway groupings, many sectional groups develop structures in which the real work is done by specialised committees or they reserve seats on their main decision-making body for particular classes of member whose interests might otherwise be neglected. Sometimes, a problem of developing a united front occurs not within a single organisation but within an entire trade or profession where several competing organisations claim representative status. British business, for example, at the moment is far from presenting a united front on the single currency, with the CBI broadly in favour whilst significant minorities inside the organisation – and outside it in the form of the Business for Sterling group – oppose Britain joining. Internal divisions also bedevil teachers' representation, where historically numerous unions have developed representing different parts of the profession, and where debate currently rages over the merits and demerits of forming one big teachers' union (Box 7.1).

Cause groups differ considerably in organisation, ranging from the central-ised, bureaucratic structure of Greenpeace to the participatory organisation of Friends of the Earth. In each case, there is a contrasting rationale. Greenpeace deliberately decided upon an 'almost military' structure with a clear-cut division between the central command, which decides upon its 'actions', a small core of 'front-line troops' who carry out the actions, and a fee-paying mass of non-participant supporters who provide the financial support. On the other hand, Friends of the Earth, whilst also posssessing a full-time national organisation, encourages its large number of local groups to undertake environmental initiatives of their own. Groups such as FoE, radical feminists and 'deep greens' like Earth First!, it is clear, favour decentralised, informal networks rather than corporate, top-down structures such as Greenpeace's, largely for ideological reasons – because that is what their members want – rather than for any considerations of effectiveness. Nonetheless, there is a strong link between such structures and effectiveness in the sense that this organisational form – or rather, in many cases, 'disorganisation' – is the one most likely to unleash members' energies on behalf of the cause. If they are prudent and lucky, groups will develop the kind of organisation that maxi-mises their effectiveness. The Campaign for Nuclear Disarmament, for example, has a formal, democratic structure in which an annual conference is responsible for defining the aims of the organisation: this has helped to keep the organisation stable and contributed to its long-term durability by enabling the membership to prevent radical or moderate minorities from swaying the peace movement in their direction (Byrne, 1997, pp. 136–9, 163–4, 168).

BOX 7.1

The question of teachers' organisation: one big union or several small ones?

Fragmentation, involving too many small unions, has often been seen as a weakness of twentieth-century trade unionism, one that the movement has steadily tried to overcome by means of mergers, such as that leading to the formation of the massive public sector union Unison in the 1990s. With teachers' representation divided among six different unions in England and Wales and a further two in Scotland, the dilemma of whether to combine to form one big union faced teachers' unions in the late 1990s when teachers' disunity contrasted sharply with the greater unity achieved by lawyers, doctors and nurses.

In November 1998, the leaders of the two largest teachers' unions debated the case for forming one large union in the profession. Doug McEvoy, general secretary of the National Union of Teachers (NUT), put the case in favour of such a move whilst Nigel de Gruchy, general secretary of the National Association of Schoolmasters/Union of Women Teachers (NASUWT), argued against it (Figure 7.1).

Figure 7.1 Pulling their punches: but discussion about unity was heated.

BOX 7.1 (CONTINUED

For:

- Unity is strength: a single union would enable teachers to put forward a united front against government criticism. Disunity made it possible for the government to pick off different unions one by one when establishing the Review Body which determines teachers' pay and conditions. Since its first report, teachers have received a real terms pay rise of just 0.2 per cent.

- Eliminate inter-union competition and bickering: at present teachers' unions spend too much time and energy competing with each other for members in a recruitment war which compels them to exaggerate the differences between them.

- Reduce the costs of administration: over three-quarters of the fee income of the unions in 1997 (£32 million out of £41.7 million) went on administration. Merging unions would enable more to be spent on protecting the best interests of teachers.

- The historical reasons for representation by different unions have disappeared as comprehensive education has largely eliminated the old class differences between grammar school and other secondary teachers and equal pay has removed the differential treatment of men and women teachers.

Against:

- The conditions for successful amalgamation do not exist: the current unions represent genuine differences of view about the purposes unions serve and the ways in which they organise themselves – one large union would be unable to maintain unity as these real differences would come to the surface.

- A single union might contain a permanent majority against strike action, which the NASUWT sees as a vital trade union right. Such an anti-strike majority could be created if NUT moderates were joined by principled opponents of industrial action in the Association of Teachers and Lecturers (ATL) and Professional Association of Teachers (PAT). On the other hand, it might also contain unrepresentative activists (i.e. left-wingers at NUT conferences) making too many calls for direct action on too many issues.

- The main concern of a teachers' union is improving the pay and conditions of its members, not educational policy. This is the priority of the NASUWT. Its ability to operate as a separate entity has brought many gains for teachers in recent years, including a reduced administrative burden, a slimmed down national curriculum, concessions on national tests following a successful boycott in 1993 and, further back in time, a reduced pension contribution to 6 per cent (1973) and a 30 per cent pay rise (1974–75).

Questions

1. Which arguments do you find more persuasive – those for or against a single large teachers' union – and why?

2. Do you agree with the NASUWT argument that strike action is a vital trade union right as well as a crucial weapon in the armoury of a group of workers or with the ATL and PAT argument that going on strike is incompatible with professional status? Give your reasons.

BOX 7.1 (CONTINUED

3. Would a single large teachers' union representing all or most of the 500 000 teachers be likely to possess as much bargaining power in its dealings with government as does the doctors' organisation, the BMA? If so, why? If not, why not?

4. How far does the case for a single teachers' union underestimate the strength of historical divisions and antagonisms within the profession?

Membership

Size of membership or extent of support, density, solidarity and quality of membership can all be significant. Size of membership obviously matters. It is a source of weakness to the trade union movement that membership declined so dramatically – by over 4 million – between 1979 and 1998, just as it was a source of strength for the Countryside March in 1998 that it could claim the participation of 280 000 supporters. Unlike sectional groups, whose membership is in an important sense 'given', and who can often be attracted by incidental 'fringe' benefits such as lower insurance costs and the like, cause groups have to build up their support from nothing. The capacity of the new social movements to develop such huge memberships has been a significant factor in their growing influence in the 1980s and 1990s. However, with regard to sectional groups, whilst *absolute* numbers of members or supporters can be a persuasive factor, *relative* numbers – i.e. of actual members compared with potential members – can be important too. The concept of *density* refers to the percentage of potential or eligible members of an organisation who actually belong to it. For example, in 1991 the density of union membership in the total labour force – the proportion of workers who joined unions – was just over 34 per cent (Butler and Butler, 1994, p. 370). The fact that unions spoke for such a relatively low proportion of workers was used by the Conservative Party after 1979 to undermine the morale of trade unionists, dent their legitimacy in public opinion and so weaken their resistance to the attack on their privileges. The solidarity of its membership is another factor in the pressure a group is able to bring upon a given situation. Divisions within the membership are a sign of weakness exploitable by opponents. For example, the breakaway of the Union of Democratic Mineworkers from the NUM in 1984–85 undermined the miners' strike. Equally, strike ballots demonstrating majority support for industrial action can strengthen the cause of striking unions.

A criterion such as density of membership can scarcely be applied to cause groups which lack a clearly identifiable potential membership. Whereas solidarity as demonstrated in support for the leadership is also a key factor in the effectiveness of sectional groups, a considerable amount of solidarity can simply be assumed amongst the cause group members who share a particular set of values. Quality of membership is what matters for cause groups in which *activism* is a primary requirement. Amnesty International, for example, asks its members to engage in letter-writing campaigns to foreign governments on behalf of dissidents. Members of social movements like peace, feminism and ecology expect to 'bear witness' to their beliefs both in direct action and in their private lives. Paul Byrne has suggested the kind of activity, requiring a sizeable investment of time and energy as well as drawing upon significant knowledge, that a member of a local FoE group might undertake to counter development of an unspoilt piece of land: in addition to both conventional tactics (e.g. lobbying local councillors and contacting the local media) and unconventional tactics (e.g. demonstrating and leafleting), this would also probably involve activities such as organising volunteers to clear the land of litter and undertaking a study of flora and fauna on the land in conjunction with local schools (Byrne, 1997, p. 137). Although often deficient in money and numbers, cause groups and social movements can draw upon other resources such as enthusiasm and expertise. Such expertise covers a broad range, with members of promotional groups often able to deploy legal, scientific, technical, medical and other expertise on behalf of their group as well as personal contacts and an understanding of 'how to get things done'.

Leadership

Good leadership matters to the success of pressure groups. But there is no single leadership style that can fit all types of group and all circumstances. A simple contrast would be between the responsible, managerial style adopted by established insiders such as business leaders or the chiefs of local authority associations and the media-friendly style of the leaders of campaigning groups. Necessarily the latter will give a higher public profile than the former: thus, few will have heard of Adair Turner, the director-general of the CBI in 1998 or even John Monks, the general secretary of the TUC, but many more will recognise the names of the green activist, Jonathan Porritt, or the former director of the housing group Shelter and campaigner for lead-free air, Des Wilson. However, common to leaders of both cause and sectional groups is the need for a well-argued case. For instance, the animal welfare campaigner, Richard Ryder, points to the need for a well-argued and balanced case with which to persuade decision-makers and remarks how much more effective the campaign against animal experimentation became after it moderated its demands from immediate and total abolition to a call for reform. He writes: 'We tried to argue our case logically and with supporting evidence . . . My own tone in *Victims of Science* also tried to be objective and scientific and thus, to a very large extent, avoided the charges of being emotional or ill-informed . . . governments are more likely to listen to calls for reform that are (a) moderate, (b) scientific and well-reasoned, and (c) argued by experienced and qualified people' (in this case former members of the scientific and medical communities) (Ryder, 1996, cited in Garner, 1996a, pp. 172–3). But even a good case does not guarantee success. Local authority professional associations, for example, were well aware of the extra costs and losses of revenue that local councils would suffer if the community charge (poll tax) were introduced, and the case was clearly put within specialist local government finance and accountancy circles. However, senior local authority finance officers were not consulted by the government of the day on the desirability of the new tax, only on how to implement it (Butler *et al.*, 1994, pp. 276–7). A particular point at which groups require astute leadership is at a change of government, when the ruling ideology sometimes changes too. At such moments group leaders need to learn to 'speak a different language' in order to have any chance of influence. An example is after the election in 1979 of the Thatcher Government with its new anti-corporatist, arm's length attitudes to business and the unions. CBI and TUC leaders may have contributed to the length of time they spent in the political wilderness, ignored by government, by their failure to adapt their strategies to the new situation.

Sanctions

Sometimes groups can employ sanctions in pursuit of their goals. Sanctions normally involve groups in blockage, disruption and non-cooperation with government policy. Because of their importance to the successful functioning of the national economy, sectional groups – business, professional, trade union – normally possess greater social and economic leverage than cause groups, and therefore greater capacity to impose effective sanctions. According to Harden and Lewis, certain sectional interests can exert a 'power to veto and at least substantially amend government policies' (cited in Weir and Beetham, 1999, p. 272). National Farmers Union muscle was shown in 1988 when it forced the sacking of the Junior Health Minister, Edwina Currie, who had with some exaggeration drawn attention to the danger of salmonella in eggs, and also forced the government to bring in a costly compensation scheme for egg-producers (Weir and Beetham, 1999, p. 280). Another important sanction is the withdrawal of labour by the strike weapon, although its effectiveness has declined in recent decades. In the early 1970s, for example, trade union militancy destroyed the Conservative Government's industrial relations legislation, but industrial action by steel and mining unions was powerless to halt Conservative industrial and trade union policies after 1979. A very expensive BMA campaign against the Conservative NHS reforms failed in the late 1980s but the teachers' boycott of national tests won some concession in the early 1990s (see Box 7.1). Early in 1999, doctors gave notice that they might defy the rationing of the anti-impotence drug, Viagra, by the Health Secretary. Obstruction and non-compliance have also been deployed effectively by cause groups in the 1990s, notably by Hunt Saboteurs, anti-poll tax protesters – who ran 'can't pay, won't pay' campaigns – and anti-roads campaigners, who used driving up the costs of road-building as a deliberate tactic (see Box 7.2). Consumer boycotts are coercive weapons against firms which in recent decades have helped to force the withdrawal of Barclays Bank from South Africa (1986) and, largely in Holland and Germany, helped force Shell to withdraw its plan for the deep sea dumping of the Brent Spar oil rig. Other boycotts have targeted Chinese toys made in labour camps, Chilean wines, South African fruit and sport, holidays in Spain under Franco or Greece under the colonels, Continental crate-reared veal, cosmetics tested on live animals and furs made of real pelts (Ascherson, *The Observer*, 19 November 1995).

Strategy

Choice of an appropriate strategy can be an important factor in pressure group success. A group's resources – and the effectiveness of its manipulation of these – normally plays a key role in its choice of strategy. The broad decision is between an insider strategy targeting government at European, national and local levels or an outsider strategy targeting public opinion but also using the courts or aiming at converting political parties. The choice of strategy depends upon the nature of the group, which means that it is often severely constrained. Thus, most business groups can realistically aim at insider status whilst ideological groups such as the Campaign for Nuclear Disarmament and oppositional groups such as the Anti-Poll Tax Federation have no alternative to adopting an outsider strategy, since their aims are in direct conflict with government policy.

Whilst no strategies could be more sharply opposed than, say, the insider strategy of the CBI and the outsider strategy of the direct action protest groups, sectional and cause group strategies can overlap to a significant degree. There are two basic underlying reasons for this. First, all groups aim at influence, government is the major decision-maker, and therefore few groups would resist a bureaucratic request for consultation. Thus, some cause groups and social movements pursue outsider and insider strategies simultaneously: for example, the major environmental groups engage in direct action but also run scientific establishments which enable them to take on government scientists on their own terms and provide a basis for conventional lobbying when the situation demands. The animal welfare movement, it has been argued, is so diverse that it benefits from the activities of both low public profile insiders and direct action outsiders. A leading animal rights campaigner has suggested that this dual, if generally unplanned and uncoordinated, strategy, 'is probably the most successful approach. Often the more moderate, the more constitutional and the more discreet actually benefit from the antics of their more extreme colleagues. Without the extremists the moderates might not be admitted to centres of influence. Occasionally it happens the other way

round ... But not for long. One may conclude that there should be some
tolerance of diversity within any movement which seeks to be effective'
(Ryder, cited in Garner, 1996, p. 178). By the same token, business organisations which normally run insider strategies often run public campaigns. Thus,
retail interests lobbied for Sunday trading, shipping and airline companies
fought to retain duty free shopping, threatened industries campaigned against
nationalisation, and sections of business resisted membership of the EEC in the
1970s and are currently opposing Britain's membership of the European single
currency. Whilst not running an extensive anti-government campaign, the CBI
was often outspokenly critical of government policy, especially high interest
rates, between 1979 and 1992.

The second reason sectional and cause group strategies often overlap is
because it is in the interest of neither to avoid a potentially useful pressure
point. Thus, as already noted in Chapters 3 and 5, both types of group often
seek good relations with the British and European parliaments, normally in
combination with other targets. Although the constitutional role of these
institutions is rather limited, good contacts can bring results in particular
circumstances, for example, when precarious government majorities prevail at
Westminster, and in particular issue areas, such as women's rights and the
environment in Strasbourg.

Sometimes groups that succeed in an outsider strategy need to decide how
to consolidate their gains. When a government is prepared to incorporate a
successful outsider group into the ring of insiders, the group faces a by no
means straightforward decision. Will it enhance or maintain its influence by
incorporation into government policy-making machinery, or will its former
cutting edge as a political outsider be blunted by being absorbed into the
policy community? Stephen Joseph, the director of the group Transport 2000,
which lobbies for public transport and against new trunk roads, faced this
dilemma before consenting to membership of the Standing Advisory Committee on Trunk Road Assessment and the UK Round Table on Sustainable
Development. Anti-road groups have to decide whether an outsider strategy is
effective to start the process of change by altering the policy image but needs
to be followed up with an insider strategy to consolidate these gains.
Environmental groups failed to do this in the 1960s but, as already noticed,
there were signs that a dual insider/outsider strategy might be operating in the
1990s (Dudley and Richardson, 1996, p. 746). The dangers for a cause group
of insider status degenerating into the impotence of 'phoney insider status', in
which groups go along with decisions they dislike for fear of losing their
insider privileges and the possibility of influencing future decisions, has been
well brought out with reference to animal welfare groups. The recommendations of animal welfare groups coopted onto the Farm Animal Welfare
Council (on factory farming and slaughterhouses) have been 'almost totally
ignored' whilst the views of the Nature Conservancy Council, which also
contained animal welfare groups, had very little influence on the 1981 Wildlife
and Countryside Bill (Garner, 1993b, p. 346).

BOX 7.2

Obstruction and non-compliance: the impact of protest on the nature of public policy

Some public campaigns or protests succeed in shaping legislation because they strike a chord with both élite and public opinion. The Snowdrop Campaign (1996–97), which was successful in winning legislation that banned handguns, was supported across the media with broadsheets and tabloids running parallel campaigns. There was also strong support from powerful groups such as the Police Federation and ACPO. Other campaigns have to rely more on 'shows of strength' or direct protest as means of exerting leverage on policy-makers.

The Countryside Alliance organised a large march on London in March 1998 involving around 280 000 people from rural Britain. The protest was organised to draw attention to the 'rural crisis' and involved concerns as diverse as opposition to any measures that outlawed hunting, farmers' grievances about BSE and falling farm incomes, the loss of countryside to urban development, and declining rural services such as transport, schools and shops. Some political commentators argued that the Labour Government could ignore the rural vote, since it won a little over quarter of the vote in the most rural constituencies and had only a dozen MPs from totally agricultural constituencies. Others, however, believed that Labour attempted to buy off the Countryside protest with policy concessions. Grant Jordan, for example, argued 'not coincidentally, there were government announcements on policy changes involving rural schools, the financing of the slaughtering of cattle, dropping the idea of banning "green top" milk, restricting the use of country lanes by lorries, improving bus services and speculation about the creation of a rural affairs ministry' (Jordan, 1998, p. 322).

The Brent Spar issue. The oil company Shell announced its intentions of dumping the redundant Brent Spar oil rig in the North Atlantic. The Conservative Government fully supported the policy of deep sea disposal. In other words, the policy community favoured this method of disposing of old oil rigs, arguing that technically it was safe. However the policy offended the environmental lobby, particularly Greenpeace, whose activists occupied the rig. Adverse publicity in Britain combined with consumer resistance in Europe persuaded Shell to abandon its plan. Greenpeace had wrested decision-making about decommissioning from the British policy community to a more open international issue network.

Animal welfare. Concern for animal welfare has a long history in Britain; the RSPCA was established in 1824 as the world's first society of its kind. Another moderate group, Compassion in World Farming, publicised the poor conditions in which many exported animals were slaughtered. In response to increasing public anxiety about the export of live animals, some ferry companies ended transporting live animals, which led to animals being exported from smaller ports like Brightlingsea and Shoreham. Up to a third of the populations of these small towns joined with more radical animal rights protesters in demonstrations (*The Observer*, 22 January 1995; *The Economist*, 19 August 1995). Despite traditionally strong links with farmers, the Conservative Government began lobbying to change EU regulations over conditions concerning animal welfare.

The roads protests of the 1990s. Much media attention focused on the protests over road building schemes in Hampshire and Berkshire. The latter involved the construction

BOX 7.2 (CONTINUED)

Figure 7.2 The Donga strategy.

of a new nine-mile bypass running around the east of Newbury. The radical protesters against the M3 construction at Twyford Down in 1992, the so-called Donga tribe, occupied many of the trees that were due to be felled to make way for the new Newbury bypass. As in the struggle against live veal exports a year earlier, radical protesters were supported by many 'respectable' citizens drawn from middle England. The Donga strategy was not to prevent the bypass being built but to cause maximum delay which would increase costs and so reduce the resources available for future road building (Figure 7.2).

The British Roads Federation had consistently argued that Britain's increasing traffic congestion could only be eased by building new roads. However, the government appeared to acknowledge that the 'roads ideology' was flawed since new roads did not end congestion but simply encouraged more traffic. The Newbury bypass was the only major new road project started in 1996 and further new road building was severely curtailed. Once again, outside challenges had disrupted the policy community

BOX 7.2 (CONTINUED)

and the debate moved to a more open issue network. The Labour Government accepts that the solution to cutting congestion is a reduction in road traffic rather than more roads, and the new roads programme has been cut to one third the size envisaged in 1989.

(Main sources: Doherty (1998); Dudley and Richardson (1996); Toke (1996))

Questions

1. To what extent do the coalitions of 'radicals' and 'moderates' on issues such as animal exports and road building represent the failure of parliamentary politics?

2. How far are those who participate in direct action justified in breaking the law?

3. What tactics would you advise any outside group to follow if it wished to disrupt a 'closed' policy community?

The external environment

In order to explain why certain policy outcomes occur it is not enough to focus on the resources and activities of groups. It is necessary to analyse the relationships between the state and groups and the interests and actions of state actors.

(Smith, 1993a, p. 6)

Professional status

Doctors' groups are relatively well resourced in terms of resources at hand, the quality of leadership, effectiveness of organisation and public image, and are generally recognised to be influential and powerful. It is rightly assumed that their professional knowledge gives them easy access to government. Yet the relative success of doctors in shaping health policy should not be attributed to these factors alone, but just as much to the context within which policy is made.

... the success or failure of the doctors in influencing health policy has not depended on their pressure group activity, but is actually the result of the interests of state actors, the forms of policy networks in health policy and the wider forces within the policy process ... the influence of doctors on health policy is not pre-ordained ... [relations with government are] highly variable and can often be conflictual.

(Smith, 1993a, p. 163)

In other words, if it serves the political ends of government to claim the support of the medical profession it will do so and doctors' groups will appear ascendant. If, however, it serves government to attack doctors as representing 'the forces of conservatism', as Labour did in 2000, previous relationships may be disturbed until it suits politicians to restore them. For the intervening period doctors may appear relatively excluded from the health policy process.

Professional power

Professional groups are potentially powerful in the policy process because of their high status which is principally based on the possession of specialist knowledge and expertise. Such groups are by nature exclusive, limiting entrants to the profession to those holding specific qualifications or able to meet specific standards in professional performance. The medical profession provides an example of such a group which has been studied by numerous academics. As mentioned above, an element of their influence is based upon government dependence on their expertise in shaping health policy. Other elements depend upon the wider needs of government policy. As Smith noted (1993a, pp. 165–6) the health policy community in Britain 'developed partly as a result of government policy, and it was this policy, rather than the intrinsic power of the medical profession, which accounts for the power of doctors'. In this sense British health policy 'developed out of a combination of state interests and medical power'. When state interests were redefined, as during the years of the Thatcher governments, the influence of the medical profession changed accordingly.

It is worth recalling that the establishment of the NHS in 1948 was essentially a compromise between government and the medical profession. Doctors were persuaded to participate in free health service through being granted professional privileges as well as acknowledgement of their consider-able influence over health policy. An essentially new policy community was established which involved doctors, civil servants and politicians. The Thatcher governments of the 1980s challenged the extent of professional power over health policy, undermining the rationale of the long-established health policy community. Policy-making became conflictual, with traditional participants such as the royal colleges becoming marginalised whilst various New Right think-tanks became increasingly involved in developing policy ideas. The BMA became less involved as a politically inspired, rather than professionally based, programme of reforms imposed purchaser–provider contractual relationships on a previously unified health service.

Government institutions

To what extent can changing orthodoxy or ideology challenge established relationships between government and pressure groups? The adherence of the Thatcher governments to promoting, or at least to proclaiming, the virtue of free market economics threatened established relationships and frequently resulted in contradiction within government. For example, Conservative consumer policy during the 1980s was based on strengthening free market forces and increasing consumer information so that free choice in the market-place would become based on more informed and rational behaviour. However, the large department charged with enhancing entrepreneurialism and competi-tion was close to the business community and not particularly sympathetic to the interests of consumer groups. In 1987 the government passed the Consumer Protection Act, a major piece of legislation making producers liable for defective goods whether or not the defect was the result of negligence. Was this Act the result of government determination to increase competition combined with a desire to improve the position of consumers in the market-place? Most commentators concluded that the Act only came into existence as a result of an EC directive, and that in shaping the legislation all possible measures were taken to 'limit the damage' that might be done to producers. A strong business lobby, which itself frequently paid lip service to free market competition and standards, was able to influence government into protecting its interests against those of the relatively weak consumer lobby.

The relative success or failure of groups in influencing the policy process can change as a result of restructuring within government. The merging of existing departments into a new 'super ministry', or the abolition of depart-ments and the creation of new ones, or even restructuring within departments can destabilise government–group relationships. Even a change in personnel, especially the minister, can lead to changes in the micro political climate, and hence the behaviour, of policy communities. Changes within the DTI in 1998 strengthened the influence of trade associations (May *et al.*, 1998) whilst the Blair Government's decision to merge the Transport and Environment depart-ments weakened the influence of the roads lobby (Doherty, 1998).

Custom and practice

Government departments continuously decide which groups should be granted access to officials but, of course, they have no published rules or protocols concerning which specific groups should be consulted or on what policy issues negotiations should take place. An interest group such as the CBI possesses near automatic access to government on any issue affecting its members' interests (Weir and Beetham, 1999, p. 275). Another group, Amnesty Inter-national, has a close working relationship with Foreign Office officials concerning human rights violations abroad but is excluded from policy formation with regard to human rights in Britain. Amnesty International has 'dual status'; it is recognised as a legitimate insider group in terms of the credibility of its information and provided the British Prime Minister with a list of Chinese 'prisoners of conscience' which he duly handed to the Chinese Government in 1991. But on domestic issues Amnesty International has only outsider status and has to rely on political campaigning and parliamentary lobbying in its attempts to get heard.

Climate of opinion

Finally, the success or failure of pressure groups may be wholly or in part the product of public opinion, temporary yet fashionable views, or publicly expressed values by opinion-formers that mark a change in direction for some previously favoured or condemned activity or cause. Richard Rose (1974, pp. 254–5) has developed a six-fold typology of relationships between pressure groups and prevailing cultural norms which embraces the vagaries of changing political values. The general rule states that the closer a group's values are to the wider cultural norms, the easier it will be for that group to equate its demands with the public interest; the greater any disparity, the harder it will be for a group to achieve its aims.

1. *Harmony between pressure group demands and general cultural norms.* Groups whose aims command immediate respect, affection and support, such as the NSPCC, fall into this category. So too do some groups that oppose cruelty to animals such as the RSPCA, although more extremist groups such as the Animal Liberation Front offend cultural norms because of their frequently violent methods.

2. *A gradual increase in the acceptability of political values supporting pressure group demands.* An example of a group benefiting from élitist and public acceptance is ASH, the anti-smoking group. In the past such groups were marginal organisations, but over time attitudes have changed and their cause has moved up the political agenda.

3. *Bargaining with fluctuating support and changing cultural norms.* Trade union membership declined sharply during the 1980s, rising marginally in 1999–2000. Public opinion has also changed from being broadly pro-union in the 1950s to being anti-union in the 1970s. Leaders of groups with fluctuating support have to be adaptable, pressing government when support is high or rising but being prepared to defend their positions when swings go against them. Gay rights groups have enjoyed a change of influence during the postwar years; once illegal, gays' behaviour was seen as deviant and consequently most were reluctant to 'come out', but with changes in both law and cultural norms, gays have increased in visibility, including prominent gays in government, and won near equality with heterosexual rights.

4. *Advocacy in the face of cultural indifference.* Little publicity has been given to the activities of the Pedestrians Association, which has a membership of approximately one thousand. Most citizens are pedestrians from time to time and likely to be inconvenienced by insufficient zebra crossings or speeding urban traffic, yet there is little explicit support for increasing pedestrian rights.

5. *Advocacy in opposition to long-term cultural trends.* Groups such as the Lord's Day Observance Society and Keep Sunday Special opposed reforms

aimed at liberalising the Sunday shopping laws. Yet public attitudes and behaviour increasingly identified Sunday as a day for leisure, including shopping. A Shops Bill announced in the Queen's Speech in 1985 was designed to end regulation on Sunday shopping but it was eventually defeated. Another attempt was made in 1993 with the Sunday Trading Bill which was successful. The legal pattern of shopping on Sundays was at last congruent with public opinion.

6. *Conflict between cultural values and pressure group goals.* Groups some-times advocate political demands that conflict with prevailing norms in the hope that eventually cultural norms will change. Groups advocating absolute values, such as pacifists, are not able to compromise and this has a major impact on their tactics. A negotiated policy outcome, which to many groups would represent at least partial success in influencing policy, is likely to appear as defeat to groups with fundamental principles deeply embedded in their goals. Some groups are successful in winning public support for some goals whilst suppressing other, unpopular goals. Animal rights groups have focused on banning field sports such as fox-hunting and hare-coursing because of high levels of popular support for such goals. However, such groups also oppose angling and horse-riding. Public opinion is not opposed to these country activities. Not wishing to risk losing support, groups have responded by playing down or de-emphasising the goals that still remain unacceptable with the wider public.

The success or otherwise of a campaign may rest on the development of an 'attentive public' which is made up of individuals who are not members of any particular group but who share to a greater or lesser extent the groups' aims (Garner, 1993b, p. 335). Partly as a result of effective campaigning and the development of an attentive public, opinion has shifted on animal rights through the 1980s, the 1990s and into the new millennium. According to polls, a build-up in public opinion occurred until there were substantial majorities opposed to killing animals for their fur; to testing cosmetics and toiletries on animals; and to fox-hunting and hare-coursing.

With reference to environmental issues on the American political agenda, Anthony Downs (1972, pp. 38–50) argued that they were subject to a five-stage cycle which would end on every occasion in their eclipse. *Stage 1* represents the pre-problem stage when some pressure groups may be concerned about the environmental significance of an issue but the media is uninterested and the public is generally unaware; *Stage 2* occurs when the problem is discovered, perhaps as the result of some particular event, and the public calls on politicians for a solution. Politicians respond by promising action on the issue; *Stage 3* is the slow realisation of the costs involved in making progress and the knowledge that sacrifices might have to be made to solve the problem; *Stage 4* sees public concern over the issue decline, either through boredom or rejection of the high costs or scale of changes necessary to solve the issue; and *Stage 5* is marked by the issue disappearing from the political agenda as the public forgets. In reality, the problem still exists. A small share of resources may be devoted to researching the problem.

Assessing the influence of groups: a cautionary note

Whiteley and Winyard have observed that the least researched aspect of pressure group politics has been their effectiveness in influencing policy (1987, p. 111). This chapter has examined factors concerning resources, political structures and aspects of the prevailing political culture, which may help some groups to influence policy whilst the same factors may militate against the influence of other groups. But assessing the influence of a group or groups in precise terms is extremely difficult. Influence involves persuasion, argument and debate, which are all difficult to assess. Also governments rarely explain why policy has changed; rather there are tendencies by government officials to conceal policy changes by down-playing them, or disguise them through the arts of spin, or present an unchanged policy as something new. British governments rarely concede in public that a particular policy outcome is the direct result of specific lobbying from a named group. Indeed, government is characterised by secrecy rather than such openness and it is the closed nature of government decision-making that obscures bargaining and negotiation from public gaze, thus concealing the balance of advantage any group or groups may secure in deal-making.

In any assessment of group influence there are dangers of attributing policy change to the successful efforts of interested groups. This may be too simplistic. For policy-making is a complex process, involving a number of parties including civil servants and special advisers, plus considerations of factors ranging from domestic public opinion to the responses of foreign governments or the EU, with pressure groups being only one factor bidding for influence in the policy debate.

Measuring influence is also a subjective assessment in which perceptions count for everything. For example, Labour's recent workplace rights legislation restored a number of privileges to trade unions; some members saw this as a major policy concession which had been won by the unions, some saw it as merely the 'best deal available' under the prevailing circumstances, whilst others believed that it represented yet another defeat for the unions since it would weaken their position through encouraging 'sweetheart' deals with employers.

What might appear to be a group campaign that has successfully influenced government need be no more than a political illusion. This occurs when a particular group and the government department concerned are thinking along the same lines. In reality the group is 'pushing at an open door' in the sense that government policy is already decided in favour of an approach favoured by the group. For example, the roads lobby may have seemed to dominate the Department of Transport during the postwar years only because its pressures fitted pre-existing departmental plans (Dudley and Richardson, 1996, p. 746). Garner (1993b, p. 346) made a similar point with reference to the influence of the animal lobby; thus concessions in the Animals (Scientific Procedures) Bill (1986) may have only been 'apparent' in that the government, swayed by public opinion, had been moving in that direction anyway.

Groups are able to exploit 'ideas', 'institutions' and 'events' when influencing policy. For example, during the 1990s green groups have been able to exploit the idea of global warming and the associated dangers of burning carbon fuels. Structures for public participation, notably Highway Inquiries, provided groups and individuals with the opportunity to question policy assumptions.

What may appear as the successful exercise of pressure group politics in one policy area may be no more than the knock-on of a Treasury decision taken elsewhere and for other non-related reasons. For example, during the mid-1990s, Conservative transport ministers began meeting representatives of Transport 2000, Greenpeace, Friends of the Earth and even Alarm UK Local expressions of public opinion regarding the M3 and A34 Newbury bypass were given considerable attention in the media. Road-building was cut back. Surely the anti-roads lobby had won the day? An equally plausible interpretation is that Treasury was looking for reductions in public spending, and the roads budget was an easy economy. Regarding the cancellation of future projects, 'Even decisions like the cancellation of Oxleas Wood, which won plaudits from environmentalists has been taken for financial rather than green reasons' (Norris, 1996b, p. 232).

The political influence of the campaign launched by STOPP (Society of Teachers Opposed to Physical Punishment) appears more straightforward to assess. This was formed in 1966 and dissolved in 1987 after achieving its goal through a free vote in Parliament on abolishing corporal punishment in schools. Part of the group's success can be attributed to its 'moderate' tactics; it kept to the single issue, it avoided extremism, it used language with subtlety and referred constantly to the distasteful act of 'child beating' rather than the more neutral sounding 'corporal punishment'. The key breakthrough for STOPP was winning decisions at teachers' conferences during the 1980s which was then followed by a favourable European Court judgment.

Byrne (1997, pp. 22–3) has argued that protest campaigns need to be assessed in terms that differ from those used when assessing social movements. This is because a 'social movement is something more than just a handful of events or actions, more than just a protest against a single act or policy ... Movements aim for societal, not just localalised change ... This does not mean that social movements cannot *contain* protest campaigns within them'. Protest movements, then, confront political authorities over policy whereas social movements are more concerned with changing society's values rather than with changing specific policies. He argued that Greenpeace and Earth First!, examples of the former, are a 'constant thorn' in the side of the authorities and as such do have an affect but ultimately as 'an irritation rather than as a serious threat'. Their main impact is 'to ensure that the issues remain in the public eye, thus creating a climate conducive to change, rather than forcing specific policy reversals' (p. 173). The impact of social movements, such as feminists, is even harder to assess. Public attitudes have changed, at least superficially, 'but it is questionable how far attitudes have been translated into practice' (p. 178). Few politicians would today challenge the idea of equality for women. Yet it took what was to be judged illegal selection procedures to get women chosen as Labour candidates in significant numbers prior to the 1997 General Election; the Conservative Party selection processes have since resulted in 80 per cent of candidates being male. Byrne concluded that the biggest impact made by social movements such as the feminists is to have successfully placed their concerns on the political agenda and changed the way in which people think about politics.

Questions

1. Identify the nature of resources likely to account for the success or failure of a pressure group.

2. What are possible benefits and possible risks for a group deciding on direct action as a means of political participation?

3. To what extent does the existence of a policy community represent the absence of public involvement with policy-making?

4. Assess the impact of the political culture on the behaviour on pressure groups.

5. Explain the difficulties political scientists face when attempting to measure the influence of pressure group activity on the making of policy.

Summary

- Groups are important but not so central to explaining policy outcomes as traditional theories have suggested. Even powerful groups like doctors only establish institutional relationships once government has decided for its own reasons to adopt a particular policy.

- Success or failure of groups can be partially explained by the prevailing political culture. When politicians are committed to increasing economic growth and raising affluence environmental groups will encounter difficulties in achieving major ecological goals. The government's political agenda will address achievable lower order goals such as recycling, unleaded petrol, and congestion charging.

- The internal organisation of a group may be a key factor in accounting for its relative success. The organisation of government is also an important factor for insider groups, and changes in departmental structure may result in a loss in influence.

- Measuring the influence of groups on policy-making is a complex and difficult task. The nature of government as well as the multiplicity of goals pursued by many groups hinders attempts at objective assessment.

Further reading

Paul Byrne (1997) *Social Movements in Britain* (London: Routledge) provides valuable accounts of the peace movement, the women's movement and the green movement. Grant Jordan and William Maloney (1997) *The Protest Business? Mobilizing Campaign Groups* (Manchester: Manchester University Press) explores the dynamics of group membership as well as the role of 'marketing' in the formation and growth of pressure groups. Robert Garner (ed.) (1996a) *Animal Rights. The Changing Debate* (London: Macmillan) examines the issue in terms of its growing political significance. Duncan Watts (1995) 'Sunday shopping: reform at last' in *Talking Politics* 8, 1 examines the reasons behind the success of the reformers. Martin Smith (1993a) *Pressure, Power and Policy* (Harlow: Prentice Hall) provides an excellent theoretical account together with useful case studies.

Pressure groups, pluralism and democracy

The final chapter of this book considers the main theories relating to the overall impact of pressure groups on the British liberal democratic political system. What is liberal democracy? How does the operation of pressure groups relate to it? Do they enhance it or undermine it? In particular, how far do pressure groups enhance political participation, increase access to government and strengthen political opposition? This chapter examines the main arguments in a continuing debate.

Modern liberal democracy

The term 'liberal democracy' refers to a form of government whose main characteristics are government satisfaction of citizen demands, political choice and widespread political participation. This is the form of democracy that has attained general acceptance in the twentieth century as a desirable model and it is the type of democracy found in contemporary advanced industrial societies and a few other countries such as India. Its main features are described in Table 8.1 but it is worth examining the concept of liberal democracy in a little more detail in order to understand how pressure groups fit into this type of government.

Bringing together the two terms 'liberal' and 'democracy' enables certain basic features of this political system to be expressed. First, there is open competition for power expressed through the machinery of at least two but usually several parties, regular elections, a representative assembly, universal voting rights and a free mass media. Second, it is a limited system of government in which the powers of rulers are restricted by a combination of law, convention and public opinion. Third, government is both derived

Table 8.1 Liberal democracy: the main features

High level of competition for power

Two-or-more party system

Universal suffrage

Free elections

Representative assembly

Widespread political participation

Legal political opposition

Free mass media

Clear state–society distinction based on a variety of voluntary groups

Legal and constitutional limits on powers of rulers and public officials

Liberal political culture involving in particular a pluralist belief in the virtue of open competition for power and in the existence of a wide range of differing beliefs, movements and groups

System legitimated in terms of doctrine of popular sovereignty, 'rule by the people'

from and accountable to the people: the government owes its existence to the popular vote, must keep in touch with public opinion between elections to get its mandate renewed and is held in check by a legally guaranteed political opposition. In modern states with large territories and sizeable populations, democracy must be representative (conducted through representatives such as MPs or Congressmen) rather than direct (conducted in face-to-face fashion by the people themselves). However, the ideal of direct democracy underlies the notion that remains continually present in modern representative democracies: that the more strongly the political system manages to incorporate popular influence, and the more extensive is popular political participation, the better it is. What is the relationship between pressure groups and liberal democracy? The broad argument for democracy is that it is the form of government most likely to secure governments sensitive to the wants of the people. Representative democracy encourages the formulation of group demands and makes governments responsive to these demands. It does so through governments' electoral sensitivity to intense minorities and to wider popular needs because of a desire to be elected: pressure groups play a key role in both processes. But democracy is also a form of government that aspires to more than the goal of satisfying wants of the widest possible range of groups. It also aspires (Lively and Lively, 1994, pp. 122–3) to a concern for the possible general good – this search encourages government and groups to justify policies and demands in terms of the general interest (p. 124).

Definition 8.1   Liberal democracy

A system of representative government in which majority rule through a representative assembly and competing parties, free elections and universal franchise is balanced by regard for the rights of the individual and of minorities. The powers of government are limited by institutional checks and balances, a legitimate political opposition, a free media, a pluralist tolerance of a wide range of groups and interests and an individualistic political culture. 'Representative democracy encourages the formulation and representation of group demands and it also makes government responsive to those demands ... the mechanisms through which these ends are achieved [are] – the electoral sensitivity of parties to intense minorities and the everyday activity of pressure groups' (Lively and Lively, 1994, p. 115).

Pluralism

Lively and Lively (1994) say pluralism is now the major defence of political practice in Western democracies:

1. Society is and must be an arena of diverse and conflicting interests.
2. All legitimate groups have a claim to be heard and taken into account in the formulation of policy.
3. Government's role is to accommodate and reconcile these group claims.

Articulation and reconciliation of group demands enhances democracy by making government responsive to the demands of the electorate and diffusing power within society.

Pluralism is both an integral aspect of liberal democratic theory and the dominant theory developed by political science to explain the distribution of political power. Whilst the main concern of this chapter is pluralism as a theory of the distribution of power and with criticisms and changes in this theory, its initial concern is with the way in which liberal democracy may also be termed pluralist democracy. Liberal democracy involves a theory of society, government and the state in which groups play a key role. Thus, according to liberal philosophy, truth is relative rather than absolute, the implication of this conception being that a wide variety of social groups expressing a multiplicity of beliefs, customs and economic interests are not only tolerated but positively encouraged (so long as their views and ways of expressing them are compatible with the norms and continued existence of a liberal democratic community). Society, then, is diverse with no individual or group holding a monopoly of the truth. The liberal democratic theory of government reflects their belief in the right to existence and free expression and association of a large variety of social groupings. Influence over political decisions is diffused over a host of organised groups – trade unions, business, churches, cause groups, etc. These organisations mediate between citizen and state and constitute an effective system of checks and balances limiting power of rulers and ensuring the liberty of citizens (Lively and Lively, 1994, p. 58). Rivalry and competition between organised groups is one guarantee of limited government. Furthermore, the liberal democratic theory of state makes a sharp distinction between the state, the area of political compulsory activity, of public affairs, and civil society, and sphere of the free practice of a wide range of voluntary activities. Finally, underpinning liberal democracy is the basically moral concept that the good society is one that involves its people in political decision-making to the maximum degree possible.

Pressure groups play a key role in the theory and practice of liberal democracies. In particular:

- They increase opportunities for citizen political participation, especially between elections. This can be defended first as a way in which group wants are forced onto the political agenda and also as a way of involving the largest possible number in determining public policies/public decision-making and hence dispersing political skills and aptitudes.
- They improve the quality of government by increasing the expertise and information available to it and assisting in policy delivery. The process of bargaining within pressure groups, between pressure groups, and between pressure groups and government educates in the spirit of compromise necessary to democracy and contributes to the effectiveness of opposition by criticisms of government policy. This provides a system of checks and balances limiting power of rulers and contribution to individual liberty; but does this mean real popular contribution or simply government checks by other élites (economic, military, etc.)? How responsible are group élites to the wider electorate (Lively and Lively, 1994, p.59)? Voluntary organisations act as countervailing powers against the state and prevent hegemony of any one social group.

Voluntary, informal institutions and pressure groups complement the role of parties in liberal democracies. Although not standing for election themselves, they perform a similar function to parties in communicating popular opinions and demands to governments. In this regard, they perform a vital function of political intermediation. They keep governments informed of a wide range of opinions, including new demands and grievances and in doing so help to keep governments responsive and accountable. The overall consequence of pressure group activity is to improve social cohesion and political stability.

Pluralism is a theory of group politics which developed in a broad sense within the body of liberal democratic theory but also to some extent as a counter to specific aspects of it and ultimately an alternative to it. It may be said to be part of liberal democratic thought because of its endorsement of liberal democratic norms and values, notably choice, competition and participation. However, pluralists rejected the individualism of nineteenth-century liberalism, positing instead a group theory of society in which individuals are represented primarily through their membership of organised groups. As it has developed throughout the twentieth century, pluralism is a theory of the distribution of power within liberal democracies. Its major tenets are:

- power in society is widely dispersed among competing groups
- this dispersal of power is desirable in a democracy
- all groups cannot be winners but groups whose interests are neglected can lobby for their interests
- policy is the consequence of a process of continuous interaction between government and a wide range of groups
- although groups have unequal resources, none becomes completely dominant
- groups are internally responsive, with leaders accountable to members.

Certain features of pluralism require further discussion. First, pluralism can be integrated into modern liberal democratic theory thus: the mechanism of parties and elections produces majority governments whilst the mechanism of pressure groups keeps government informed, responsive and publicly accountable between elections. Second, pluralism has been plausibly described less as a theory than an 'anti-theory', the main thrust of its vision of a complex political process with multiple participants and uncertain outcomes being to deny élitist and Marxist theories which perceive the political process in term of the rule of an élite or ruling class. Where these theories see minority rule, pluralism sees rule by minorities. But it can also be seen as a theory of rule by minorities, rule not by the majority but by the many, composed of a range of minority groups (Hague *et al.*, 1992, p. 14; Heywood, 1997, p. 77). Finally, traditional pluralists believe no single group dominates decision-making. Despite their unequal resources, no single group becomes dominant: first, because powerful groups counterbalance each other, for example, business by the unions, pro-hunting by anti-hunting, supporters of abortion by opponents, and so on; second, because no group seeks influence across the whole range of policy-making, a particular group's influence in one sphere of policy is offset by that of another group in a different area; third, because membership of groups overlaps, for example, many people are both workers and consumers, it is in the interest of neither section that the other becomes dominant; and finally, even if an interest is not organised, its 'potential' for organisation makes government wary of threatening it.

This chapter aims to examine three key propositions of pluralism in the light of recent criticisms:

- That pressure groups increase political participation. In particular, they enable the intensity of public feeling on issues to be expressed and despite the unequal distribution of political resources they facilitate lobbying by the poor and disadvantaged in society. Their responsiveness to their members' wishes and opinions enhances democracy.

- That pressure groups provide access to government for a wide variety of groups – none of which, because the influence of one is offset by the sway of another, and because no group seeks influence in more than a limited sphere of policy, becomes totally dominant.

- That pressure groups help to control and limit governmental power, thereby enhancing the critical function of the political opposition.

Pressure groups and participation

Participation is justified in terms of forcing more demands on the political agenda and involving more in policy-making, but (1) how socially limited or extensive is ever increased participation and (2) how far do new pressure groups bring active involvement in running them? If not, can they still be defended in terms of delivering what members want? The upsurge in popular political involvement in citizen groups in Britain and other Western democracies in the postwar period has been widely perceived as a welcome step towards a genuinely participatory democracy. In particular, the growth of direct action protest and more broadly of new social movements are said to herald a 'new politics' of decentralised, non-hierarchical grass-roots activity. This section subjects this claim to close examination. It focuses on the extent of the expansion in political participation and the validity of the depiction of the peace, environmental and women's movements as new social movements constituting a 'new politics'. How far does this expansion of participation reflect a real increase in political involvement? How far does it involve a wide cross-section of society, and how far is it limited to a better off, well-educated minority? How far specifically does it involve the poor and disadvantaged and take place for their benefit or disadvantage them?

There seems little doubt in general terms that British politics has become more pluralist and participatory with a greater number and variety of groups and a larger overall group membership. This postwar expansion of pressure groups is often contrasted with the contemporary decline in political parties. The 1980s and 1990s saw the development of campaigning pressure politics (CND, Greenpeace, gay groups), self-help network politics, local exchange and trading schemes, credit union, the homeless and pensioners, including disabled groups, and a new eco-cultural politics (youth groups, travellers, anti-poll tax, freedom network). Traditionally, political scientists focused on parties as superior agencies of representation to pressure groups, often also tending to see the strength of parties and groups as in inverse relationship, strong parties shutting out weak groups and vice versa. In today's society, it is usually argued that declining parties are being steadily displaced by expanding pressure groups. Whilst clearly not true of all kinds of groups – for example, trade unions have declined hugely in membership and influence since 1979 – it does seem that the often narrow and intensely held concerns of many people can be better expressed through single-issue groups than through parties with their need to develop a broad range of policies often involving compromise (Jordan and Maloney, 1997, p. 177). Seyd and Whitely sum up this line of argument in their comment that 'alternative forms of participation (including) single issue pressure groups ... and new social movements ... provide a more rewarding type of political participation for many people than membership of a political party' (Seyd and Whiteley, 1992, p. 204). There is much truth in the declining parties/expanding groups contention but nonetheless it does need some qualification. First, whilst the major parties have experienced a severe decline in membership between the early 1950s and the early 1990s, with combined Labour and Conservative losses perhaps approaching 3 million, it should also be noted that since then the Labour Party has reversed this decline, attracting an additional 150 000 members between 1992 and 1996 whilst over the 1950s to 1990s period major party decline was at least partially offset by the rise in the membership (and electoral support) for the minor parties, especially the nationalists and Liberals. This contrasts, however, with the really dramatic increase in the membership of groups; membership of the green movement for example was approximately 5 million in the mid-1990s, compared with 2.5–3 million in 1980 and under 1.5 million in 1970. There was also a large increase in ecology groups and conservation groups (Jordan and Maloney, 1997, p. 121) with 1600 environmental groups in the 1994 *Directory for the Environment* (p. 12). Writing in 1995, Jonathan Porritt described the membership of environmental organisations as 'massively outweighing the collective membership of all political parties combined' (cited in Jordan and Maloney, 1997, p. 178). Second, the membership of social movements and groups within such movements is unstable, fluctuating and subject to downturns as well as increases. For example, membership of national CND expanded massively from just over 4000 to 100 000 members between 1979 and 1984 but then fell sharply to 47 000 in 1994 (Byrne, 1997, p. 91). Equally significantly, environmental and other public interest groups experience very high membership turnover rates, which in many cases average between 30 and 40 per cent a year (Jordan and Maloney, 1997, p. 16). Finally, there may be signs that growth in the environmental movement is levelling out but also that the ecological side may be declining: thus, whilst membership of the conservationist National Trust and RSPB continued to rise between 1990 and 1994, the membership of Greenpeace, Friends of the Earth and World Wildlife Fund for Nature all fell (Jordan and Maloney, 1997, p. 13).

Second, how valid is the new social movement perspective that the environmental, peace and women's movements constitute a 'new politics'?

Membership of new social movement organisations has been seen as 'élite-challenging' participation in which individuals are directly involved in specific political decisions and/or use unconventional and sometimes illegal actions to influence decision-making (Poguntke, 1993, cited in Jordan and Maloney, 1997, p. 179). This may be compared to the élite-directed political participation more characteristic of traditional political parties. Groups within new social movements have non-hierarchical, decentralised, participatory forms of organisation. However, this thesis has been contested by Jordan and Maloney who argue that political participation through certain campaigning pressure groups may involve no greater activity from the average member than do political parties. Parties, on this view, expect merely broad allegiance to their principles and a modest financial contribution from their members. 'The leadership of Friends of the Earth and Greenpeace want the same kind of vicarious "commitment" from their "supporters", they want to limit their participation to sending in the cash to support campaigns selected by the organisation – *supporters should be seen and not heard*' (Jordan and Maloney, 1997, p. 188; italics in original). Many campaigning organisations, the authors contend, are similar to Friends of the Earth and Amnesty International, the groups on which their research centres. Such organisations offer 'astroturf' rather than 'grass-roots' opportunities for participation. Bureau-cratised and hierarchically controlled, these groups are run by small, centralised, metropolitan-based leaderships who decide the campaign strategies mainly with an eye to attracting the kind of publicity that will bring in fee-paying members, whose role, however, is a limited one of sending in funds, selling raffle tickets or buying goods from catalogues. As in most large-scale groups, decisions in groups such as Friends of the Earth 'are made by the few on behalf of the mass within a framework which the *few* believe will be popular enough to maintain support'. This is 'anticipatory oligarchy' rather than 'participatory democracy'. Rather than being engaged in a new type of politics, such groups are engaged in the 'protest business'. The only 'voice' possessed by their supporters is that of 'exit'. They can literally take it (the campaigning policy) or leave it (i.e. the group). As one Friends of the Earth organiser told Jordan and Maloney in 1995: 'Members have to decide whether to back us or not. We make policy and if they don't like it they can join some other group' (cited in Jordan and Maloney, 1997, p. 188). Membership surveys are used to inform the leaderships of these groups what their members can 'live with'.

Jordan and Maloney conclude that: 'public interest/campaigning/protest group politics do not significantly extend participatory democracy'. Rather than providing opportunities for member participation and control of a democratically accountable leadership such groups possess 'no internal democracy'. Indeed, rather than providing an antidote to élite oligarchy, as is sometimes contended, 'Amnesty and Friends of the Earth (and we suspect other similar organisations, e.g. Greenpeace) seem just as affected by Michels' "iron law of oligarchy" as are political parties'. Not only are these campaigning groups hierarchically organised with few concessions to democracy in their internal structure, their members largely approve this situation. Over 70 per cent of the membership of Amnesty and Friends of the Earth said that 'being politically active' was 'not very important/played no role whatsoever' in their decision to join these organisations. Jordan and Maloney consider that this passively suggests that they are more appropriately termed 'customers' or 'subscribers' than 'members' and that 'people now appear to prefer to do very little in public interest groups as opposed to doing very little in political parties' (Jordan and Maloney, 1997, p. 192).

This argument clearly contains some truth with regard to the organisations described by Jordan and Maloney and no doubt applies even more accurately to conservationist organisations within the environmental movement such as the National Trust and Civic Trust. But in itself it merely qualifies and adds a note of caution to the contention that the postwar emergence of new social movements has significantly enhanced grass-roots political participation. Thus, large numbers do enlist in social movements because they wish to be politically active, and go on to practise it. For example, *within* both the environmental and feminist movements, significant minorities – deep greens and radical feminists – favour a radically different style of politics. Thus, Paul Byrne contends that these elements 'want an end to hierarchical, élitist politics. Deep greens favour a dramatic decentralisation of decision-making in society; radical feminists want society to give them the freedom to realise a different and autonomous lifestyle ... "democracy" for the mainstream means representative democracy; for the social movements, it means direct democracy' (Byrne, 1997, p. 175). Further, significant numbers especially in the peace movement and parts of the environmental movement engage in direct, sometimes illegal, action and willingness to engage in such actions outside the normal institutional and/or legal channels has been seen as a key characteristic of a social movement, setting it apart from other types of political activity (Byrne, 1997, pp. 19–20). Jordan and Maloney (1997) accept that small activist groups may be more unconventional, anti-establishment, decentralised, anti-bureaucratic and participatory than the older-established organisations they studied, with some internal democracy (p. 71). As already noted (Chapter 6), large numbers of activists have been mobilised in the 1990s, by animal rights campaigns and anti-motorway protests, many of which 'new wave' protesters scorn the more traditionalist groupings. Again, although the Campaign for Nuclear Disarmament, the dominant peace organisation in Britain, has a formal structure, it is a federal one with much freedom for local groups to adopt their own tactics and with members having voting rights at annual conferences, which is the ultimate arbiter of policy. Moreover, it has been the archetypal outsider organisation, with large numbers turning out year after year in mass demonstrations of which the largest was of 400 000 in 1982 (Byrne, 1997, pp. 93–4). Moreover, CND, with its formal structure, is not typical of social movements as a whole which are rather 'networks of interaction' than formal organisations. In this sense, the women's movement is 'about as close as you can get to a "pure" social movement in Britain'. Thus, not only does it have 'no single, over-arching organisation', it has 'little in the way of any formal organisation at all'. Indeed, rather than build a national organisation that could engage in dialogue with policy-makers at national level, the women's movement in Britain has remained 'localised rather than national; non-hierarchical rather than bureaucratic; loosely-networked rather than co-ordinated by a "peak" organisation...; and purist rather than pragmatic' (Byrne, 1997, pp. 108, 124–5).

> As networks rather than formal organisations, movements attract supporters or adherents rather than members. Although those supporters are often more committed than those who have formal membership of political parties (being prepared, for example, to risk hardship and/or punishment by undertaking direct action), decisions on what to do are taken locally or individually. It is rare for any significant effort to be made to co-ordinate supporters' efforts nationally, and even rarer for such efforts to succeed. *Autonomy*, then is an important defining feature of social movements, and one which ... reflects the strong beliefs about democracy and participation which are held by most social movement supporters.
>
> (Byrne, 1997, p. 15)

Finally, supporters of social movements are involved in *expressive* politics in which getting their values accepted through society in the long term is a key feature. They eschew the bargaining and compromise involved in normal day-to-day *instrumental* politics, in favour of a purer form of politics in which values are non-negotiable and goals not achievable short of a total trans-formation of society. Involvement in a social movement for its adherents is a central way of defining their personal identity (Byrne, 1997, pp. 13–14). Byrne distinguishes 'protest movements' such as CND, Greenpeace, liberal and socialist feminists which are sometimes helped by formalised structures from 'social movements' which have a radical ideology rejecting prevailing social, economic and political norms and also conventional ways of practising politics. Examples include the radical feminists and deep greens mentioned above. Deep greens, according to Byrne, include not only the Green Party but also Friends of the Earth, which he describes in fundamentally different terms to Jordan and Maloney as a non-hierarchical radical organisation consisting of autonomous local groups controlling their own budgets and deciding on their own activities whose supporters are expected to live out the cause in their own lives' (Byrne, 1997, pp. 133, 166). Even Jordan and Maloney (1997) accept that membership of groups such as Amnesty International and Friends of the Earth has an *expressive* function. What they term 'the mail order group' are 'a means to allow the individual to relate to the political system and make a personal statement about concerns' (p. 193). They found that most Amnesty International and Friends of the Earth members were very committed to their organisations, believed themselves to be politically efficacious and joined for non-material reasons (p. 142). Membership of such groups fitted in with members' aims, which is to support a cause, not obtain a constitutional relationship with it, involving time and effort. People joined for diverse reasons including the need to stand up and be counted, supporting a worthwhile cause and the recognition that the larger the group, the more clout it had with government (p. 129).

In conclusion, it seems incontestable that political participation has increased in recent decades as a consequence of more numerous and larger groups, and a broad trend involving popular desertion of parties for groups. Unquestionably a significant proportion of public campaigning groups lack internal democracy. But liberal pluralist theory remains more or less undented. More numerous groups do provide greater opportunities for participation (even though participation in internal decision-making is often minimal), for the expression of political identity and the building up of a sense of political efficacy in more people.

Pressure groups and pluralism

This section asks whether and how far it is true that groups provide wide access to government, with no group becoming dominant. More specifically, it surveys three views which suggest that power in modern British society is more concentrated and less dispersed, more élitist and less democratic, and less socially beneficial than classical pluralism maintains. These are the New Right, reformed pluralist and neo-pluralist perspectives. The neo-liberal New Right in the 1970s and 1980s advanced two main arguments about the form interest group representation had taken in Britain. These are important arguments because they draw critical attention to the consequences of interest group activities for the parliamentary system and the economy as a whole. The emergence of the neo-liberal critique had as its background the tripartite relationship between British government and the two main producer groups which arose in the 1960s and 1970s as a result of growing state economic intervention. Incomes and industrial policies depended for their success upon closer 'corporatist'-style relations between state, business and unions in which the two major sectional groups, in return for close consultation in policy-making, were expected to control their members and ensure that they complied with the 'deals' their leaders struck with government. Corporatism with its stress on economic groups only, may best be seen as a sub-type of policy networks theory (Marsh and Rhodes, 1992, p. 211). Neo-liberals criticised this neo-corporatist process on two main grounds, political and economic: first, for bypassing, and thereby weakening, parliamentary government; and second, for blocking economic growth.

The undermining of parliamentary democracy

The thesis that tripartism weakened parliamentary democracy was endorsed in the 1970s by both New Right Conservatives and by academics. The New Right disliked the way in which the process of secret government consultation followed by deals with the main sectional interests shut out parliament, and what it regarded as the excessive power achieved by the trade unions as a result. Thus, the 1979 Conservative manifesto maintained that 'outside groups have been allowed to usurp some of its (i.e. parliament's) democratic functions' whilst its 1976 policy document *The Right Approach* asserted that 'the trade unions are *not* the government of the country ... It is Parliament, and no other body, which is elected to run the ... country in the best interests of the people' (cited in Judge, 1993, p. 119). The bypassing of parliament thesis was further supported by the historian Keith Middlemas who argued that as a consequence of the elevation of trade unions and employers' associations from interest groups to governing institutions, the political system as a whole had lurched into 'corporate bias' with a consequent reduction in the importance of the role played by the political parties and parliament in the political system (Middlemas, 1979, pp. 374, 381–3). As already noted (Chapter 2), Conservative governments between 1979 and 1997 themselves destroyed the corporatist or tripartite thesis by adopting an arm's length attitude to the CBI and TUC, by abolishing institutions of corporatist consultation and by severely curtailing trade union privileges by legislation. Hence, in the 1990s 'few remnants of tripartite structures remain at the core of the central state in Britain' (Judge, 1993, p. 118). However, the problem of the bypassing of parliamentary institutions did not disappear with the ending of corporatism as policy networks analysis has also been seen as a form of group representation which shuts out parliament from the policy-making arena (see below).

Economic stagnation

Other neo-liberal theorists see the close linkages of major producer interests with government as a serious blockage on wealth creation and national economic growth and an excessive claim on government spending. For these analysts, the organised interests are part of democratic pathology rather than of a healthy democracy (as they are perceived in social democratic accounts of the political process). Special interests, according to one liberal critique, are 'harmful to growth, full employment, coherent government, equal opportunity and social mobility' (Olsen, 1971, cited in Grant, 1995, p. 43). The strength of special interest organisations led to an 'institutional sclerosis' in Britain which slows its adaptation to changing circumstances and new technologies. On this view, pressure groups operate, in Douglas Hurd's phrase, as 'strangling serpents' on the body politic, stifling social and economic progress. A similar analysis was put forward by Samuel Brittan, for whom 'the entrenched position of industrial, economic and political interest groups will limit what can be achieved by any form of economic management, new or old' (Brittan, 1987, cited in Grant, 1995, pp. 41–2). As with the argument that the strength of producer interests undermines parliamentary democracy, the thesis that special interest groups act as barriers to economic progress did not necessarily disappear with the abandonment of corporatist arrangements by the Conservative governments between 1979 and 1997. Special interests remained embedded in policy-making, with the power on occasion to thwart governments and block progress, as for example with middle-class privileges such as tax relief on mortgage interest, the concessions to farmers, the BSE scandal and the failure of a Food Standards Agency, and the continued failure of government to investigate the large gulf in new car prices between Britain and the rest of Europe.

> Interest groups do not merely reduce the national income when they become embedded in the political process. They embody rival claims which more than exhaust the national product and threaten the survival of liberal democracy itself.
>
> (Brittan, 1987)

It can still be argued that group opposition can slow down or block desirable changes, thereby reducing social and economic progress.

Reformed pluralism: policy networks and policy communities

Policy networks analysis (see especially Chapters 2 and 4) developed within the pluralist tradition and constitutes a broadly accurate picture of how decisions are made in British government. But how far is its notion of the segmentation of policy-making with each segment dominated by its own group of top bureaucrats and leading, mainly sectional group, representatives a pluralist and democratic one? The argument has two prongs: first, to what extent does a decision-making process that is compartmentalised into separate policy networks marginalise parliament? The leading exponents of policy networks analysis argue that Britain has become a 'post-parliamentary democracy'. The 'normal' policy style in Britain is best described as 'bureaucratic accommodation', its main feature being a constant process of bargaining and negotiation between government and groups. This process of accommodation between mainly insider groups and Whitehall departments is closed, private and insulated from both parliament and public. It is 'a system of private government subject to only the most tenuous forms of accountability'. There is little opportunity for parliamentary participation in the group–parliament world. Decisions made in behind-the-scenes consultations between civil servants and group representatives are beyond effective check or even proper discussion by parliament. In reality, decision-making is beyond parliament, and most of it beyond party and Cabinet too. Rather than being a parliamentary democracy, Britain is more aptly described as an 'organised democracy' (Jordan and Richardson, 1987b, p. 287).

This argument has been challenged by David Judge who maintains that parliament retains a vital role in British democracy for several reasons. First, parliament legitimates the outcomes of group–bureaucracy negotiations. The authority of public officials in negotiating with groups is delegated from representative institutions. Public policy decisions emanating from policy networks and policy communities are legitimised by a presumption of the ultimate authority of parliament. Second, whilst agreeing with Jordan and Richardson that 'bureaucratic accommodation' is the 'normal style' of policy-making, Judge argues that the independence of the covert policy-makers is politically constrained by the need 'to consider wider partisan/parliamentary/public concerns – even if only in the limited sense of seeking to forestall possible future criticism in Parliament' (Judge, 1993, p. 32). The independence of policy communities is further limited by Cabinet coordination of policy-making, direction of policy-making within departments by Prime Minister and Cabinet and even on occasion by the direct involvement of parliament itself. Parliament can become involved when normal bureaucracy–group accommodation is disrupted by, for example, a change of government, especially if impelled by a new ideology, e.g. Thatcherism, or by the intrusion of outside forces such as the IMF or EU. Parliament remains a crucial arena for three reasons: first, because outcomes of the group–civil servant negotiating process need to secure parliamentary consent 'in the last instance'; second, because parliament can be useful to groups in 'climate setting', insider as well as outsider, even where no immediate benefits can be expected; and third, because no other system of representation, including group/functional/pluralist representation, has the legitimacy of parliamentary representation (Judge, 1993, p. 39). Thus, whilst true as far as it goes, the group–bureaucrat process needs to be placed within the framework of parliamentary democracy rather than set against it. The theory of parliamentary representation can accommodate group theory. Britain remains a parliamentary rather than a 'post-parliamentary democracy'. The 'post-parliamentary' theorists are right that the great majority of policy decisions in the British system are made in Whitehall rather than in Westminster but go too far in claiming that the system has therefore become one of 'organised' or 'post-parliamentary' democracy in view both of the key legitimating role – and the more modest capacity for policy influence – residing in parliament.

Second, whilst less vulnerable than corporatism to the charge that policy-making is élitist because it is dominated by a very restricted number of sectional groups, reformed pluralism (policy networks theory) is also open to this accusation. Although more extensive than the peak organisations of business and unions, the participation of groups in policy-making in the policy networks theory is still mainly confined to sectional insiders. Its major exponents argue that, although their analysis appears to move away from the pluralist tradition, its conclusions remain compatible with it. Thus, different groups are influential within different segments of the policy-making universe and no group is able to dominate decision-making across all the various sectors of policy-making. Whitehall pluralism with each sector dominated by a different constellation of groups can be seen as containing inbuilt safeguards against concentration of power. Moreover, as already shown in Chapter 4, policy networks consist of dynamic sets of relationships, are constantly changing, subject to entry by new groups and therefore more open than they often seem. However, it has been argued against this that policy networks and especially policy communities exclude all but a few favoured insider groups so that this version of pluralism starts to degenerate into something resembling 'an élite political cartel' (Grant, 1993, p. 25). Reformed pluralism can also be criticised as confusing 'a large number of groups being involved in policy-making with a large number of groups being influential'. Groups may be consulted but may still lack influence (Smith, 1995, p. 221). Moreover, access is less open than reformed pluralisms imply, with many groups consistently and for lengthy periods excluded from policy-making.

Another recent version of pluralist theory – neo-pluralism – stresses the privileged position of business. Its paramount influence stems from two factors: first, its power as an interest stems from government's need, in order to achieve political and electoral success, for a successful economy; the second source of its special influence flows from the influence of its decisions on the economy directly. It can thus use its political clout to gain concessions for itself beyond the capacity of less powerful groups to achieve and its economic clout to shape the environment with which governments must deal. According to this theory, government and business decide the big issues between them leaving other groups to compete for influence over areas of secondary importance. According to Grant, Britain is a 'company state' in which the most important form of government–business contact is between government and the individual company. Thus, the corporatist-style state of the 1970s was consigned to limbo in the 1980s and 1990s but in its place the civil service increasingly emphasised direct dealings with firms (Grant, 1993, p. 15). Neo-pluralism or élite pluralism can be criticised both for failing to give sufficient weight to the conflicts within it, for example, between manufacturing and finance, and presenting it as too monolithic and also for failing to consider countervailing influences such as the trade unions, consumers and environmentalists (see Boxes 8.2 and 8.3). In addition, business is influential only over a relatively small range of policy-making, not the entire spectrum, and although business groups possess greater resources and superior access to government than their rivals, poorer groups are not without resources and can, as noted in earlier chapters, use the media and run public campaigns.

But the main argument against the idea – found in corporatist, reformed pluralist (policy networks) and neo-pluralist theories alike – that group competition leads to excessive concentration of power in one or a few groups is that of the 'arbiter state' (Lively, 1978, cited in Grant, 1993, p. 23). This is the notion that the state stands above the group battle, draws up the rules for it and decides whom it wishes to consult with and whom it does not, thereby conferring legitimacy on some groups, and denying it to others. The state can help to create a rough balance of power between groups, checking those threatening to become too powerful (e.g. the pruning of trade union powers in the 1980s) and raising up the less powerful (e.g. consumers and the disabled). Increasingly, within agricultural policy-making, for example, governments have been forced to respond positively to the concern of consumers at the expense of producers. Clearly, the government's relative position with regard to the groups varies – it sometimes needs to make concessions to groups; it may also decide to favour one or more groups against the rest. But it is not co-equal, it does not share power with the groups, largely for the reason already noted – its possession of democratic legitimacy via the machinery of elections, parties and parliament. Even with regard to business, the most powerful interest, the state, establishes a regulatory framework and also ensures business compliance with rules relating to equal opportunities, and workers' health and safety (Grant, 1993, p. 203).

Marsh and Rhodes, in their case studies 'describe a system of private government subject to only the most tenuous form of accountability'. 'Professional expertise and effective service delivery legitimize', they contend, 'the oligarchy of the policy network' (Marsh and Rhodes, 1992, pp. 22, 65). The system is one of 'private government' by interest groups.

> The mystique of scientists and of doctors serves not only to reinforce their role in the nuclear and health networks respectively, but also to strengthen the relevant network's claim of rendering policy free from the 'irritating' constraint of political, especially electoral, legitimacy.
>
> (Marsh and Rhodes, 1992, p. 265)

Moreover, the government is constantly under pressure from a large number of sources including parties, parliament, public opinion and foreign governments as well as groups, which therefore provide only one set of inputs into a very complex decision-making process. However, groups do form a very important influence on policy-making and the insights that both policy networks and élite pluralists bring out is the structural inequality in, access to, and influence over, government policy-making (Rhodes and Marsh, 1996, p. 220).

> It may be that different professional or producer groups and different sections of Government departments, or different Government agencies, dominate in different policy areas. You would hardly expect the BMA to play a key role in sea-drainage

policy or the NFU to play a key role in the abortion issue. However, there is clearly structural inequality in the access of interests to, and their influence over, Government policy-making.

(Rhodes and Marsh, 1996, p. 220)

The conclusion is that the operation of pressure groups disperses power less than classical pluralists believed. They considered that power was unevenly distributed under pluralism but reformed pluralism (policy networks theory) and neo-pluralism has made clear that the effect of groups is to concentrate power rather than disperse it. Some groups such as business clearly enjoy greater access and more influence than others. Some groups such as the major financial institutions in the City enjoy structural power in that governments check economic policies against the anticipated reactions of the City and adjust in order to maximise the chances of gaining City approval. The financial interests do not have to lobby in order to receive such favoured treatment. Finally, the formal legitimation process advantages some and excludes others, often for long periods. However, as noticed in earlier chapters, even the most tightly drawn policy communities can break up under external pressures, which may come from changes of government, ministerial reshuffles, public resistance or the EU. Although uneven, the distribution of power fluctuates, reflecting a dynamic, changeful and unpredictable situation.

Pressure groups, opposition and countervailing power

When one power is set against another, power itself will be tamed, civilised, controlled and limited to decent human purposes.

(Dahl, 1967, p. 24)

A key feature of the modern liberal state is diversity. It consists of a wide range of interests, none of which has a monopoly of the truth and consequent claim to exclusive domination. In liberal democratic theory, social and political pressures are brought together (aggregated), sifted and presented to electorates as comprehensive policy packages by political parties at general elections. The victorious party at a general election forms the government, the losing parties go into opposition, the largest party in the British system becoming the loyal opposition in parliament. The main source of regularised, official opposition in Britain is therefore parliament just as in other Western democracies it is the representative assembly. It is based on party, whose role it is in the democratic system to offer continuous criticism. The right to disagree is thus built into democracy and is one of its fundamental principals. The knowledge that it is likely to be criticised is a formidable check on governments who operate to some extent by the law of anticipated reactions in an atmosphere that has been compared to a continuous election campaign. This form of political opposition, whilst essential to a democratic system, and long resisted by opponents of democracy as factious and even unpatriotic, operates within strict limits set by the government's majority. Possession of a majority in the British unitary system of government means that the government almost always prevails. Government defeats on votes of confidence which lead to a general election are extremely rare and depend on an unusual combination of circumstances, usually involving a minority government together with the preparedness of the opposition to bring it down, as in the 1979 fall of the Labour Government. More usually, British governments do possess a viable or good majority and cannot be brought down by parliamentary means. This is generally accepted as right – after all, the government has won a general election and may therefore be said to possess a popular mandate to carry out its programme. On the other hand, the British electoral system has in recent time thrown up lengthy phases of single party government, as between 1979 and 1997, followed by government with a massive majority relatively unchecked by a weak and demoralised opposition, as after 1997. In these circumstances, criticism from outside the parliamentary arena becomes even more important for the effective functioning of a healthy democracy.

Liberal democratic theory is pluralist in allocating an important role to extra-parliamentary sources as checks on modern governments. Of these, most commentators would argue that the media (television, radio and the press combined) are the major source of criticism to governments. Fear of harmful publicity keeps government within bounds, a theory well-supported by the prominence given by contemporary governments to press officers, 'spin doctors' and the like, officers charged with the task of ensuring favourable media coverage and of putting the best gloss possible on government decisions and policies. However, the situation is rather less straightforward in that media and pressure group activities are interlinked: groups need the media for life-giving publicity, the media need groups for vital information and dramatic 'events'. Groups play a key role in the political system as critics of government in the extra-parliamentary arena. How may this role be best described?

The existence of powerful voluntary institutions is important to political freedom in two main ways – first, as serving as a counterweight to the growth of excessive state power and second, as preventing the emergence of a totally dominant group in society. Pressure groups then provide checks on the state and in the government by the following:

- *Political surveillance.* Pressure groups continually monitor government decisions in the areas of their concern. Has the government kept to its manifesto promises? Environmentalists, consumers, welfare lobbyists, constitutional reformers will want to know the reason if it hasn't. Is the government acting in accordance with its treaty obligations and with European Union regulations and directives? If not, it will be picked up and censured. In this way, the total effect of groups is to direct a stream of informed and often impassioned criticism at government. The groups' action may even be more effective than the official opposition in parliament for being sharply focused and specialised. Sometimes, they will actually contribute significant details to bolster the parliamentary opposition's case. Whatever the case, acting independently or in concert with it, criticisms by groups considerably enhance the effectiveness of opposition in general.

- *Public campaigns.* Most commonly, group criticism of government proceeds by way of swift reactions to government pronouncements and policy developments – the politics of the 'soundbite'. A good example is the quick responses of a range of groups to how far the Chancellor's proposals benefit or damage the interests of their clients on Budget Day. However, groups also provide the mechanism for keeping debate going on issues: they possess longer attention spans than parliament and the media and are often able to maintain public focus on important matters which are, however, of only transitory concern to the media and official parliamentary opposition. On occasion, they can mobilise opinion in public campaigns and even bring about the defeat of government policy. The most prominent example of this was the anti-poll tax campaign (see Box 8.1) but, as noted in Chapter 6, direct action opposition to government road-building plans in the early 1990s was a significant factor alongside cost considerations in forcing the scaling down of government plans. Government normally prevails in the end, and it is right that they should do so but it is also right that intense feeling should be expressed and that on occasion it should force governments to think again, as over the poll tax.

Both in classical pluralism and contemporary radical democratic theory, voluntary organisations are seen as playing a vital role in controlling the tendencies to concentration of power in the state (Smith, 1995, p. 225).

The second countervailing power argument with reference to pressure groups is that a diversity of interests provides checks upon each other. Antagonistic groups prevent any one of them gaining too much power. Thus, trade unions set limits on business power, and vice versa, pro-abortion groups' influence is constrained by anti-abortionists, and so on. However, against this theory, it has been urged that in practice, in Britain as in other liberal democracies, no group, either single or in combination with other groups, possesses the resources to stand up to business interests. How effectively do trade unions, consumers and environmentalists separately or together restrain employers and manufacturers? In general terms, the answer would be less at present than between the 1940s and 1970s in the case of the unions, rather more in the case of consumers and environmentalists. Detailed empirical investigation would be necessary over a range of episodes. But the evidence over the past two decades suggests that the increasing power of business in modern society has not been matched by other interests. Moreover, modern pluralist analysis has been forced by criticisms to accept the significance of a

---

BOX 8.1

The defeat of the poll tax

The poll tax was a 'policy disaster' of the first magnitude. Introduced in England and Wales in 1990–91, the tax aroused huge public opposition, caused massive dislocation in local government, played a significant part in the downfall of Margaret Thatcher as Prime Minister in November 1990, proved impossible to administer, was scheduled for replacement and had to be replaced by a new local tax within five years (1991), a year after its introduction; it cost £1.5 billion to set up, administer and replace as well as much larger costs to the national taxpayer. Its historians estimate that had it not been introduced and abandoned, income tax would have been about 4p in the pound lower in 1994–95 than it actually was or VAT about 4 per cent lower. But why was the disaster not foreseen? and prevented? The answer lies in the way in which a British government with a reasonable (or better) majority functions as an 'elective dictatorship' with the so-called checks and balances of the parliamentary system powerless to check, let alone arrest the 'executive steamroller'. The Conservative Government was warned at a relatively early stage of the policy process of the likelihood of severe difficulties – for example, soon after the Green Paper on the Community Charge appeared (January 1986), an article appeared in the house journal of the Chartered Institute of Public Finance and Accountancy, the professional body representing local authority finance, detailing the extra costs and losses of revenue that would occur if the community charge was introduced whilst a consultancy report commissioned by the Department of the Environment also predicted that the tax would cost very considerable sums to administer. However, given that the tax was likely to impose a significant additional burden not only on the poorest but also on middle income households, it was a political disaster in waiting from the time it received the backing of the Prime Minister, and wide support of the Cabinet. It was estimated that a mere 8 million households gained from the tax whilst 27 million households were 'losers'.

Not only did opposition within parliament fail, opposition parties failed to realise the potential of the issue for a concerted national campaign.

1. *'Parliament was a rubber stamp'.* The best chance of seriously amending the legislation lay with back-bench Conservatives where the bill had many enemies and few friends. With a government majority of 100, at least 50 rebels would have been needed to carry any amendment against the government, but in fact only 39 Conservative MPs voted against the government on one or more of the three critical votes and on a back-bench amendment which would have introduced a banded poll tax, the government majority was a comfortable 25. The House of Lords proved even less able to challenge the tax with the government defeating a key amendment relating the poll tax to ability to pay with a majority of 134.

   None of the opposition parties proved capable of warning the public of the disaster ahead. Underestimating the degree of likely public opposition, unable to appreciate the scale of losses for middle income earners, and anxious to dissociate itself from its 'loony left' image, Labour was determined to play down rather than highlight the issue. In the years between 1987 and 1990, the Liberal–Social Democrat Alliance had little time for anything apart from the resolution of its own bitter internal divisions. The opposition parties in general failed to appreciate the enormous potential of the poll tax as an issue around which to build a national,

BOX 8.1 (CONTINUED)

single-issue crusade against the government which would embrace everyone from the opposition parties to non-aligned interest groups, professional associations, and the media.

2. *The media.* Itself distracted for some of the time by the Westland affair and its aftermath, the media gave little attention to the poll tax during its Cabinet government gestation and legislative phase. Indeed coverage was very limited until the issue suddenly leaped to enormous prominence in early 1990.

3. *Public opposition.* The poll tax collapsed because it was introduced at too high a level, represented too large a tax for large numbers of people, especially the poor and not quite poor, provoked considerable evasion and was generally regarded as unfair. It failed because it was massively unpopular and provoked widespread opposition, including non-payment and popular disturbances. Opposition came mainly from fringe far left parties and groups such as Militant Tendency and the Socialist Workers Party which formed the British Anti-Poll Tax Federation (APTF) in 1989. Also involved was the 3-D Network (Don't Pay, Don't Collect, Don't Implement), a loose network of smaller groups. The Federation organised a non-payment campaign and played a significant role in 'the biggest mass agitation since the war' which included nationwide anti-poll tax rallies and a mass demonstration in Trafalgar Square on 31 March 1990 which was initially good-humoured but turned into full-scale, bloody riot, with 339 arrested, and 374 policemen, 86 members of the public and 20 police horses injured. Other participants in the movement included anarchists, greens and the non-politicised middle class including a variety of housewives groups. Although strengthening the government's resolve in the short term, in the slightly longer term the APTF gave considerable assistance to the defeat of the tax. It focused and strengthened public resistance, including the provision of legal assistance on the tax and the powers of the bailiffs, encouraged civil disobedience in the form of non-payment, and altogether by its activities intensified the sense of political crisis which engulfed the poll tax. In particular it strengthened Conservative MPs' resolve to get the tax abolished, a point reflected in its prominence in the 1990 leadership campaign.

(Sources: Butler *et al.* (1994); Barr (1992))

Questions

1. Would it be accurate to describe the British Anti-Poll Tax Federation as an 'ideological outsider group' because it had a simple non-negotiable principle – abandon the poll tax?

2. Why was parliamentary opposition to the poll tax so weak?

3. In view of public hostility including minority non-payment of the poll tax, how significant was extra-parliamentary opposition in bringing about its downfall?

4. Is this episode best characterised as a legitimate defence of the weakest, most vulnerable members of the community against an overmighty government or as the illegitimate thwarting of an elected government by a group of extremists?

second dimension of power beyond formal decision-making. This is 'non-decision-making', the process by which a powerful interest such as business can keep policy issues that it regards as potentially damaging off the political agenda. In addition, élitist pluralists have argued that the structural power of business in the economy means that governments will always take business interests into account, whether or not it lobbies directly for them, because it needs business to be flourishing in order to enhance its chances of re-election. However, all of this analysis goes to show only that business occupies a privileged position, not that its position is completely or even largely unrestrained by other groups. Rival groups may not have matched its growth of influence in recent decades but as environmental, animal welfare and pro-consumer as well as post-1997 pro-union legislation demonstrates, business does not always have its own way. In this slightly qualified sense, the concept of countervailing power amongst social groups undoubtedly exists.

BOX 8.2

Business as a sectional interest

Groups representing capital are major players, if not *the* major players, in British politics. But does this make business 'a privileged interest'? On the one hand, business has immense structural power flowing from the basic fact that in a free enterprise, capitalist economy, government must give priority to the achievement of a prosperous economy. At the level of overt policy-making, this means that in order to get re-elected, governments must broadly sympathise with the demands of business and do nothing to damage them. At the level of covert policy, or non-decision-making, it means that issues damaging to private property will not appear on the political agenda at all. On the other hand, business itself is not a monolithic bloc, but rather contains many internal divisions, between manufacturing industry, finance and retailing, for example, and between large and small businesses. Second, business is not always a cohesive political force: in Grant's words, it 'has not been able to get its political act together' (Grant, 1993, p. 19). Third, business faces opposition and whilst some emanates from declining forces such as the unions, other opposition stems from groups whose influence has increased steadily in recent decades such as environmentalists and consumers.

Contacts between business and government can take place directly through individual companies or through an intermediary – a representative organisation of employers (e.g. the Engineering Employers' Federation), a trade association (e.g. the Society of Motor Traders and Manufacturers) or a 'peak' organisation such as the Confederation of British Industry (CBI). In some countries, e.g. Germany, business–state relations are conducted mainly through a peak organisation, in some mainly through a political party, e.g. Italy. In Britain, whilst significant business–state contacts take place via representative business groupings and via parties, the most important form of contact is between individual companies and government. This has led to the description of Britain as 'a company state'. Companies such as ICI, Rover, British Aerospace and British Airways are very familiar in 'the corridors of power'. Reasons for the paramount importance in Britain of company–government contacts include the high degree of

BOX 8.2 (CONTINUED)

concentration in British industry: it makes sense for the large firms which predominate to deal directly with government, and this is a trend that has increased rapidly since the 1970s, with many large companies setting up special divisions to handle relations with government. Large and medium firms have also made increased use of political consultancies (specialist lobbying companies) in recent years. The establishment by government of 'task forces' to advise on particular aspects of public policy underlined the significance of relations between government and prominent businessmen who headed and staffed the task forces. Thus, Martin Tyler, chief executive of Barclays Bank, heads the Tax and Benefits task force whilst Sir Peter Davis, chief executive of the Prudential, heads the Welfare to Work task force and Sir Richard Sykes, chairman of Glaxo, is a prominent figure on the Competitiveness task force. A key part of Labour's strategy (by August 1998, it had set up over 75 such bodies), task forces appointments gave businesses useful access to government and in August 1998 it was reported that 350 business people were serving on task forces. In late 1998, it appeared that task force appointments were favouring companies that had made political donations to Labour or used lobbying firms run by people who had worked for Labour. Tesco and BP have seats on six task forces, Zeneca on five, Marks & Spencer, Ford and Northern Foods on three (The Guardian, 22 July 1998; The Observer, 9 August 1998; Grant, 1993, pp. 14, 55, 201). Task forces, it was argued, had now become even more important than quangos since they went 'right to the heart of government'. At the same time, some trade union leaders complained about the domination of task forces by businessmen. The two major reasons that business is rarely able to present a united front to government are first its internal divisions and second, real differences of opinion amongst businessmen over the policy that best serves its interests. Internal divisions have dogged the CBI's efforts to represent the whole of British business by increasing its membership from the financial sector. Complaints that it was not lobbying forcefully enough for manufacturing industry during the early 1980s and early 1990s recessions led to it establishing a National Manufacturing Council in 1991 within its organisation. The dominance of large firms within the CBI led small firms to secede from it in 1971 to set up their own organisation, the Smaller Businesses Association. As well as internal divisions within the main 'umbrella' organisation, business is institutionally divided between a wide range of organisations, including the Association of British Chambers of Commerce (small business), the Retail Consortium (retailing), the British Bankers' Association (banking), and the Association of British Insurers (insurance).

Historically, there have been – and remain – divisions of interest between industry and finance (over the strength of the pound and high interest rates, for example) but these should not be exaggerated. The City has a stronger bargaining hand with government than industry and stronger sanctions, including a concerted refusal to buy government stock, a gilt-edged strike, if it feels its interests to be threatened.

A good illustration of the way in which business can fail to develop a united front is the current division within the business community over whether Britain should join the single European currency. The Labour Government's decision to join the Euro (although not in the first wave) gained favour with the CBI, but a significant and vocal minority opposed or was sceptical about the benefits to Britain of European monetary union. This minority included the Institute of Directors, the so-called bosses' trade union, and a new pro-maintenance of sterling pressure group, Business for Sterling, set up in 1998 to

BOX 8.2 (CONTINUED)

challenge the CBI stance. The European Research Group published *The Euro: Bad for Business* in July 1998 and it was reported that the group was planning a mass demonstration to save the pound modelled on the Countryside March. Other differences within business in 1998 arose over the CBI negotiations with government and unions over an extension of employee rights, with the Engineering Employers' Federation and other leading trade association members believing the CBI had made too many concessions; in particular, many companies were worried that workers winning unfair dismissal cases might gain unlimited payouts (*Daily Telegraph*, 4 July 1998; *The Guardian*, 28 June, 7 July 1998).

Business's relations with government are made through individual companies and business associations rather than through political parties. Nonetheless, parties receive very large amounts of money from corporate donors and individual businessmen: for example, the Conservatives, traditionally the business party, received 17 donations of over £1 million between 1992 and 1997 whilst Labour, traditionally a trade union party but increasingly downgrading its union links and courting business, received four gifts of over £1 million from businessmen in 1997, including one from Lord Sainsbury, and 10 more donations in the £100 000–700 000 range (Neill Report: *The Guardian*, 14 October 1998). Supporters of the system argue that financial support of political parties by business gives 'a solid ballast to parties, a link to the realities of political life which parties might otherwise lack' (Grant, 1993, p. 145), but many people are concerned that business may expect political favours – policies for cash – in return for its gifts. In 1998 the parties were increasingly seeking sponsorship deals rather than donations, with Labour's 1998 Conference sponsored by a US power corporation, Euron, and the largest European drug company, Novartis, but the Neill Report on party funding is likely to make political gifts more open and possibly also smaller. Two recommendations were full disclosure by parties of all gifts over £5000 and that shareholders should decide on company donations or sponsorship.

Labour gained the broad support of business in its first period of office by implementing its pre-election promises of a low tax, low inflation regime, maintenance of Conservative public spending levels for two years, flexible labour markets and help for small business. Its appointment of leading businessmen to ministerial office as well as to quangos and task forces reinforced the impression of a pro-business government. Close relations between parties and businessmen did not arise solely over donations. The influence of tabloid newspapers over voters was widely seen as underlying Labour's close relationship with the media mogul Rupert Murdoch, with whom a suspected deal was the support or neutrality of *The Sun* in return for light media regulation, especially over BSkyB's domination of sports rights and the introduction of digital TV.

Questions

1. 'Even if not "privileged", business is by far the most powerful interest'. Is this the case? Give reasons.

2. Why has Britain been described as 'a company state'?

3. What limitations do you find on the political influence of business?

4. How may financial support of business for political parties be defended and criticised in a democracy?

BOX 8.3

Trade unions as a sectional interest

Trade unions experienced a severe reduction in influence under the Conservatives between 1979 and 1997. However, although Labour made it clear there would be no repeal of Conservative anti-union legislation and that the party would continue its efforts to distance itself from the unions, there were early signs that the unions were undergoing a modest revival in influence under New Labour.

Decline of trade unionism

Trade unionism declined for three main reasons in the 1980s and 1990s.

Conservative anti-unionism

The Conservatives came to power in 1979 determined to curb what they perceived as excessive union power. Their assault on union privileges and influence operated over a broad front and included:

- *Anti-union legislation.* Key points were the removal of immunity for secondary picketing, the abolition of the closed shop and the introduction of secret ballots before strikes and in the election of union leaderships. The government also engaged in a massive confrontation with the miners' union and won.
- *The abandonment of tripartism.* The Conservatives ended the system of neo-corporatist consultation over economic policy-making, adopting instead an arm's length approach to business and the unions. It downgraded and eventually abolished (1992) the National Economic Development Council.
- *Higher unemployment.* The Conservatives gave priority to the control of inflation over reducing unemployment, allowing unemployment to increase rapidly from 1.3 million (1979) to 3.4 million (1986).

Economic change

The continuing decline of the industrial base, intensified by recessions at the beginning of the 1980s and 1990s, was a key factor in the sharp fall in union membership from over 12 million (1979) to 6.6 million (1998). There are significant sectoral and regional disparities in the extent of unionisation: thus, a mere 21 per cent of the private sector compared with 61 per cent of the public sector is unionised whilst over 40 per cent of the workforce in Scotland, Wales and Northern England are members of unions compared with under 30 per cent in the south-east.

The combined impact of deindustrialisation, the rise of the more lightly unionised service sector, higher unemployment and casualisation of the workforce leading to increasing uncertainty of job tenure was a very significant reduction in the strike rate. Days lost to strike action declined from 29.5 million in 1979 to a mere 415 000 in 1995.

Relations with the Labour Party

Down to the late 1980s, the unions dominated the party. They provided over three-quarters of the party's income, dominated Conference, had a 40 per cent share (from 1981) in the election of the leader and between 1983 and 1992 sponsored over half of the party's MPs. However, Labour leaders Neil Kinnock, John Smith and Tony Blair saw a

BOX 8.3 (CONTINUED)

reduction in the role of the unions within the party as essential to winning the vote of the middle class, especially in southern England. Accordingly, they introduced reforms which scaled down union influence:

- *Finance*. The share of party funds provided by the unions shrank to about half by 1996, with higher income from a rising membership and from business to some extent offsetting the decline in union funding.

- *Conference*. The union share of the vote at Conference was steadily reduced from 90 per cent to 50 per cent by a rule change beginning from 1991; from 1994 the votes of affiliated unions were no longer cast as a block but divided up among union delegations.

- *National Executive Committee*. Previously electing 12 and in a position to sway the election of six more members of the 32-strong NEC, the unions now elect 12 members only.

- *Leadership election*. From 1993, the union share of the electoral college electing the leader and deputy-leader was reduced from 40 per cent to 33 per cent whilst the share of the other two sections, MPs and Constituency Labour Parties, was raised from 30 per cent to 33 per cent.

- *Candidate selection and sponsorship*. Previously the unions played an important role in the selection of candidates and individually sponsored about one third of candidates between 1945 and 1979, and over one half – in a smaller parliamentary party – between 1983 and 1992. However, from 1993, the final selection of Labour Party candidates has been by one member one vote (OMOV) in a full meeting of each CLP and direct union sponsorship of candidates was ended in 1995. In its place were constituency plan agreements which supported the local parties by paying money into a central pool and in return gained representation on CLP general committees.

Trade unions and the Blair Government

Trade unions have a reduced but still significant role in the Labour Party and despite continually being warned by the Labour leadership that there would be no repeal of Conservative anti-union legislation and no return to the cosy government–union relationship of the 1970s, they continue to harbour expectations that a Labour Government will help them, even if to a limited extent only. In its first two years, the Blair Government continued the Conservative policy of encouraging flexible labour markets but also pleased the unions by certain measures including removal of the ban on trade union membership at the government surveillance agency, GCHQ; signing the EU Social Chapter, and moving towards the adoption of a minimum wage (although the rates of £3.60 an hour for over 21s and £3.20 an hour for 18–21s fell below the £4 an hour minimum wage favoured by the unions); and enhancing employee rights at work. Strong lobbying by both TUC and CBI preceded and followed the Government White Paper 'Fairness at Work' (May 1998) which formed the basis of the Fairness at Work Bill promised in the Queen's Speech of November 1998. Key steps included: the grant of automatic union recognition in all firms employing 20 or more workers if more than half of the workforce are already union members, or the grant of union recognition where a majority, and at least 40 per cent of those eligible, vote in favour; the

BOX 8.3 (CONTINUED)

enablement of workers to claim unfair dismissal at an industrial tribunal after one year rather than two years; and the extension to parents of the right to 12 weeks unpaid leave while their child is under 8, time off for family emergencies and an increase of maternity leave to 18 weeks. These measures represented a modest concession to the unions after nearly two decades in which the flow of influence had been wholly in the employers' favour. Like many large organisations, the Trades Union Congress (TUC) is difficult to manage (affiliated unions retain their power of independent action) but it is still the largest membership organisation in the UK (despite its drastic fall in membership) and it still has very significant representation in industry, possessing recognition agreements with 44 out of Britain's top 50 companies. It is at least being listened to again by government and, as the promised 'fairness at work' legislation indicates, wielding a measure of influence on some matters even if many of its demands fall on deaf ears. So far the request by its General Secretary for 'social partnership' – a dialogue with government and employers over pay and economic policy – and its appeals for government action to protect manufacturing jobs have made no headway and the Blair Government has actually opposed EU legislation to require employers to set up consultation procedures involving the workforce.

(Sources: *Politics Review*, 3, 4, April 1994; *The Guardian*, 17 March, 22 May, 18 September, 25 November 1998)

Questions

1. In what ways and why did trade union political influence weaken in the 1980s and early 1990s?

2. Why did recent Labour leaders seek to reduce the influence of the unions within the party and how successful have they been in doing so?

3. What signs are there that union influence over government is reviving in the late 1990s? In so far as its influence is increasing, why is this?

4. 'The trade unions' role is a strictly subaltern one in the current climate. Business has far greater clout in New Labour's most powerful circles and private corporate donors have been getting a great deal more bang for their bucks than the trade unions' (Seumas Milne, *The Guardian*, 18 September 1998). How far do you agree with this argument? Give your reasons.

Summary

- Pressure groups are forms of voluntary association which play a key role in contemporary/modern liberal democratic theory. In particular, organised groups assist in the governmental process by articulating the demands of a wide cross-section of society; helping to control and limit governmental power by enhancing society's and the political opposition's critical faculty; and by increasing political participation.

- The New Right, reformed pluralist and neo-pluralist perspectives suggest that power is in effect concentrated, being dispersed only among several largely economic élites. In New Right theory, power is dominated by the major sectional interest (business and the trade unions); in reformed pluralism (policy networks), it is compartmentalised into a series of vertical segments; whilst in neo-pluralism, business is a 'privileged interest'. All three theories are concerned about the extent to which pluralism now functions anti-democratically by shutting out parliament, blocking progress and privileging certain sectional interests, especially business, above the rest.

- The 1980s, the 1990s and the new millennium have brought a reassertion of the will of democratically elected governments over sectional interests, a trend echoed in the reminder from political science that power in Britain is legitimated through the democratic process and remains in the hands of the PM and Cabinet responsible to parliament, in turn responsible to the electorate. Britain is therefore best described as a parliamentary rather than post-parliamentary democracy and the elected political élite as supreme arbiter over the non-elected sectional élites.

- Whilst opposition is performed by parties within the parliamentary system, groups play an important role alongside the official opposition and media in criticism of government in a democratic society. Groups exercise counter-vailing power, both as checks against an over mighty state and against the emergence of an excessively powerful group. Groups are reasonably effective in checking government (anti-poll tax campaign) but rather less successful in curbing the power of business. However, although close to a privileged interest, business is not monolithic in nature; it is neither well-organised nor politically effective, speaking rarely with one voice. Trade union power was exaggerated in the 1970s, seriously diminished in the 1980s, but in the 1990s was more significant whilst remaining less so than business.

- Groups contribute to democracy by encouraging participation and this has surged in recent decades. The extent to which rising political participation through pressure groups has enhanced democracy is qualified by: (1) the way in which the increased participation is disproportionately represented by a particular social group: the well-educated public sector middle class from the educated and caring professions; and (2) the extent to which many campaigning groups lack internal democracy, being run by small, bureau-cratic, metropolitan-based leaderships. However, this argument in turn should not be exaggerated since the sheer number of contemporary groups has increased participation compared with 30 years ago; they do extend participation of lower social groups to some extent; and some groups are participatory in mobilising women and youth to a significant degree.

Further reading

Martin Smith (1995) 'Pluralism' in D. Marsh and G. Stoker (eds) *Theory and Methods in Political Science* (London: Macmillan) provides an excellent account of modern pluralist theory; whilst A.A. Birch (1993) *The Concepts and Theories of Modern Democracy* (London: Routledge) supplies a thoughtful discussion of the role of pressure group pluralism in modern democracy. Paul Byrne (1997) *Social Movements in Britain* (London: Routledge) contains a valuable analysis of the social components of new social movements. G. Jordan and W. Maloney (1997) *The Protest Business? Mobilizing Campaign Groups* (Manchester: Manchester University Press) suggest that some campaign groups enhance participation less than they appear to do at first glance. For further critical accounts of pluralism, see M.J. Smith (1990) 'Pluralism, reformed pluralism and neo pluralism: the role of pressure groups in policy-making', *Political Studies*, XXXVIII; D. Marsh and R.A.W. Rhodes (eds) (1992) *Policy Networks in British Government* (Oxford: Clarendon Press); and R.A.W. Rhodes and D. Marsh (1996) 'The concept of policy networks in British political science: its development and utility', *Teaching Politics*, 8, 3, Spring.

Bibliography

Adonis, A. (1993) *Parliament Today*, 2nd edition, Manchester: Manchester University Press.

Baggott, R. (1992) 'Measurement of change in pressure group politics', *Talking Politics*, 5, 1.

Baggott, R. (1995) *Pressure Groups Today*, Manchester: Manchester University Press.

Baggott, R. (1996) 'Where is the beef? The BSE crisis and the British policy process', *Talking Politics*, 9, 1.

Baggott, R. (1998) 'Nuclear power at Druridge Bay', *Parliamentary Affairs*, 51, 3.

Barr, G. (1992) 'The anti-poll tax movement: an insider's view of an outsider group', *Talking Politics*, 4, 3, Summer.

Beer, S. (1965) *Modern British Politics*, London: Faber and Faber.

Bennett, R.J. (1997) 'The impact of European economic integration on business associations: the UK case', *West European Politics*, 20, 3.

Bennie, L. (1998) 'Brent Spar, Atlantic Oil and Greenpeace', *Parliamentary Affairs*, 51, 3.

Berrington, H. (1995) 'Political ethics: the Nolan Report', *Government and Opposition*, 30, 4, Autumn.

Birch, A.A. (1993) *The Concepts and Theories of Modern Democracy*, London: Routledge.

Brittan, S. (1987) 'The economic contradictions of democracy revisited', *Political Quarterly*, 60, 2.

Brown, A. (1998) 'Representing women in Scotland', *Parliamentary Affairs*, 51, 3.

Butler, D. and Butler, G. (eds) (1994) *British Political Facts 1900–1994*, 7th edition, London: Macmillan.

Butler, D., Adonis, A. and Travers, T. (1994) *Failure in British Government. The Politics of the Poll Tax*, Oxford: Oxford University Press.

Butler, D. and Kavanagh, D. (1997) *The British General Election of 1997*, London: Macmillan.

Byrne, P. (1994) 'Pressure groups and popular campaigns' in Johnson, P. (ed.) *Twentieth Century Britain*, London: Longman.

Byrne, P. (1997) *Social Movements in Britain*, London: Routledge.

Carter, N., Evans, M., Alderman, K. and Gorham, S. (1998) 'Europe, Goldsmith and the Referendum Party', *Parliamentary Affairs*, 51, 3.

Christianson, L. and Dowding, K. (1994) 'Pluralism or state autonomy? The case of Amnesty International (British Section): the insider/outsider group', *Political Studies*, XLII.

Cockett, R. (1995) *Thinking the Unthinkable: Think-Tanks and the Economic Counter-Revolution, 1931–1983*, London: Fontana.

Coxall, B. and Robins, L. (1998) *Contemporary British Politics*, 3rd edition, London: Macmillan.

Curtice, J. and Jowell, R. (1995) 'The sceptical electorate' in Jowell, R., Curtice, J., Park, A., Brook, L. and Ahrendt, D. (eds) *British Social Attitudes: The Twelfth Report*, Aldershot: Dartmouth.

Dahl, R. (1967) *Pluralist Democracy in the United States*, Chicago: Rand McNally.

Davies, M. (1985) *The Politics of Pressure: The Art of Lobbying*, London: BBC.

Doherty, B. (1998) 'Opposition to road building', *Parliamentary Affairs*, 51, 3, July.

Doig, A. (1995) 'Continuing cause for concern? Probity in local government', *Local Government Studies*, 21, 1.

Doig, A. (1997) 'Cash for questions: Parliament's response', *Parliamentary Affairs*, 51, 1, January.

Dorey, P. (1995) *British Politics Since 1945*, Oxford: Blackwell.

Downs, A. (1972) 'Up and down with ecology – the "issue attention cycle"', *Public Interest*, 28.

Drewry, G. (1989) *The New Select Committees*, 2nd edition, Oxford: Blackwell.

Dudley, G. and Richardson, J.J. (1996) 'Promiscuous and celibate ministerial styles: policy change, policy networks and British roads policy', *Parliamentary Affairs*, 49, 4, October.

Garner, R. (1993a) *Animals, Politics and Morality*, Manchester: Manchester University Press.

Garner, R. (1993b) 'Political animals: a survey of the animal protection movement in Britain, *Parliamentary Affairs*, 46, 3.

Garner, R. (1996) *Environmental Politics*, London: Palgrave.

Garner, R. (ed.) (1996a) *Animal Rights. The Changing Debate*, London: Macmillan.

Garner, R. (1998) 'Defending animal rights', *Parliamentary Affairs*, 51, 3.

George, S. and Sowemimo, M. (1996) 'Conservative foreign policy towards the European Union' in Ludlam, S. and Smith, M.J. (eds) *Contemporary British Conservatism*, London: Macmillan.

Glennerster, H. (1995) *British Social Policy Since 1945*, Oxford: Blackwell.

Grant, W. (1993) *Business and Politics in Britain*, 2nd edition, London: Macmillan.

Grant, W. (1995) *Pressure Groups, Politics and Democracy in Britain*, 2nd edition, London: Macmillan.

Greenwood, J. (1997) *Representing Interests in the European Union*, London: Macmillan.

Greer, A. (1998) 'Pesticides, sheep dips and science', *Parliamentary Affairs*, 51, 3.

Griggs, S., Howarth, D. and Jacobs, B. (1998) 'Second runway at Manchester', *Parliamentary Affairs*, 51, 3.

Hague, R., Harrop, M. and Breslin, S. (1992) *Comparative Government and Politics*, 3rd edition, London: Macmillan.

Heywood, A. (1997) *Politics*, London: Macmillan.

Jordan, A.G. and Richardson, J.J. (1987a) *Government and Pressure Groups in Britain*, Oxford: Clarendon Press.

Jordan, A.G. and Richardson, J.J. (1987b) *British Politics and the Policy Process*, London: Allen and Unwin.

Jordan, A.G. (ed.) (1991) *The Commercial Lobbyists: Politics for Profit in Britain*, Aberdeen: Aberdeen University Press.

Jordan, G. (1998) 'Politics without parties', *Parliamentary Affairs*, 51, 3.

Jordan, G. and Maloney, W. (1997) *The Protest Business? Mobilizing Campaign Groups*, Manchester: Manchester University Press.

Judge, D. (1993) *The Parliamentary State*, London: Sage.

Kavanagh, D. and Morris, P. (1994) *Consensus Politics from Attlee to Thatcher*, 2nd edition, Oxford: Blackwell.

King, A. (ed.) (1976) *Why is Britain Becoming Harder to Govern?* London: BBC.

Linton, M. (1994) *Money and Votes*, London: Institute for Public Policy Research.

Lively, J. and Lively, A. (eds) (1994) *Democracy in Britain: a Reader*, Oxford: Blackwell.

Lovenduski, J. and Randall, V. (1993) *Contemporary Feminist Politics*, Oxford: Oxford University Press.

Lowe, P. and Goyder, J. (1983) *Environmental Groups in Politics*, London: Allen and Unwin.

Lowe, R. (1993) *The Welfare State in Britain since 1945*, London: Macmillan.

Marsh, D. (1992) *The New Politics of British Trade Unionism*, London: Macmillan.

Marsh, D. and Read, M. (1988) *Private Members' Bills*, Cambridge: Cambridge University Press.

Marsh, D. and Rhodes, R.A.W. (eds) (1992) *Policy Networks in British Government*, Oxford: Clarendon Press.

Marsh, D. and Stoker, G. (eds) (1995) *Theory and Methods in Political Science*, London: Macmillan.

May, T.C., McHugh, J. and Taylor, T. (1998) 'Business representation in the UK since 1979: the case of trade associations', *Political Studies*, XLVI.

May, T. and Nugent, N. (1982) 'Insiders, outsiders and thresholders', PSA, University of Kent.

Mazey, S. and Richardson, J.J. (1992) 'Pressure groups and the European Community', *Parliamentary Affairs*, 45, 1.

Mazey, S. and Richardson, J.J. (eds) (1993) *Lobbying in the European Community*, Oxford: Oxford University Press.

Mazey, S. and Richardson, J.J. (1993a) 'Pressure groups and the EC', *Politics Review*, 3, 1, September.

Mazey, S. and Richardson, J.J. (1997) 'Policy framing: interest groups and the lead up to the 1996 Inter-Governmental Conference', *West European Politics*, 20, 3, July.

McLeod, R. (1998) 'Calf exports at Brightlingsea', *Parliamentary Affairs*, 51, 3.

Middlemas, K. (1979) *Politics in Industrial Society*, London: Andre Deutsch.

Miller, C. (1990) *Lobbying Government: Understanding and Influencing in the Corridors of Power*, 2nd edition, Oxford: Blackwell.

Miller, C. (1991) 'Lobbying' in Jordan, G. (ed.) *The Commercial Lobbyists: Politics for Profit in Britain*, Aberdeen: Aberdeen University Press.

Newton, K. (1976) *Second City Politics*, Oxford: Oxford University Press.

Norris, P. (1996a) 'The Nolan Committee: financial interests and constituency service', *Government and Opposition*, 31, 4, Autumn.

Norris, S. (1996b) *Changing Trains*, London: Hutchinson.

Norton, P. (ed.) (1990) *Legislatures*, Oxford: Oxford University Press.

Norton, P. (1993) *Does Parliament Matter?* Hemel Hempstead: Harvester Wheatsheaf.

Nugent, N. (1994) *The Government and Politics of the European Community*, London: Macmillan.

Oliver, D. (1997) 'Regulating the conduct of MPs. The British experience of combating corruption', *Political Studies*, XLV.

Olsen, M. (1971) *The Logic of Collective Action*, Cambridge, Mass.: Harvard University Press.

Parry, G. and Moyser, G. (1993) 'Political participation in Britain', *Politics Review*, 3, 2.

Parry, G., Moyser, G. and Day, N. (1992) *Political Participation and Democracy in Britain*, Cambridge: Cambridge University Press.

Peterson, J. (1997) 'States, societies and the European Union', *West European Politics*, 20, 3, July.

Read, M. (1992) 'Policy networks and issue networks: the politics of smoking' in Marsh, D. and Rhodes, R.A.W. (eds) *Policy Networks in British Government*, Oxford: Clarendon Press.

Read, M. (1998) 'The pro-life movement', *Parliamentary Affairs*, 51, 3.

Rhodes, R.A.W. and Marsh, D. (1996) 'The concept of policy networks in British political science: its development and utility', *Talking Politics*, 8, 3, Spring.

Richardson, J.J. (ed.) (1993) *Pressure Groups*, Oxford: Oxford University Press.

Richardson, J.J. and Jordan, A.G. (1979) *Governing Under Pressure*, Oxford: Blackwell.

Ridley, F.F. and Doig, A. (eds) (1995) *Sleaze: Politicians, Private Interests and Public Reaction*, Oxford: Oxford University Press.

Rose, R. (1974) *Politics in England Today: An Interpretation*, London: Faber and Faber.

Rush, M. (ed.) (1990) *Parliament and Pressure Politics*, Oxford: Clarendon Press.

Ryder, R. (1975) *Victims of Science*, London: Davis-Poynter.

Ryder, R. (ed.) (1992) *Animal Welfare and the Environment*, London: Duckworth.

Ryder, R.D. (1996) 'Putting animals into politics' in Garner, R. (ed.) *Animal Rights. The Changing Debate*, London: Macmillan.

Seyd, P. and Whiteley, P. (1992) *Labour's Grass Roots: The Politics of Party Membership*, Oxford: Clarendon Press.

Smith, M.J. (1990) 'Pluralism, reformed pluralism and neo pluralism: the role of pressure groups in policy-making', *Political Studies*, XXXVIII.

Smith, M.J. (1993a) *Pressure, Power and Policy*, Harlow: Prentice Hall.

Smith, M.J. (1993b) 'Consumer policy and the New Right' in Ashford, N. and Jordan, G. (eds) *Public Policy and the New Right*, London: Pinter.

Smith, M.J. (1995) *Pressure Politics*, Manchester: Baseline Books.

Stoker, G. (1991) *The Politics of Local Government*, London: Macmillan.

Stone, D. (1996) *Capturing the Political Imagination: Think Tanks and the Policy Process*, London: Cass.

Taylor, R. (1993) *The Trade Union Question in British Politics*, Oxford: Blackwell.

Thane, P. (1994) 'Women since 1945' in Johnson, P. (ed.) *Twentieth Century Britain*, London: Longman.

Thomson, S., Stancich, L. and Dickson, L. (1998) 'Gun control and Snowdrop', *Parliamentary Affairs*, 5, 3.

Toke, D. (1996) 'Power and environmental pressure groups', *Talking Politics*, 9, 2, Winter.

Vandermark, A. (1994) 'Lobbying and registration: biting the bullet or shifting the focus?', *Talking Politics*, 7, 1, Autumn.

Walkland, S.A. and Ryle, M. (eds) (1981) *The Commons Today*, London: Fontana.

Watts, D. (1995) 'Sunday shopping: reform at last', *Talking Politics*, 8, 1.

Weir, S. and Beetham, D. (1999) *Political Power and Democratic Control in Britain*, London: Routledge.

Whiteley, P. and Winyard, S. (1987) *Pressure for the Poor*, London: Methuen.

Woodhouse, D. (1997) ' "Cash for questions": Commissioner's Inquiry', *Parliamentary Affairs*, 51, 1.

Index